D1806251

A Conservative's
Manifesto

A Conservative's Manifesto

A Brief Discussion of some Principles

Daniel Hannan MEP

Keep the struggle going

Eric Hines

Copyright © 2012 by Eric Hines.

Library of Congress Control Number: 2012901745
ISBN: Hardcover   978-1-4691-6032-0
                 Softcover   978-1-4691-6031-3
                 Ebook   978-1-4691-6033-7

All rights reserved. No part of this book may be reproduced or transmitted in any form or by any means, electronic or mechanical, including photocopying, recording, or by any information storage and retrieval system, without permission in writing from the copyright owner.

This book was printed in the United States of America.

To order additional copies of this book, contact:
Xlibris Corporation
1-888-795-4274
www.Xlibris.com
Orders@Xlibris.com

CONTENTS

ACKNOWLEDGMENTS

I want to thank the following for the help they provided in getting this book done, whether or not they knew they had a role in this effort. In no particular order, they are:

Daniel Rembert (http://danielrembert.com/)

> He did the book's excellent cover imagery, and his advice and encouragement generally were invaluable to my getting this book done.

Cassandra, of Villainous Company (http://villainouscompany.com/vcblog/).

Grim, of Grim's Hall (http://www.grimbeorn.blogspot.com/)

> These two bloggers did not know they were helping me write a book, because at the time I began participating in their blogs, I did not know I was going to write a book. However, the discussions they moderate and in which I participated, together with all the other conversation participants, helped me to crystallize some of my thoughts on key aspects of this effort. My decision to commit my thoughts to writing came lately.

My friend Kelly Shackleford, Chief Counsel of Liberty Institute, (http://libertyinstitute.org/)

> His critiques of my legal histories and cases and his feedback and analysis helped me clarify my argument and keep my facts straight.

My friend, Deborah Wang

> Her hard-nosed inputs also contributed to my thinking.

My wife, whose existence is my reason for being.

Her cold-blooded, clear-eyed, rational look at the world and at the various iterations of this book's drafts is critical to me and were critical to this book becoming what it is.

For all of that, though, I am the author, and any errors or misconceptions in this book are mine alone.

Finally, this book is written, first, for my daughter and son-in-law and for my grandson, who is their son, because these, and others of these two generations, are our nation's future. Secondly, I write this book for my wife, and for others of our generation, for we are the present and the generation responsible for our nation's present pass. Finally, I write this book for all Americans, for I am firmly convinced that the tenets described are the foundation of our nation's greatness, the foundation of that greatness' timelessness, and the basis on which we can preserve that greatness.

PREFACE

I'm writing this because what passes for conservatism, as it is constituted today, has strayed too far from its roots and fundamental tenets. The primary formal claimant to conservatism, the Republican Party, has been complicit, until very recently, in excessive government spending, excessive taxing, irresponsible borrowing, and excessive intrusion by the government into matters that properly belong in the province of the states and in the hands of the individual citizen. They have provided only the politest of brakes to the modern Liberals' and Progressives' rapid push of our nation to the left in favor of a powerful central government that seeks increasingly to do for us, for our own good. This intrusion into the lives of ordinary citizens, which intrusion completely bypasses state jurisdiction and individual freedoms, has become a threat to the national weal. The associated explosive deficit and debt, despite marvelously intrusive and Byzantine taxes and tax increases, are astronomical in their magnitude, and still growing. The Republicans' present conservative fervor has occurred only lately, during this explosion and expanding wave front; their newfound fervor has much of the foxhole conversion about it and so is entirely suspect in its durability.

As a result, there seems to be no reliable counterweight to the profligacy of the liberal/progressive faction. The nascent Tea Party movement has not been around long enough to have confidence in its durability. We have, instead, a new and out of control American aristocracy—our own American Patrician class, which consists of those who are convinced they're better educated, better informed, and blessed with greater clarity of thought. This class also possesses the larger egos associated with this view: its denizens insist that the unwashed masses—us plebes—should listen to our betters and do as we're told; after all, if only we were better informed, or could think more clearly, or weren't such racist and religious bigots, we would, of course, see things their way.

And so we have our Patricians embarking, in the most unfettered way, on one of the most destructive agendas ever inflicted on the United States. We get:

- Obamacare;
- nationalization of major industries, both manufacturing and financial;
- government bureaucrats dictating what products a private company can or cannot sell, and at what price (insurance, banking);
- government bureaucrats dictating what private companies can or cannot pay their employees—never mind what that company's owners (its stockholders) or their representatives (its management) might think is appropriate;
- a Justice Department refusing to prosecute crimes (just for instance, voter intimidation) when the victims are of a particular group;
- massive bailouts of unions at the expense of taxpayers, at a time when unions are unable to support themselves or produce quality products (our public schools, for instance) without government handouts (a redistribution of your and my money); and
- a president who denies American exceptionalism and who says, with an absolutely straight face, that an American citizen has made enough money and should give the rest to a government that knows better how that citizen's money should be spent.

How did we come to this pass? I think we, as a people, have drifted too far from our foundational beliefs. I think we have become spoiled by our success, both as a nation and as a people. Certainly my generation, the generation of Baby Boomers, is the wealthiest generation in the history of humanity; however, we never learned how to handle that wealth. We've become a nation of consumers for the sake of consumption, and since we can buy anything we want with unprecedented ease, we've became gluttonous. And we've failed to teach our children to do better. Thus, we as a people have become separated, morally, from the underlying need for hard work to achieve that success and from the personal responsibility associated with that success, and we have begun to shrink from the need to take risks in order to continue to progress, we've drifted into a mental state of victimhood. We want, and therefore it's government's job to provide. We've allowed our politicians to spend our money with ever decreasing oversight by us, their bosses, so long as they satisfy our demands for this or that "protection." No more. We simply can't afford to be so spendthrift and so spoiled, not with our material wealth, not with our moral wealth. Our grandchildren's grandchildren will still be paying the bills for our behavior.

It's time to return to the basics that let us accumulate so much success in the first place so that our progeny, and theirs, can have a chance to enjoy the same prosperity we had, with the same degree of progress, if not more, from today as we've produced and enjoyed from 200 years ago, and with better responsibility than we're demonstrating.

In this book, I hope to remind us all of what those core values are—one man's view of conservatism, founded on 18th Century Liberalism.

A couple of administrative notes are in order now.

First, the American War of Independence also is often referred to as the American Revolutionary War. Throughout this book, I'll use the two terms, or simply, Revolution, interchangeably.

Second, the United States is a Federal Republic, which means, simply, that it is a federation of States that has a governing set of documents, our social contract, that creates a Federal government with limited powers and authorities and that preserves the rights of those constituent States, each with its unique and individual approach to life within it, and that also preserves the rights of the citizens, both as individuals and as Sovereign over their government. Throughout this book, unless I explicitly say otherwise, I will be talking about the Federal government and not the governments of the States.

Third, for those more interested in the superficiality of the Politically Correct than in the substance of the message: throughout this book, I use "man," "he," and similar words generically to refer to individual humans and/or to humanity generally. Context will make clear whether it's necessary to refer explicitly to man vs. woman; when such breakout is needed, I shall do so. I would expect a female author, similarly, to use "woman," "she," and the like with a similar rejection of the distortions of American grammar or vocabulary necessary to achieve political correctness. I will not waste further distraction on this, or other, political correctness red herrings.

INTRODUCTION

def: *manifesto*: a public declaration of principles, policies, or intentions, especially of a political nature

def: *conservatism*: a philosophy calling for lower taxes, limited government regulation of business and investing, a strong national defense, and individual financial responsibility for personal needs[1]

I intend to lay out a declaration of my version of the principles of an 18th Century Liberal, which I consider to be the basis of modern conservatism. I also will show the applications of these principles to the various components of our national polity, and then I will show how these principles translate into the imperatives that a modern Conservative must follow.

"But society has now fairly got the better of individuality; and the danger which threatens human nature is not the excess, but the deficiency, of personal impulses and preferences…everyone lives as under the eye of a hostile and dreaded censorship. Not only in what concerns others, but in what concerns only themselves, the individual or the family do not ask themselves: what do I prefer?…or, what would allow the best and highest in me to have fair play, and enable it to grow and thrive?…. Thus the mind itself is bowed to the yoke: even in what people do for pleasure, conformity is the first thing thought of; they like in crowds…their human capacities are withered and starved…." These words are a clear description of today, and yet they were written 150 years ago by John Stuart Mill (**On Liberty**). This is, thus, a danger of long standing. And we have class structure being (re)created in the United States. We have a group of people—a minority of no insignificant power—who have claimed for themselves the ability to tell the rest of us what they know to be our welfare. This group presumes to tell us what we should do, what we should eat, what is acceptable compensation for our labors, on what we should spend our money, what are our appropriate charities, what are our morals. In the typical fashion of these, our modern Liberal overseers, our Patricians, the class structure which they are attempting to force is at once

---

1   from Merriam-Webster Online

muddled and carefully crafted. We have, on the one hand, the rich, who must be sorely taxed to pay for, on the other hand, the rest of us, who are too poor and too incapable of doing responsibly for ourselves, thus having legitimate demand on the resources and on the wealth and the assets earned by others. Benignly overseeing all this redistribution of the fruits of others' labor, we have the Liberal class, these modern Progressives who are our self-professed natural leaders, our Patricians, who Know Better and will instruct the rest of us. We have only to heed their instructions, and we will be taken care of. In return, rather than reveling in our erstwhile individuality, we allow ourselves to be crammed, Procrustean-like, into the pigeonholes defined by our Patricians, bereft of that greatest of values, our individuality.

And so here we are. We, "the rest of us," are seen by these Patricians as ill-informed, misled, and regretfully bigoted. We must be led by our Betters, these Patricians insist, and we are entitled to live off the fat of the rich rather than the wealth and the power and the morality of our own efforts and of our own creativity.

What happens, though, to our moral fabric, if we allow this descent into government dependency, this sheep-like surrender of our initiative and of our sense of self to "guidance" of the Patricians, to continue? What happens to our self respect, if we allow this to continue? What happens to that which made us American if we allow this to continue? What happens to our nation's standing on the world stage, and to that which made our nation the envy of the world, if we allow this to continue? If we become a people of helplessness, a people dependent on others for our welfare, we will have lost everything. And worse, we will have destroyed our children's futures before they can have a chance to form their own.

Modern Conservatives, instead, luxuriate in individualism and the personal responsibility that is the reverse of this coin. Bobby Seals, and his "Power to the People" mantra had nothing on Thomas Paine with his "power to the individual, and responsibility to the individual" tenet. We enjoy our own work and the fruits of our own labors. Our charities are our own, and they are many, and we need no Patrician or government agency to dictate them to us. We are in need of very little in the way of handouts, and we band together as necessary to help each other, and strangers, with hands up. Our nation remains great, free, and a beacon and example for the rest of the world so long as it adheres to its conservative (18th Century Liberal) roots.

The basic principles from which I write, then, are these:

— individual freedom,
— individual responsibility, and
— the primacy of the individual over the state, which means
— the state works for us, not the other way around, and not with a Patrician class as intermediary for us.

"[T]he sole end for which mankind are warranted, individually or collectively, in interfering with the liberty of any of their number is self protection. The only purpose for which power can rightfully be exercised over an individual citizen, against his will, is to prevent harm to others. His own good, either physical or moral, is not a sufficient warrant." Mill (**On Liberty**) said this, too, 150 years ago. It's as true today as it has ever been.

One might ask whether I am a politician or a philosopher that I would write on this subject. Of course, I am neither; I am an ordinary citizen of my country, and so it is my duty to write on this matter. Were I a politician, I would stand for office and work within that limited sphere in the halls of the relevant capital to achieve my own ends, claiming them to be those of the ones who elected me to that office. Were I a philosopher, I would preach from the podium of an academic hall, again reaching only a limited few, and via the copious arcane papers such a career requires to be published, reaching a few more. As I do not live in those august heights, but rather am a simple citizen, I hope my reach is far broader—my fellow citizens.

In summation of this Introduction, I offer the following:

> "We hold these truths to be self-evident, that all men are created equal, that they are endowed by their Creator with certain unalienable Rights, that among these are Life, Liberty and the pursuit of Happiness. — That to secure these rights, Governments are instituted among Men, deriving their just powers from the consent of the governed...."

Notice that there is nothing in these clauses, nor anywhere else in our Declaration of Independence, that suggests that others have any means of claiming authority over us, save with our explicit consent. 18th century liberalism—modern conservatism—is an attribute of individuals, it is not a product of groupthink or of cubbyholed collections of us in accordance with someone else's definition of the appropriateness of a category.

CHAPTER 1—18TH CENTURY LIBERALISM

*In general, the art of government consists of taking as much money
as possible from one party of the citizens to give to the other.*

— **Voltaire**

In broad, general terms, a Liberal wants marked, often radical, often rapid change from the *status quo*. This is, of course, a highly simplified description; I'll elaborate in the coming chapters. With this in mind, though, I offer now a description of the conditions in the 17th to late-18th centuries as the *status quo* of interest for the events leading up to, and including, the time frame of the American War of Independence. It is the change from this *status quo* that will inform my definition of an 18th Century Liberal, and it is this definition that underlies the rest of this book.

Although there are other and earlier thinkers on the nature of man and his relationship with his fellows (Thomas Hobbes comes to mind), I'll begin my effort from the premises of John Locke and Jean-Jacques Rousseau. These men wrote in a world of monarchy where the ruler governed by Divine Right or by force of arms, and in either event, succession was by inheritance. The concept of heritability of a "right to rule" becomes especially important whenever the first of a line takes power by force, as William of Normandy did over Saxon England. Heritability is the only justification for a usurper, a tyrant in the classic Greek sense, to maintain power in his own line through succeeding generations.

This was a world, also, where the church either was a major state organ ranking as highly as the king or queen, or it was a religious government operating separately from and in parallel with the monarchical government. In both situations, the church provided the affirmation of the divinity of that political rule and guaranteed it, and the church exercised its own control over the lives of all men. Locke and Rousseau, although they wrote the works of interest here (**Second Treatise** and **Social Contract**, respectively)

100 years apart, both essentially said that, instead, certain rights are of man and are not granted by government, and they further said that these rights were morally indivisible from man. The rights recognized by these philosophers consisted, very simply, of the right of any man to do as he will as far as he will, and to own and dispose of his own private property, right up to the point where it interferes with another man's right to do the same. Thus, Locke's and Rousseau's were very liberal, if not radical, ideas, whose time had come, but whose implementation possibly was not yet to be.

I'll provide, first, a brief overview of the religious persecutions extant in Europe and then an equally brief overview of the political conditions of the time. I'll follow these with a look at conditions in the colonies[1] as the regime within which our own Revolution took place. Much of the outright radicalism that resulted originated during the Revolution and in its immediate aftermath as the new American republican government was formed and then populated through an unprecedentedly broad reach of voting and office holding eligibility. Note that what follows in this and the next chapter is not a history lesson. It is, instead, a broad overview, with great simplification, and with a vast array of details that others might find interesting, or important, glossed over or ignored. The point of this broad brush treatment has these components only: to offer a description of the conditions that informed our Founders; to set the stage for a discussion of the liberal, if not radical, nature of the principles that guided our Revolution and the formation both of our particular form of government and of the society that resulted from the success of that Revolution; and to provide the basis for my definition of an 18th Century Liberal.

Religious persecutions and outright conflict actually began, for our purposes, with the Protestant Reformation, formally set as beginning early in the 16th century when Martin Luther nailed his 95 theses to the Castle Church door in Wittenberg. The religious wars that followed didn't end until nearly 150 years later with the Peace of Westphalia that also formally ended the Thirty Years' War[2]. However, the persecutions and associated

---

1   The centuries following the discovery of the New World by European explorers is replete with colonization by those same Europeans all over the globe. However, for the purposes of this document, I will refer to the colonies and territories of North America that ultimately became the United States as "the colonies" from here forward.

2   The Treaty of Osnabruck, part of the Peace of Westphalia, specified three acceptable types of worship, "domestic devotion," public religious services, and communal worship by minority faiths in

violence did not end: these continued for another 150+ years, spilling over into the colonies, where they didn't end (or at least become vastly abated) until the American Revolution was successfully concluded (a confluence of timing; our revolution was about the nature of liberty generally, which included religious liberty). The causes and points of conflict were many, but one theme running throughout the fighting was exemplified by the argument between those who insisted man was permanently fallen as a result of Adam's original sin and those who viewed man as fallen from the same cause, but redeemable by his own action (with God's help), as Jesuits and Pelagianists, among others, held. Another theme, held by the Puritans of the times, was that man had fallen so far, so hard, that he could not reason clearly or make free choices, even naturalistically—man had no free will. This particular argument was in full flower in the 17th century and not much resolved by the late 18th; indeed, the matter isn't resolved today, but the disagreement is far more peaceable.

Following are some examples, selected more or less at random solely to illustrate the depth of this conflict and of its violence.

In England, the persecutions initially were between the Anglican Church and the Catholic Church, as the English monarchy changed from one to the other according to the desires of each newly ascendant monarch. This resulted in the routine imprisonment and murder of adherents to the church not supported by the current monarchy. Three hundred Protestants were burned at the stake by Mary I, and Jesuits were imprisoned, tortured, and executed under James I, for instance[3]. Puritans suffered at the hands of both Catholic and Anglican churches (although Puritan emigrants to the colonies showed no greater tolerance on their arrival). These unfortunates were threatened with "extirpation" if they did not adhere to the approved religion in England. Overt torture for their beliefs was not uncommon. As a result, Puritans began emigrating to Ireland, the Netherlands, and thence to the colonies in search of freedom to practice their religion (the Mayflower carried an early group of these Puritans, along with a collection

---

clandestine churches or as private or family affairs. Even these were honored more in the breach.

3   The burnings also included Thomas Cranmer, originally Anne Boleyn's chaplain, and later Archbishop of Canterbury and a leader of the English Reformation (the creation of the Anglican Church) under Henry VIII. The Jesuit persecutions included seizing priests at prayer and beating them to the point they died of their injuries while imprisoned or executing them outright for insisting on professing their faith according to Jesuit precepts.

of adventurers). Ireland was an uncertain haven, however. During the mid-17th century Catholic Irish revolt against then-Protestant English rule, 30,000 Protestants, including large numbers of the emigrated Puritans, were murdered[4]. Conditions in the Netherlands proved not much better. Here, they felt their very sense of self threatened, leading many to make additional moves, to the colonies. The pacifist Quakers were treated no more gently. By 1680, 10,000 Quakers had been imprisoned in England, and 243 had died of torture and mistreatment in the King's jails.

English treatment of adherents of the "wrong" religion was typical for Europe as a whole. French Calvinists (Huguenots) and French Catholics routinely drove each other out of the areas each controlled, appropriated each other's' property, and murdered the recalcitrant, the Edict of Nantes[5] notwithstanding. Following a series of increasingly confining restrictions on Huguenot freedoms and the revocation of the Edict of Nantes and its replacement by the Edict of Fontainebleau[6], though, Huguenots were subjected everywhere to forced Catholic baptism, even more widespread seizure of their property, and even more zealous threats to their person. As a result of the ensuing bloodshed, Huguenots, and Protestants generally, fled France by the hundreds of thousands. Conditions were just as lethal in the German principalities, where Lutherans, Calvinists, Puritans, and Presbyterians each tortured and killed the others, always for the sake of the victim's soul.

While religious strife was stripping men of their freedom of thought and of belief, monarchist governments were robbing them of their freedom of action and of all the rest of their liberties. Liberty, as described by Locke and Rousseau—again, this liberty to do as one wishes, without needing the permission of any other, including that of any higher authority, right up to the point of interfering with another's right to do the same—simply did not exist in these times. Instead, governments granted to men certain "rights," and these same governments granted men such freedoms as those

---

4   For example, one man was sentenced to life imprisonment, had his property confiscated, his nose slit, an ear cut off, and his forehead branded "S.S." (sower of sedition). An incident in Ireland had 100 Protestants driven "like hogs" by their Catholic captors to a bridge over the River Bann near Portadown, Ulster, where they were stripped naked and forced into the water below at sword point. Survivors were shot.

5   The Edict officially granted Huguenots religious and political parity with the Catholics.

6   This new Edict eliminated all pretense of Huguenot religious freedom.

governments saw fit to grant in order for these men, these commoners, to operate within those rights.

These limits were social as well as political, for in usurping men's rights and stealing from them their liberty, governments had also merged the social into the political. Men were heavily influenced, if not outright enjoined, in how they could sell their wares, to whom they could sell their labor, and at what price for either (among other activities), by their station in both political and social hierarchies. A few examples illustrate. Men associated with each other in easy intercourse in the local tavern, and they conversed freely with their peers in other places, as well. But the master of a household had no such relaxed relationship with the men who worked his fields or in his tinker's shop. These men were supplicants to this master. Similarly, this same man had no relaxed relationship with his mayor or his priest, except this time the household master was supplicant to his mayor or to his priest. A town's mayor had the authority to command a man's services for various purposes solely on the mayor's demand. Even more, the very right and authority to marry, and to whom, was controlled, not by the man and woman involved, but by others at various levels of this hierarchical chain. For women, this control was explicit: women were owned by their fathers until they married, and then they were owned by their husbands. In all cases, they were viewed mostly as objects of barter for social, economic, and/ or political gain by the family or by other interested parties up through the hierarchy to the monarch[7] himself. The sons, being used for and entering into these arrangements, themselves were merely objects of the same barter, however voluntarily they thought they were entering into it. These authorities, these superior/subordinate relationships, I repeat, extended up the chain of command [sic] all the way through to the monarch.

Thus, a man's "rights" and "freedoms" came from his monarch as his government, and as they descended this command hierarchy to the individual, they were heavily influenced by whom he knew and to whom he was related in one or another guise. The social and political lives of men were closely intertwined, and governance itself was as much social as political. Through this interlocking of relationships, a man's first allegiance, ultimately, was to his king as sovereign and father.

---

7   I am using the term "monarch" in this book to indicate the political head (of either gender) of a polity, whether that person was a king, an emperor, or a prince.

Some will argue that these monarchs were well-intentioned, and much about these interpersonal relationships stemmed from the brother- and sisterhood even strangers shared as subjects (childlike, to an extent) of a kindly *pater familias* king. However, the attitude at this pinnacle, in fact, was nothing but tyranny and arrogance in the monarch, and this had practical effects with an immediacy that destroyed lives.

For example, Charles I's struggles with his nobility, through the intermediary of the English Parliament, to preserve and enhance his own power, in the face of actions taken by that Parliament, such as the Petition of Right[8] and the Triennial Act[9], caused a series of civil wars that led to the destruction of the monarchy and its (brief) replacement with a Commonwealth.

Louis XIV's reign in France was marked by a similar struggle for power, this time directly between himself and his nobility. The *Fronde*[10] civil war, unlike the English wars, though, left power concentrated in the hands of the monarchy, and the nobility were reduced even further. Caught in the middle was the French peasantry, whose value to their "superiors" was only as cannon fodder for the fighting.

The monarchical system also led these tyrants to interfere directly and personally in their subjects' religious lives. Formally, from the Peace of Augsburg in the middle of the 16th century onward, a monarch was authorized, or so the Peace averred, to require his own subjects to adhere to his religious beliefs and to ban all others: *cuius regio, eius religio*. This authority, granted specifically by several princes of German principalities and Charles V, of the Holy Roman Empire, to themselves, but by extension to all monarchs, also applied only to Lutherans and Catholics and excluded the newly developing Calvinist or Anabaptist Protestant sects[11]. Further,

---

8   The Petition laid out, among other things, the requirement that taxes could be levied only by Parliament and established the principle of *habeas corpus*.
9   The Act attempted to limit royal power by demanding that Parliament be summoned into session at least every three years.
10   The *Fronde* was an effort to protect the liberties that had been gained from the king over the preceding centuries and to protect the prerogatives and powers of the French *parlements*, or courts of appeal, that could functionally overturn royal decrees that ran "contrary to custom."
11   Some will note that the Peace did not have England as signatory, and so it would seem to exclude the Anglican Church, also. However, the English functionally had been practicing *cuius regio, eius religio* since the Reformation that created the Anglican Church.

it functionally authorized the execution all who refused to adopt that monarch's religion[12].

The claim of heritability of the monarchy—this assertion that a small group of people could claim legal and moral superiority in perpetuity, without any consideration by these future generations of that perpetuity—also led to realized problems in the lives of men, including in the interaction of secular and religious governance. The English Glorious Revolution was precipitated by whether a sitting Catholic king would pass his monarchy to his Protestant daughter or to his newly born Catholic son. The struggle was between nobility and the monarch; the common man had no say, he had only to fight and to die in the nobles' wars.

The monarchical system led to serious economic and legal failures. The English economy was devastated by their civil wars, for instance, and their interventionist conflicts (*vis.*, the Thirty Years' War[13]). Charles I's dubious efforts at raising revenue, given Parliament's reluctance to do so,[14] coupled with his intervention in the continental Thirty Years' War, left the English economy deeply in debt and generally unproductive as output went to satisfying that debt and not to improving lives.

Taxes imposed in France to support both a weak economy and French involvement in the Thirty Years' War and its separate war with Spain were large and economically destructive. By the end of Louis' reign, the French government owed 2 billion livres ($21 billion today), and the taxes imposed—on the peasant, since the nobility and clergy were largely exempt from taxation—were both usurious and unfairly applied. Even 100 years later, in the 1770s and 1780s, two ministers attempting to reform the system of taxation in France were summarily dismissed from their

---

12   Although the Peace formally allowed migration after a (brief) decision period, a refusal to accept the monarch's religion exposed the subject to charges of heresy, which itself often was a death sentence.

13   Although England generally stayed out of this war, Charles authorized a force to aid the Elector Palatine in the latter's war efforts, subsequently declared war on Spain in support of this, and sent a large fleet to Rochelle in support of the Protestants there.

14   Bypassing Parliament by reviving the Distraint of Knighthood and then fining those who failed to appear in court, reviving the Ship Money tax and making it nationwide instead of its original coastal application, using the Monopolies Act to grant monopolies and collect revenues from these grants.

posts, so entrenched was the system's protection of the secular and religious aristocracy.

In legal matters, the common man's rights, such as were given him by his government, were equally precarious. Although the English were evolving a jury system, as recently as the 1600s English judges had the authority, in the event a jury returned the "wrong" verdict, to jail that jury until it changed course and returned the "correct" verdict.

There is a recurring theme here, the view by the aristocracy, whether religious or secular, that the common man is incapable of reason, is unable to decide what is best for himself; and the man's acquiescence in this: we see this in the following paragraphs. The moral failure of this had impacts at all levels of the monarchist hierarchy, but it was most apparent at the bottom, with the common man, and at the top, in the person and office of the monarch himself. The monarch's assumption of a nonexistent superiority caused widespread moral damage across entire nations and at all levels of society and politics.

The very existence of their reigns, by denying their subjects any choice in the matter and manner of their governance, gave monarchs an attitude of the "natural" subordination of a man to a higher sovereign, the despot himself. This immorality was identified by the theft from these individuals of their liberties and the arrogation of these liberties to the sole possession of the person of the monarch. This created the monarch as the arrogant tyrant described above, as he viewed his subjects as mere pawns in his personal power struggles with his nobility and fellow monarchs. The monarch came to view himself as fully justified in directing the behaviors, the very beliefs, of his subjects.

At the bottom of the hierarchy, a man was viewed, and he viewed himself, as needing to be led by his betters. This moral damage issued from his seeming dependency on his government, on his monarch and his command chain from there all the way down through his mayor and his employer and his priest, for everything in his life, including life itself. This attitude in which the common man was steeped pushed him toward a belief within himself as well as in his "superiors," that he not merely need not, but could not, think for himself or determine for himself what is best for himself. He was not qualified to determine for himself his circumstance or what he might do, or need to do, about that circumstance. Such a man became, in his outlook on the world around him, increasingly dependent on this hierarchy to make his decisions for him, in the way a child is dependent on the parent for answers. More, he came to view himself as absolved of responsibility for his own actions, since each man's actions, in fact, were not his own. The severity of this damage is illustrated, at the individual's level, by the marriage sham of the times. The bartering for the "hand" of a woman in marriage was morally destructive both for men and for women, since it reduced the woman to the status of chattel property, and the voluntary nature of the man's entry into these arrangements made each man complicit in this chattel property creation and use, thus turning each man into a tyrant over each woman in exactly the same way as the monarchical tyrant controlled lesser men.

And so we have a morally depressed monarch controlling morally depressed men. Both were coming to believe in the man's inadequacy, even as the man's resentment of this status built. As a result, men left for the New World in increasing numbers, both to escape the physical assaults on their persons for their religious and political views and to escape the moral assaults, even though few if any could yet clearly articulate these even to himself.

Turning to the colonies themselves, we see them evolving while their Mother country did not. Though they began as rife with persecution and secular dominance as was the Old World, their deliberate separation from that world as self-selected refugees from it enabled them to examine and reject many of the Old World's practices. This growing estrangement progressed into an evolving colonial aristocracy,[15] and these men, together with the colonial common man,[16] were ready to find a way to break away from those

---

15   Colonial aristocracy (as opposed to English and continental aristocrats transplanted) were characterized by ownership of large tracts of land; higher education; and the gentleman's status of not working, but living off his rents, instead. Further, this status was not heritable, and primogeniture generally did not obtain. Property and wealth were passed on with far less regard to birth orders. Even more critically, anyone could join this "aristocracy" from below through hard work and accumulation of the trappings of this new class—larger tracts of land and education.

16   Colonial commoners, apart from being political or religious refugees, were characterized by small land ownership; frequently earning their passage to the colonies and subsequent freedom through a period of indentured servitude; operating small businesses; or working for others—all as did their English or continental counterparts. However, the difference for the colonials was their ability to sell their wares and/or their labor (after satisfying any indenture requirements) to whom they wished. They were not bound by the limits of relationships under an Old World monarchy.

old abuses, to find their own solutions, and to understand and recover their liberties and freedoms of choice and actions.

I'll provide a few examples of the continued attacks on liberty in the colonies, and then I'll close this chapter with a description of the evolution of the American 18th Century Liberal.

At end of 17th century, various of the colonial governments were actively pushing greater church authority over existing members and actively seeking to bring those who were not active members into the church, whether the newly incorporated wanted to become members or not. This occurred in parallel with growing crown authority in the colonies as the English monarchies increasingly saw the colonies as economic, geographic, and military tools for their struggles with the continental monarchies over political and economic supremacy.[17]

The Puritan Massachusetts colony provides one set of examples of colonial assault on liberty. In the early 17th century, Roger Williams was expelled from the colony, in mid-winter, for leaving the Puritan church. In the late 17th century, hundreds of people were accused of witchcraft and at least 45 were executed, while more died in prison before trial and at least one was crushed to death for refusing even to enter a plea in the matter.

In the mid 17th century, the Virginia colony began enacting anti-Quaker laws, forcing them to convert to the Anglican Church, or effectively driving them out of the colony: Quakers were subject to execution for refusing to convert if they stayed. Although the Quakers were singled out, Virginian persecution applied to all non-Anglicans. Everyone was required to attend the Anglican church and to be catechized by an Anglican minister, and those who refused could be executed or sent to the galleys. When the House of Burgesses was established, it enacted religious laws that "were a match for anything to be found in the Puritan societies."[18] This House from the early

---

17   The details of the struggle are not relevant here, beyond stating that the English bid was for outright naval and commercial supremacy and control of New World trade on the one hand, and sufficient meddling in continental affairs to prevent any single power from gaining hegemony over the continent and so becoming a threat to England on the other hand. These two goals were mutually supporting and were viewed as such by the English.

18   These and other quotes from the colonies are contained in "Religion and the Founding of the American Republic, I. America as a Religious Refuge: The Seventeenth Century," Library of

17th century on specifically required that there be a "uniformitie throughout this colony both in substance and circumstance to the cannons [*sic*] and constitution of the Church of England."

Crown abuses ranged from the 17th century seizure of Rhode Island[19] to the economic and political abuses well described by other sources. Questions of taxation, control of trade, and even whether a colony's laws had legitimacy outside of the English Parliament's approval, however, are some of the better known abuses.

There was growing reaction to these abuses, however, and other colonies created governing charters that pushed for religious tolerance. Rhode Island was founded (with the aid of Roger Williams) on the principle of actual religious tolerance, and in direct response to the depredations of Massachusetts (the other founders also were refugees from the Massachusetts colony).

Pennsylvania was created in direct response to Anglican Virginia attacks on religious freedom. The Quakers resembled Puritans in some religious beliefs and practices, but they disagreed strongly over the necessity of compelling religious uniformity in society. Indeed, one feature of Quaker religious practice that especially enraged other religious orders was Quaker insistence on equality for women, including the right to speak in Meeting for Worship and to preach the Gospel. Pennsylvania's charter of religious freedom explicitly guaranteed freedom of worship, albeit only for some religions: all citizens who believe in "One Almighty and eternal God . . . shall in no wayes be molested or prejudiced for their Religious Perswasion or Practice in matters of Faith and Worship, nor shall they be compelled at any time to frequent or maintain any Religious Worship, Place or Ministry whatever."

Colonial (and Catholic) Maryland enacted a law stipulating that no Trinitarian Christian "shall from henceforth be any waies troubled,

---

Congress, http://www.loc.gov/exhibits/religion/rel01.html at the time of this writing in Fall 2011.

19   Originally the Colony of Rhode Island and Providence Plantations, it joined the United States as the State of Rhode Island and Providence Plantations. The colony was founded as in independent colony on land bought from the local Indians. In the late 17th century, the English monarchy seized the colony and incorporated it into its North American Empire. Although it gained a measure of freedom under a Royal Charter, it remained a crown entity until the Revolution's success.

molested, or discountenanced, for, or in respect of his or her religion nor in the free exercise thereof within this Province."

In the immediate aftermath of the Revolution, Thomas Jefferson decried his Virginia's attitude toward religious freedom, complaining that "If no capital execution took place here, as did in New-England, it was not owing to the moderation of the church, or spirit of the legislature, as may be inferred from the law itself; but to historical circumstances which have not been handed down to us."[20] Further, Pennsylvania increasingly was seen as a model by those opposing plans for government-supported religion. We have this statement from a group of Virginians to its House of Delegates in a 1785 <u>Petition Against Assessment for Paying Teachers of Religion</u>: "Witness the state of Pennsylvania wherein no such establishment hath taken place; their Government stands firm and can any of the neighboring states boast of man of better morals and more upright character."

Notice the theme in the colonies is the continued view that some men are better than others, and others are born to be led—they have no liberty, only those "freedoms" and "rights" handed down from on high by the government that rules over them. The common man is incapable of reason, is unable to decide what is best for himself, must be led by his betters. Of course, this governance always is for only the best of reasons: "We know better," and "It's for your own good."

We have now, though, a growing rejection of this tyranny with its moral and other abuses. The colonial population, having already selected itself according to the characteristic of being able to seek something better for themselves, had begun to understand what "better" might be and to pursue it. The Revolution began when two major groups of people got fed up. It began when the gentleman farmers, the lawyers, and the well-educated (most of them church school educated, church schools being the dominant source of secondary education), many of whom were men of the cloth—this colonial aristocracy, this American gentry—finally had had enough interference from a monarchy distant and remote, not only geographically, but psychologically and morally, as well. These men knew Locke and Rousseau, and their classical education also had taught them Roman and Greek ideas of law and polity.

---

20   **Notes on the State of Virginia**, 1781-1782

The Revolution also began when the merchants, the businessmen, the small farmers, the laborers, these men who *worked* for a living (with no pejorative intended toward the American gentry) had had enough interference with their business, with their pocketbooks, with their livelihoods, with their ability simply to do as they wished, from a monarchy distant and remote, not only geographically, but psychologically and morally, as well. These two groups of colonials, one perhaps articulating the problems more crisply than the other, had done with the crown's trampling on individual liberties, had done with the crown's separation of man's natural rights from the men themselves—rights that Locke had recognized and described 100 years prior and that Rousseau was articulating simultaneously with the growing colonial rejection of crown abuses of them. Although the proximate causes of the Revolution were economic and political, the Revolution was broader and more far reaching. With a firm reliance on the protection of Divine Providence, the gentlemen mutually pledged to each other their Lives, their Fortunes, and their sacred Honor, and they enlisted the common man to the cause of freedom, as well. Thus, the second paragraph of the Declaration of Independence contains an explicit reaffirmation of these natural rights as elucidated by Locke and Rousseau:

> We hold these truths to be self-evident, that all men are created equal, that they are endowed by their Creator with certain unalienable Rights, that among these are Life, Liberty and the pursuit of Happiness. — That to secure these rights, Governments are instituted among Men, deriving their just powers from the consent of the governed, — That whenever any Form of Government becomes destructive of these ends, it is the Right of the People to alter or to abolish it, and to institute new Government, laying its foundation on such principles and organizing its powers in such form, as to them shall seem most likely to effect their Safety and Happiness.

And here is the gauntlet thrown down, and the basis for 18th century liberalism made manifest. A man has rights that are indivisible from that man because they are inherent in his humanity, in his very existence. Government exists to protect these rights and for no other purpose. When such a government strays too far from this duty, the citizens of this wholly voluntary polity, which has authorized, created, and hired this government to serve them, have an equally inalienable right (later in the Declaration, our Founders aver a duty, as did Locke) to do whatsoever is necessary to bring that government to heel or to replace it with a more obedient one. This is the very antithesis of the world of governance extant in the Old World at the time of the Revolution. Governments, said the Conservatives of the time, who were generally monarchists, exist, and the rights of the people are those granted by these governments[21]. Those governed are to satisfy the needs of that government. The right to govern is an inheritable right, but only by those already comprising that government, for their superior fitness to govern is demonstrated by their being part of the government.

As Locke and Rousseau wrote, and as our Founders repeated, the relationship between the citizens of a polity and that polity's government is a social contract that is originated by the citizens, among the citizens, and that is maintained by the citizens. The government is an instrument of the people, not the other way around. I'll repeat this theme often, for it bears repeating as often as necessary.

Thomas Paine wrote in **Common Sense** during the winter of 1776 while actively fomenting rebellion, "A government of our own is our natural right…." Paine repeated this in 1791 in his **Rights of Man**:

> There never did, there never will, and there never can exist
> a parliament, or any description of men, or any generation
> of men, in any country, possessed of the right or the power
> of binding and controuling posterity to the "*end of time*," or
> of commanding for ever how the world shall be governed
> or who shall govern it: and therefore all such clauses, acts
> or declarations, by which the makers of them attempt to do
> what they have neither the right nor the power to do, nor the
> power to execute, are in themselves null and void.

Further, as Locke and Rousseau emphasized, and as our Founders acknowledged in word and their action of the Rebellion, these natural rights

---

21   As a side note, and in the context of a prolonged discussion about the French Revolution, Thomas Paine, in his **Rights of Man**, had some very choice words about Sir Edmund Burke, a major Irish proponent of this monarchist philosophy.

cannot be given up by man to a government; they are God's gift to man and so are indivisible from us.

Our Founders went further. Not only is a government the servant of the people, the direction of this relationship utterly determines and controls the nature of the powers that the government has. This government, this object of the social contract that men have *with each other to create that government* has only those powers, only those authorities and permissions, explicitly granted to that government by the people in their social contract with each other; and that government has no other such powers, authorities, or permissions whatsoever. And so the social contract which our Founders wrote and which Americans approved among themselves and for themselves, includes the Constitution of the United States, which created a government with the following structure, carefully crafted to correct the deficiencies, both moral and physical, of the monarchy being replaced.

- an assemblage of representatives of the people, elected by the people.[22]
- to counterbalance this assemblage, a national executive officer, also elected by the people (albeit indirectly; the choice is made by an Electoral College, but the electors of a particular State are chosen by a mechanism determined by that State's legislature, and these legislatures are elected by the citizens of the respective State).
- counterbalancing these two is an independent judiciary as an equal branch of the government, whose purpose is to try matters of law, both civil and criminal, as created by the representatives and carried out by the executive officer. The Supreme Court of the United States also determines, when particular cases rise through the appellate process to it, the Constitutionality,[23] the legitimacy, of any law.

It originally was envisioned that gentlemen would become the elected officials. The thinking here was that gentlemen, having no pecuniary interest in the world, were best suited to govern because they would do so disinterestedly and solely with the best interests of the nation at heart

---

22   Originally, one part of this assemblage, the Senate, had its members chosen by the States' elected assemblies. This part of the Constitution was changed to direct election by the people of each State with the 17th Amendment.

23   This authority first was asserted by the Supreme Court in *Marbury v Madison* in 1803.

(centuries old habits die hard, even in the fire of Revolution). Here is where the radicalism of our Revolution enters. The citizen soldiers, the common man, who did most of the actual fighting (through their sheer numbers in the continental forces; this is not to denigrate the sacrifices of gentry, who fought with every bit as much courage and sacrifice), took the American aristocracy, the gentlemen of the Declaration of Independence, Thomas Paine with his pamphleteering, *et al.*, at their word: government should flow up from the people and not down from the pinnacle of an aristocracy. These private citizens and these pecuniary merchants and businessmen voted in earnest in the elections subsequent to victory, and more radically, they stood for office and got elected, to city governments and to State and Federal legislatures, in competition with the gentlemen.

Thus, this liberal/radical movement, for this is what it was, even though it was not so organized, brings us to the major outcome of the Revolution. Society, politics, and the underlying conceptualization of these were changed completely in the new nation compared to the English colonies of just a few short years prior:

- A completely new social contract among the citizens of the new country was created, one which laid out the new nation's principles of liberty and which created a republican government subordinate to the people, who are sovereign in that new nation, and which removed all monarchy from the polity.
- Religious tolerance (not merely nominal freedom) replaced persecution, and the new government-as-people's-servant was explicitly enjoined from taking any action that might even begin to seem like taking a stand on religion.
- Perhaps most importantly, the individual was recognized as politically superior to government, in control of government, with national sovereignty acknowledged as residing solely in the people and not at all in the government.
- Related to this, government was recognized to be, and created as, an instrument of the people with the sole purpose of protecting the individual's natural rights.
- Society was severed from government. Perquisites of social standing, business deals, honors, and the like no longer flowed

from a monarchical peak downward through a pyramid of class relationships.

- Society itself changed and was no longer hierarchical. Who one was or could ever be, was no longer defined by to whom one was connected or where one lived. Who one was or could become, was defined by the character and characteristics of that person.
- More than not merely not hierarchical, society became truly classless:
    - The relationship between a common man and a gentleman changed. One might work for the other (it was, indeed, a two way relationship, as many of the gentleman were economically ruined by the war and others were unable to collect enough in rents to cover expenses, and so these gentlemen had to work for pay, as well), but each was the equal of the other where it most mattered—in the eyes of the law and in open court.
    - Businessmen and merchants were getting elected to legislatures at all levels of government jurisdiction; government service no longer was the sole province of disinterested gentlemen.
- Central government was limited to a very few, explicitly identified powers. If the Federal government didn't have these powers, the people did or their State governments did, and neither needed any permission from the Federal government to exercise them. Further, the non-named powers were not government's to give or to withhold; they resided solely in the people or their state governments—which, being closer to the people, were even more directly under their control.

And so we come now to my definition of an 18th Century Liberal. The Liberal movement had succeeded in withdrawing government from its absolute control over life, and the movement had replaced that with a government that was subordinated to free men as a product of a social contract among free men, with the sole function of preserving the individual liberty of free men, and with powers limited to exactly those necessary to achieve that end and no more. This Liberal movement also had changed the state of mind of man from that of a dependent whose worth, whose very definition, depended on his connection to others in a governing hierarchy, and restored him to his proper status as a free and sovereign individual and thereby restored to him his understanding of his own true worth. This movement had restored man, with his rights morally inseparable from his person. This movement had restored to the individual man his own morality, his own responsibility to act and to accept the consequences of those actions. This movement had restored to the individual man his freedom of choice. This movement had restored to him the actual ability to enter into agreements, of his own free will, with his fellow man, and to engage those agreements for any purpose he would—including the purpose of forming a government that can, and can be required to, devote itself to the preservation of his abilities and of his freedoms.

In sum, this movement had restored to the individual man his rights to Life, Liberty, and the pursuit of Happiness. This movement was consummated by these men, now finally freed of a government thrust upon them against their will (a government which tended to deny the very freedom of that will), reaching an agreement among themselves on the proper nature of a government working for them as sovereign, and then by their establishing that government.

An 18th Century Liberal, then, is a person who recognizes and acts to achieve and to support the following:

- The individual man is sovereign over his person and his beliefs.
- The individual man, acting in concert with his fellows, is sovereign over their common polity.
- The individual man is the sole decision maker as to what he will or will not do, and is acknowledged to have a rationality and freedom of will to do so.
- The individual man is the sole person responsible for the outcomes of his actions.
- The individual man is fallen and imperfect but can take his own steps to improve himself, both in physical circumstance and morally, without government mandating those improvements or their means of achievement.
- The government formed through the mutual agreement of these free men is subordinate to, responsible to, and has only those powers explicitly granted it by, those free men.

- The government formed through the mutual agreement of these free men must be kept small and limited to, and in, the powers granted it by those free men.
- The government formed through the mutual agreement of these free men has as its sole purpose the preservation of the liberties of those free men.

CHAPTER 2—CONSERVATISM VS. MODERN LIBERALISM

Democracy must be something more than two wolves
and a sheep voting on what to have for dinner.

— *James Bovard*

I offered a (very) brief description of a Liberal at the outset of Chapter 1, and I closed that chapter with my definition of an 18th Century Liberal, in particular. In this chapter, we fast forward to the period encompassing the early 20th Century through to our present time in the early 21st, and I offer an equally brief description of a Conservative: a person who, in recognizing the need for change as the *status quo* evolves, works for carefully considered, deliberate change. He's *conservative* because he's not willing to lose that which is good in search of something which may, but is not known to be, better. He conserves as well as changes.

I also closed the preceding chapter with a description of the social contract that we Americans developed for ourselves, a contract consisting of our Declaration of Independence and our Constitution of the United States. The Declaration is our principles statement, and it carries a brief discussion of our inalienable rights and duties: particularly identifying Life, Liberty, and the pursuit of Happiness as among of the rights endowed in all Americans[1] by our Creator, and our right—and duty—to rid ourselves of any government that too badly exceeds or abuses the authorities we have granted it. Our Constitution, agreed to after extensive debate among a broad reach of all Americans, sets out the structure and rules within which our Federal government can function in order to protect those rights and form an environment within which we may satisfy those duties, and then it animates that government.

---

1   These are endowments of all men, but I'm writing about the United States here.

Notice, further, that our social contract hews close to the heart of the social contract described by Locke and Rousseau in that it

- Maintains the freedom of a citizen to do as he will and to own, and dispose of his own private property according to his own wishes, so long as these do not interfere with the freedom of another to do the same, and
- It maintains the sovereignty of American citizens over our nation and over the government we've hired to run it in our name.

Our social contract also proudly proclaims that no government may assume responsibility for the outcomes of an individual's actions and decisions, nor can an individual's neighbors, nor any strangers: the individual alone has that responsibility. This is why our contract acknowledges that we begin life equal—created equal, equal under law, with equal opportunity—while protecting our freedoms to pursue our own interests and to achieve our own goals without government interference. This is key: freedom to do as we will and sole ownership of our private property are inseparable from our responsibility for our actions; if we cannot act freely, if we do not own our property exclusive of all other claims, then we cannot assume that full responsibility. Finally, within the deliberately broad framework of "all other rights and powers," our Constitution singles out for special mention a non-exhaustive list of specific freedoms that all Americans, as sovereign individuals, have—our Bill of Rights.

From the other side of this acknowledgment of individual rights, our contract also specifically limits our government to a short list of specific authorities, and it explicitly states that all other powers and authorities not specifically named for the Federal government belong to our American States and to we American citizens.

Among the powers authorized our Federal government, for instance, is the authority to regulate the interstate aspect of the commerce of businesses. These clauses in our Constitution,

- Article I, Section 8, Clause 3 (the "Commerce Clause"),
- Article I, Section 9, Clauses 1, 5, and 6, and
- Article I, Section 10

taken as a whole, authorize the government to regulate what the States may do with respect to commerce across their boundaries. These limits were applied by our Founders with a view to reminding the States that they were no longer mutually competitive independent nation-type polities but were now cooperative, equal members of a larger Union, the United States. These Sections and Clauses did not authorize the government to do any other thing concerning the commerce of Americans, either directly among themselves or indirectly through the agency of businesses they might form.[2]

More generally, Article I, Sections 8 and 9, together with the 10th Amendment, set out quite clearly the limits of Federal authority, in our commerce, and in our affairs generally. The "general welfare" clause can only be read in the context in which it is provided: to enact laws within the powers specifically enumerated in the rest of Article I, Section 8. This limited set of authorizations and the broader set of limitations on the government's powers is, in part, a recognition that when a government regulates business, it also regulates what a citizen may do. To tell a business what it may or may not produce, how much it may produce, and at what price it may sell what it produces is to tell the citizens who are the business how they must comport themselves in their private business. Further, it is to tell every other citizen what he may or may not buy; how much he may, or may not, buy; and at what price he will buy. Regulating business thus regulates, and abridges, the natural right of a citizen to enter into his own arrangement for an exchange of goods and services with his fellow citizens.

Concerning a citizen's relationship with his fellows and with the government that works for him, and the specific rights flowing from these relationships, consider the following. Since our founding, one of the truths we've held to be self-evident is that all men are created equal, not just some of us. We hold, further, that all men have inalienable rights to Life, Liberty, and the pursuit of Happiness. We animated these natural rights via, among other vehicles, the Bill of Rights in our Constitution, which also emphasizes the essential subordination of the government to the citizen. These rights and liberties of men, that should have been self-evident from our social contract, turned out

---

2   At bottom a business is nothing more than an agency of men. Although a business has legal status as a separate entity, this status exists only in certain narrowly prescribed areas. Any business gets its purpose and animation from the men who form it and populate it, and from no other source.

not to be so, or were ignored outright, and this failure drove us into the Civil War. In the aftermath of that tragedy, then, we modified our social contract, in accordance with the rules we had set out for doing this, and we made these rights and liberties explicit via the 13th, 14th, and 15th Amendments to our Constitution: that no man may own, or otherwise coerce, another; that all citizens are equal under the law, not just some of us; and that all citizens can, and may, vote—not just some of us. All men truly are created equal, with natural rights that cannot be severed from us by any agency of man.

This recognition, finally achieved, that our fundamental rights are inherent in each of our very existences, and with that recognition that the citizens are sovereign, and government is limited in its powers; is subordinate to; responsible to; and works for that sovereign, makes the United States unique, indeed exceptional, on the global stage.

Despite the (clarified) tenets of our social contract, though, we are seeing the Federal government's increasing involvement in the lives and affairs of American citizens in contravention of its authorized role. In general, the expansion of government and of government's insertion into the affairs of the citizens have occurred in conjunction with major economic dislocations (thus one of those expansions has been economic: increasing encroachment of our freedoms through increasing regulation of our commerce). The modern Liberals and Progressives driving these encroachments, of course, have always asserted the best of intentions, trying to do well by us and by our nation; in general, there is little reason to doubt their claims. *So are they all, all honorable men,—*[3].

What follows, now, is a brief description of that move away from our foundational principles of individual responsibility, individual morality, returns to the individual of the results of his actions. As with Chapter 1, it's important to note that this is not a history lesson, it is, instead, a very broad overview, with a vast array of details glossed over or ignored. The examples offered here are selected more or less at random (again) in order to illustrate the increasing encroachment of government into the lives of individual American citizens; to illustrate the increasing blurring of the constitutionally mandated lines drawn between the powers of the

---

3   Marc Antony, **Julius Caesar**, Act III, scene ii, William Shakespeare

Federal government and those of the several States and between the Federal government and those of citizens; and to show the outright crossing of these lines, in direct contravention of the structure and rules for governance which our Constitution provides. Following this survey, I'll offer a more complete description of a modern Conservative.

The general tenor of the Liberal/Progressive attitude is apparent from their own words. Theodore Roosevelt, operating in the aftermath of the Panic of 1893 and with the memory of the Panic of 1873 still strong, held that business was to blame for all the economic problems of the nation, and so businesses were not to be trusted. Instead, they needed to be controlled by the Executive branch of government, as he made clear in speaking about the railroads in particular: "The Government must in increasing degree supervise and regulate the workings of the railways engaged in interstate commerce. ... Such increased supervision is the only alternative to an increase of the present evils on the one hand or a still more radical policy on the other."[4]

That he was, in fact, intending to reach all businesses is apparent in his 1908 Annual Message to Congress, wherein he said,

> The chief reason, among the many sound and compelling reasons, that led to the formation of the National Government was the absolute need that the Union, and not the several States, should deal with interstate and foreign commerce; and the power to deal with interstate commerce was granted absolutely and plenarily to the central government.... The proposal to make the National Government supreme over, and therefore to give it complete control over, the railroads and other instruments of interstate commerce is merely a proposal to carry out to the letter one of the prime purposes, if not the prime purpose, for which the Constitution was founded.

This is an enormous leap of logic that attempts to clear a vast chasm of fact between what the Founders wrote for the Commerce Clause, and those

---

4   Annual Message to Congress, 1904

turn-of-the-century Progressives' attempts to use it to gain government control over citizens' commerce. Although he failed, several Supreme Court decisions supported his attempts,[5] and Woodrow Wilson later did succeed in expanding this intrusion.

Franklin Delano Roosevelt, governing during the Great Depression, shared his second cousin's disdain for business. Business was to blame this time, he asserted, for the Depression. However, FDR broadened this to include a view of the inherent incapacity of American citizens. He led the evolution of the modern Liberal's perspective to the point that Americans were considered incapable of seeing to their own ends and needs, and we must, instead, have government provide welfare benefits for us. FDR said, in his 1932 nomination acceptance speech, "Throughout the nation men and women, forgotten in the political philosophy of the Government, look to us here for guidance and for more equitable opportunity to share in the distribution of national wealth...." Within this claim that government knows better is FDR's belief in taking wealth from the successful and transferring it to others by government fiat.

In the 21st century, the Progressive Obama administration has extended this attitude. His Progressives know better than the common American, government is the only proper vehicle for determining the efforts and rewards of American citizens and of who should garner the rewards from those efforts, and so these Progressives push for an ever-increasing dependency of Americans on government. The Obama administration explicitly disparages an American citizen's right to control his own property, including his own money and his own path to creating his own wealth. In October 2008, Candidate Obama, responding to a citizen questioner in Toledo, OH, who asked "Your new tax plan is going to tax me more, isn't it?" said, "I think when you spread the wealth around, it's good for everybody." And President Obama said at a rally in Quincy, IL in April 2010, "I think at a certain point, you've made enough money." Here is the Progressive saying in so many words that an American's wealth—an American's property—isn't the individual's; Progressives in government know better how to dispose

---

5   One such was *United States v Delaware & Hudson Co.*, 213 U. S. 366 (1909), which placed interstate railroad companies themselves within the purview of Congressional control under the Commerce Clause.

this property, how this money should be spent, what constitutes sufficient wealth.

Despite repeated town hall meetings beginning in the Congressional recess of August 2009, in which Americans vociferously expressed their objections to the Patient Protection and Affordable Care Act (PPACA), and despite repeated polls (Schoen, Rasmussen, Gallup, *et al.*,) showing overall, and steadily growing, disapproval of the bill, the Democratic Party passed it unilaterally. Indeed, the legislation was so unpopular, that it had to be assembled in the back offices of the Senate Majority Leader's Senate office suite, with the President present and the doors locked explicitly against the minority party. When the bill finally was presented for floor vote in both houses of Congress, amendments were not allowed, debate was extremely limited, and Democratic Party Representatives and Senators admitted they had not even read the 2,000-plus pages of the Act before they voted for it in 2010. Indeed, at one point, the Democratic Party Speaker of the House announced that the Congress would "have to pass the bill so that you can find out what is in it."[6] And as information came out on what these Progressives had put "in it," the uproar increased.

The following examples show, within that Liberal/Progressive, Patrician vs. commoner mindset, various administrations have steadily eroded Americans' ability to act for themselves and worked diligently to create— and then to enhance—a dependency on government for our welfare. In FDR's first presidential term, he seized the property of private citizens— their privately held gold—in direct contravention of our social contract, and without even the fig leaf of legislative action: he did this by diktat.[7] He instituted price controls on farm products, at prices higher than extant in the market at the time, and at higher prices than Americans, already suffering massive unemployment, could afford to pay.[8] He instituted price,

---

6   "Pelosi Remarks at the 2010 Legislative Conference for National Association of Counties," Press Release, 03/09/2010, available from Rep. Pelosi's Web site, http://www.speaker.gov/newsroom/pressreleases?id=1576, as I write this in Fall 2011.

7   **Executive Order** 6102, signed in April 1933, made all privately held gold of American citizens property of the US Treasury. That citizens were paid $20.67 for each ounce seized in no way makes this less confiscatory. Americans did not have the opportunity to voluntarily enter into, or to decline, the exchange; failure to comply put them at risk of a $10,000 (over $97,000 today) fine and/or 10 years in prison. Further, the duplicity of the exchange is demonstrated by the administration's subsequent debasement of the dollar from $20.67/oz. of gold to $35/oz.

8   Agricultural Adjustment Administration (AAA). The AAA also tried to force higher prices by

wage, and work rule controls in other industries (*vis.*, refined petroleum products and their transportation, electric utilities, and steel).[9] All of these worked to limit citizens' choices in the market, prevent them even from controlling their own labor, and to increase both the government's role in citizen decisions and the citizen's dependency on government for those decisions.

In his second term, with the Supreme Court having ruled that key parts of his New Deal legislation were unconstitutional, FDR overtly attacked this third, equal, branch of the Federal government and tried to pack the Court with an additional five Justices, all to be appointed by him. Although his Judiciary Reorganization Bill ultimately failed, he succeeded in cowing the Court, and it was much more compliant to his legislation thereafter (we'll see specific examples later in this book). This now willing subordination was solidified by FDR's ultimate ability to pack the court, anyway; by 1941, eight of the nine Justices had died or retired, and their replacements were his appointees.

The Lyndon Johnson administration continued this encroachment, initiating as dangerous an attack on explicit Constitutional rights as any of FDR's. The Gun Control Act of 1968 attempted to limit a critical clause of our Constitution,[10] agreed to by our Founders explicitly in response to the need to guard against an overweening central government. This act, among other things, gave control over the sale of firearms to the government, it reserved to the government the sole authority to determine who should be allowed to act as intermediary in any interstate purchase or sale of a citizen's firearm, and it gave the Federal government, in place of individual Americans, the power to determine the legitimate purposes of owning weapons.[11] It's important to note that this 2nd Amendment infringement also represents an expansion of government intrusion into Americans' ability to engage freely in commerce with each other by asserting government authority to determine what products are fit for interstate commerce at all.

---

paying farmers to take land out of crop production.

9   National Industrial Recovery Act (NIRA) of 1933

10   2nd Amendment: "A well regulated Militia, being necessary to the security of a free State, the right of the people to keep and bear Arms, shall not be infringed."

11   The government decided the weapons had to be "sporting" weapons before they could be imported, and it was the government's definition of "sporting" that was to be enforced.

Turning now specifically to a citizen's ability to engage in commerce with his fellows, and the government's encroachment on that ability, we see the following sequence of events. Theodore Roosevelt inaugurated an early expansion of government regulation/control of business with the Elkins and Hepburn Acts.[12] Roosevelt's rationale for these was that specific customers and railroads colluded too much at the expense of competing railroads and customers, which was a valid concern, as far as it went. That he was actually outright Federal control is made clear from his decision not to act under existing law (*vis.*, the Sherman Antitrust Act) to break up these collusions, and his remarks cited above.

Woodrow Wilson continued this liberal trend of government intrusion into commerce with his support of the Clayton Antitrust Act. This law was claimed to benefit the economy and the citizens by reducing the likelihood that monopoly abuses even would get started. However, Section 7 of the Act allows the Federal Trade Commission and the Department of Justice to regulate all business mergers, and it gives the government discretion to approve or reject a merger, solely on the speculation that monopoly abuses might occur[13]—legalizing prior restraint. Additionally, the businesses involved could appeal such a decision, and the legal burden was shifted from the government having to prove an abuse actually exists to the prospective, newly merged business having to prove that a violation *will not* occur. Further, Clayton specifically excludes unions from the antitrust provisions of Sherman, which has the effect not only of overturning *Loewe v Lawlor*,[14] concerning the right of unions to engage in strike activity, it allows union monopoly control of labor to exist and allows unions to use that monopoly power to coerce business.

---

12   1903 and 1906, respectively. These two acts worked to give the Federal government increased control over the business decisions of rates to be charged by railroads, with the Hepburn Act extending these fee controls to several other modes of interstate transportation, as well.

13   This despite the fact that the Supreme Court, in 1911, had established the doctrine of the "rule of reason:" not all big companies, and not all monopolies, are evil; and the courts (not the Executive branch) are to make that decision. To be harmful, a trust had somehow actually to damage the economic environment of its competitors. The application of the rule of reason, further, flew in the face of the liberal assumption that decisions concerning the potentiality of—much less actual—abuses by "big" businesses belonged in the Executive, not the Judicial, branch.

14   *Loewe v Lawlor*, 208 U.S. 274 (1908) (also referred to as the *Danbury Hatters' Case.*) In this case, a business had declared itself to be an open shop (union membership not a requirement for employment), resulting in union boycotting and striking against the business in an attempt to coerce a change to a union shop. Ultimately, the Supreme Court ruled that the unions' behavior was a violation of the Sherman Antitrust Act and disallowed boycotts and strikes having such purposes.

During FDR's administration, *Nebbia v New York*[15] demonstrated a developing erosion of the Supreme Court's understanding of the Commerce Clause, even though the Court had held that New York state could implement price controls on milk, in accordance with that state's right to manage its own internal affairs. Associate Justice Owen Roberts's opinion for the court acquiesced to the administration in this way: "[T]his court from the early days affirmed that the power to promote the general welfare is inherent in government," thus beginning the distortion of the general welfare clause into giving the Federal government authority to intervene in intrastate commerce, rather than remaining limited strictly to national affairs.

In 1942, the successfully packed Supreme Court, a willing accomplice in the Roosevelt administration's arrogation of the rights of individual citizens to make their own commercial decisions, showed its full complicity with its *Wickard v Filburn*[16] ruling. The magnitude of this blow to our freedoms under our social contract can be seen by looking at prior rulings of the Supreme Court, from a time when it was an equal branch of the Federal government, and not simply an arm of the Roosevelt administration. Since our nation's birth, Supreme Court rulings had specifically acknowledged the Constitutional limits to the Federal government's power to regulate commerce: the Commerce Clause, the related Section 9 clauses, and Section 10 were well understood to regulate commerce solely among the several States and to regulate only the commerce of a product in being, explicitly excluding the original production of that product, regardless of the purpose of producing it (*e.g.*, for interstate trafficking). *Kidd v Pearson* and *United States v E. C. Knight Co.*,[17] for instance, had held explicitly that production activities were separate from commerce activities, and so were not subject to regulation under the Commerce clause. *Wickard*, at a stroke, reversed

---

15   291 US 502 (1934).

16   *Wickard v Filburn*, 317 US 111 (1942), dramatically increased the power of the federal government to regulate individual economic activity. A farmer, Roscoe Filburn, was growing wheat to feed his chickens. The U.S. government had imposed limits on wheat production for interstate commerce, in order to manipulate wheat prices during the Great Depression, and Filburn was growing more than the limits permitted. Filburn was ordered to destroy his crops and pay a fine, even though he was producing the "excess" wheat for his own use and had no intention of selling it. The Supreme Court, reinterpreting the United States Constitution's Commerce Clause, decided that because Filburn's wheat growing activities reduced the amount of wheat he would buy for chicken feed on the open market, and because wheat was traded nationally, Filburn's production for personal use was affecting interstate commerce, and so could be regulated by the federal government.

17   128 U.S. 1 (1888) and 156 U.S. 1 (1895), respectively.

over a century of interstate commerce practice and Supreme Court rulings. *Wickard* now placed farm production, *in toto*, under government control and removed that control from the farmers' own—or the State's—hands.

The Eisenhower administration continued this erosion, albeit at a slower pace. This administration expanded the New Deal with its Soil Bank and acreage retirement programs. The Soil Bank, in particular, far from supporting farming and farmers, as was actually intended, actually inhibited individuals from entering farming.[18]

The Progressive Obama administration has expanded the claimed powers of the Commerce clause beyond all recognition. The PPACA, also known as Obamacare, includes a mandate that all Americans buy health insurance, whether we want it or not, and whether we need it or not. In a breathtaking expansion of the claimed authorities of the Commerce Clause, Americans now are instructed that we must take part in this commerce as a condition of being an American. No longer is the government "merely" instructing an American as to what he may or may not buy; now the government is demanding—coercing—that the citizen *must* buy.

Additionally, commerce rights, and rights generally, are completely abrogated by the Obama administration's Environmental Protection Agency (EPA). When Congress explicitly rejected carbon tax legislation, President Obama's EPA functionally overruled the people's representatives and ignored legitimate commercial concerns to enact its own regulations to tax these emissions.[19]

The Dodd–Frank Wall Street Reform and Consumer Protection Act of 2010 is another example of the Progressives' goal of taking business decisions out of the hands of business and courts and placing them in the hands of Federal

---

18   See, for instance, an interview with Terry Schrick, who said he was unable to enter farming at all due to the unavailability of land, published at http://www.livinghistoryfarm.org/farminginthe50s/movies/schrick_money_05.html# as I write this in Fall 2011. The Soil Bank system also worked, counterintuitively, to suppress prices the remaining farmers could get by not allowing market forces to operate free from government restraint. By paying people to idle their land, rather than renting it out, land was made unavailable to new farmers.

19   "EPA Formally Announces Phase-in of Clean Air Act Permitting for Greenhouse Gases/Agency reiterates no stationary source requirements until 2011," Release date: 03/29/2010; and "DOT, EPA Set Aggressive National Standards for Fuel Economy and First Ever Greenhouse Gas Emission Levels For Passenger Cars and Light Trucks," Release date: 04/01/2010

bureaucrats, who presume to know better what decisions need to be made. The Act, for instance, sets up an Executive bureaucracy, a "resolution regime," ostensibly complementing existing FDIC authority to "allow for orderly winding down of bankrupt firms." This denigrates the existing regime, whereby business' owners were making their own decisions concerning their business' recovery and/or entry into bankruptcy proceedings. This also deprecates the judiciary's bankruptcy courts, which had been overseeing the "orderly winding down," or emergence from bankruptcy, for those businesses whose owners had chosen this route.

The Act intrudes into freedoms in other ways. It includes provisions for the Federal Reserve Bank (the "Fed") to receive authorization from the United States Treasury Department for extensions of credit in "unusual or exigent circumstances," thereby encoding a concept of "too big to fail in the market" into US law and making individuals unrelated to those "failing" businesses pay for those "failures" with Federal tax revenue to guarantee that credit. This Fed (selective) extension of credit also overrules business decisions and legitimate market forces, placing success or failure itself squarely in the hands of Federal bureaucrats. Further, the Act specifically authorizes the bureaucratic regime, with no oversight by our elected representatives, to nationalize broad sectors of the American financial industry should the victim companies be viewed by these bureaucrats to be threats to our economy—and the bureaucrats are the ones who will define of "threat."

When we look at the Liberals' and Progressives' view of the American citizen, of an individual's relationship with his fellows and with his government, and of his individual rights—these 20th century-styled civil rights—we find an appalling and highly restrictive record. Woodrow Wilson, for instance, openly ignored the 14th Amendment with his blatantly segregationist policies. Indeed, he reversed the trend toward integration of blacks into the Federal government, a trend which had been accelerated by Theodore Roosevelt and William Howard Taft, by actively supporting his Cabinet Secretaries in their (re)establishment of official policies of segregation in their government offices, including offices that had been integrated since the middle of the Civil War. Wilson went so far as to spend public money to build separate buildings for black employees. When called on this, Wilson responded, "…segregation is not a humiliation but a benefit, and ought to be so regarded by you gentlemen."[20] He later told the *New York Times*, "If the colored people made a mistake in voting for me, they ought to correct it,"[21] or, as a President would echo in a later time, with similar arrogant self-importance, "That's what elections are for." President Wilson, this Liberal, actively denied a significant portion of American citizens their rights under our social contract because he knew better what those rights should be and who should have them.

FDR's performance on civil rights, and the applicability of our social contract to all Americans, was at best hypocritical, with the practical effect that he continued Wilson's racist policies. Although his mouth said the words that lynching was "a vile form of collective murder,"[22] he actively opposed anti-lynching legislation: his New Deal legislation was more important than actually enforcing equality for all Americans, and he thought he needed the support of Southern Jim Crow Democrats to get his New Deal legislation through Congress. Although he ruled by fiat[23] (not legislation) that the defense industry could not use "race, creed, color, or national origin" as hiring criteria, he refused to desegregate our armed forces, denying the men and women called upon to die in defense of our social contract the equal standing that this contract should have provided them. In 1942, Roosevelt announced, in so many words, that Americans, in fact, are not all equal.[24] He seized and imprisoned until 1945 some 120,000 Americans of Japanese descent, 11,000 Americans of German descent, 3,000 Americans of Italian descent; he further applied strict freedom of movement restrictions to 600,000 more Americans of Italian descent, although these restrictions were lifted in late 1942.

The Obama administration and the Progressive Congress of 2008 moved further to marginalize us Americans, and to make us outright wards of the government. These Progressives are direct descendants of the Wilson and

---

20   Quoted by Mary Beth Norton, Carol Sheriff, David M. Katzman, David W. Blight, Howard P. Chudacoff in **A People And A Nation: A History of the United States, Since 1865**. Since Wilson regarded blacks as inherently inferior, he considered segregation to be a means of according them the special protections they needed.

21   *New York Times* November 13, 1914.

22   Cited in University Publications of America, **The Documentary History of the Franklin D. Roosevelt Presidency**, Vol. 11, "FDR and Protection from Lynching, 1934-1945."

23   **Executive Order 8802**,the **Fair Employment Act**, 1941.

24   **Executive Order 9066**, 1942.

Roosevelt Liberals, with a similar disregard for our civil rights as individuals, although in a different manner from their predecessors. Our Progressives regard themselves as a modern Patrician class who know better than we do how we should comport ourselves, what our rights should be, and above all how we should be governed. The logical outcome of the individual mandate in Obamacare (itself a direct result of *Wickard*), for instance, is this. If the Federal government can require, under the Commerce Clause or any other rationale, an individual to buy one product (for instance, health insurance), then that government can require that same American to buy another product, also (a particular automobile, perhaps). That government can require that American to not buy yet another product (a firearm, perhaps). And generally that government can require that American to buy, or not buy, on the government's schedule and at the government's dictated price. We will have lost our freedom of choice, and our control over our own property with this single act, which is the pride and joy of the Obama Progressives: they passed it even at the expense of recovering our economy during the present, ongoing economic crisis.

These Progressives, these Patricians, further demonstrate their belief in their own superiority with their penchant for rule by Executive fiat, their slander of the American people, and by their naked extortion of businesses and of Americans themselves. We have Department of Homeland Security Secretary Janet Napolitano, in the context of excessive airport security protocols involving the "choice" of being imaged nude or being physically searched (including handling of breasts and groins) as a requirement of being allowed to travel by air saying, "Look, everybody has a role to play. And if people don't want to play that role, if they want to travel by some other means, of course that's their right. This is the United States...."[25] (Benjamin Franklin knew better than this false choice.[26]) We have President Obama recess appointing Dr. Donald Berwick to serve as Administrator of the Centers for Medicare and Medicaid Services, bypassing the Senate and its advice and consent role. Mr. Obama's stated reason for bypassing the Senate—after leaving the position vacant for 15 months before nominating

---

25   Her statement, 15 Nov 2010, in response to the hue and cry from a traveler advising a TSA agent (and filming a portion of the incident), "If you touch my junk, I'll have you arrested."

26   Those who would give up Essential Liberty to purchase a little Temporary Safety, deserve neither Liberty nor Safety.

any one at all—makes his disdain for the people's representatives clear.[27] As a result, we have a man in control of health services who sees health care as necessarily a transfer of wealth from one person to another by government diktat.[28]

The Obama administration and its allies have kept up a steady drumbeat of slanderous attacks against us, the American people, their bosses. During and after the town hall meetings of late summer/early fall 2009, then Democratic Party Speaker of the House Nancy Pelosi referred to the Tea Party attendees of the town halls as Astroturfers and as swastika-carriers, then Democratic Party Majority Leader Steny Hoyer dismissed American protestors of Obamacare as Un-American, then Democratic Party Senate Majority Leader Harry Reid compared objections to the breathtaking speed with which Obamacare was being rammed through to objections to ending slavery, the news media[29] dismissed Obamacare protestors as fundamentally racist, the President himself dismissed American citizens as too stupid to understand his message, or alternatively, he hadn't dumbed down his message enough for us to understand.[30]

Kathleen Sebelius, Obama's Secretary of Health and Human Services, threatened to lock insurance companies out of Obamacare's health insurance markets if they persisted in criticizing it and raising their premiums in response to the increased costs engendered by it.[31] When several large

---

27   Through the Obama's then White House Communications Director, Dan Pfeiffer, in July 2010: "In April, President Obama nominated Dr. Donald Berwick to serve as Administrator of the Centers for Medicare and Medicaid Services (CMS). Many Republicans in Congress have made it clear in recent weeks that they were going to stall the nomination as long as they could, solely to score political points.

"But with the agency facing new responsibilities to protect seniors' care under the Affordable Care Act, there's no time to waste with Washington game-playing. That's why tomorrow the President will use a recess appointment to put Dr. Berwick at the agency's helm and provide strong leadership for the Medicare program without delay."

28   "Excellent health care is by definition redistributional." 2008 speech celebrating the 60th anniversary of the U.K.'s National Health Service.

29   http://www.huffingtonpost.com/ray-hanania/opposition-to-obama-healt_b_242938.html, for instance, in as I write this in Fall 2011.

30   "Part of the reason that our politics seems so tough right now, and facts and science and argument do not seem to be winning the day all the time, is because we're hard-wired not to always think clearly when we're scared" October 2010 fundraiser; "Making an argument that people can understand, I think that we haven't always been successful at that." CBS **60 Minutes** interview, November 2010.

31   Letter to America's Health Insurance Plans, September 2009.

companies filed SEC documentation announcing extra charges against their revenues that were directly caused by Obamacare-related increased costs, the then Democratic Party Chairman of the House Energy and Commerce Committee threatened to summon them to his hearings to explain their inappropriate actions.[32] Following one American's objection to the new TSA airport security procedure mentioned above, the TSA's head of the San Diego office called a press conference specifically to announce the opening of an investigation of the American and to threaten to fine him thousands of dollars.[33] The TSA later retracted the threat to fine, but they cannot remove the threat created by their investigation and the prior existence of their threat to punish a dissent. It is clear from all of this that Progressives view Americans' civil rights, our freedoms, our liberties, as stemming from the wisdom of their governance, in the finest tradition of Edmund Burke, rather than as inherent in our very being.

Furthermore, the Progressive movement have completely changed the landscape of the American economy, where individual citizens should be free to trade with each other solely in accordance with agreements they make with each other. For instance, the insurance industry has been transformed over the past two decades or more from a voluntary, fee-based business of risk transfer into a mandatory, privately funded, government controlled welfare entitlement program. This enlarges the moral hazard for Americans by increasing our dependence on government and decreasing our responsibility for our own actions—as well as decreasing our ability to enjoy the rewards of our own actions. Dodd-Frank, as I've stated earlier, encodes the ability to be "too big to fail" into law. It also takes the definition of "too big" out of the hands of the market of citizens interacting of their own accord, and for those businesses which are allowed to fail, it takes the terms of failure away from the business owners, its creditors, and the courts, and gives control to government bureaucrats, who will determine for themselves who will fail and who will succeed. This makes it extremely difficult for investors to value businesses accurately for investments, and this further

---

32   For instance, March 26, 2010 Waxman letter to Mr Randall Stephenson, Chairman, President, CEO of AT&T. A copy can be found at http://democrats.energycommerce.house.gov/Press_111/20100326/Stephenson.Letter.pdf as I write this in Fall 2011.

33   **The San Diego Union-Tribune**, 15 November 2010, has one version of this story at http://www.signonsandiego.com/news/2010/nov/15/tsa-probe-scan-resistor/ as I write this in Fall 2011.

restricts economic growth and the freedoms and rights of Americans as actors in the economy and as investors in our businesses.

This intrusion of government and its usurpation of Americans' liberties extends the moral hazard to our children. Obamacare, for instance, encourages retention of Americans on their parents' health plans until these "children" are 26 years old. This not only artificially inflates parents' costs at a time when they should be accumulating wealth and assets for their own retirement (rather than depending on direct wealth transfers from the children of strangers, as the current Social Security/Medicare miasma requires), but it denies, also, these "adult" children the opportunity to step out on their own, to seek their own fortune, to have the responsibilities and benefits of their own success.

We see, in the end, these results. The *Nebbia* argument confuses individual, inalienable rights to liberty with "the general welfare" and uses the "general welfare" rubric to drive a government wedge between an American citizen and his inalienable rights. *Nebbia* also has significance as a case in which the Court abandoned its distinction between the "public" and "private" spheres of economic activity: both now are within the government's purview. This decision then flowed, leading to creation of a government power to control wages, a citizen's labor generally, and assertively expand the power of the U.S. Congress to regulate commerce. *Nebbia* also denied the individual the freedom to set his price at a lower level than that mandated by the government. A minority of Justices understood the dangers of this; Justice James C. McReynolds dissented, providing a lengthy discussion of the history and application of the Due Process Clause, ultimately concluding that although "regulation to prevent recognized evils in business has long been upheld as permissible legislative action … fixation of the price at which A, engaged in an ordinary business, may sell, in order to enable B, a producer, to improve his condition, has not been regarded as within legislative power," adding "This is not regulation, but management, control, dictation." His dissent was joined by Justice Willis Van Devanter, Justice George Sutherland, and Justice Pierce Butler. However, by the time of *Wickard*, they had retired or died, and so they no longer could hope to keep the Court's understanding of the purpose of the Commerce Clause intact.

Wickard expanded on this encroachment. With this ruling, the Supreme

Court decided that when examining whether some activity was considered "commerce" under the Constitution, the Court now must speculate on the future and estimate the total effect the activity might have on interstate commerce. Intrastate activities, specifically including production now, could fall within the scope of the Commerce Clause, if those activities could have some possible effect on interstate commerce. Justice Robert Jackson said [emphasis mine],

> Whether the subject of the regulation in question was "production," "consumption," or "marketing" is, therefore, not material for purposes of deciding the question of federal power before us.... But **even if appellee's activity be local and though it may not be regarded as commerce, it may still**, whatever its nature, **be reached by Congress** if it exerts a substantial economic effect on interstate commerce and this **irrespective of whether such effect is what might at some earlier time have been defined as "direct" or "indirect."**

Wickard thus rendered farmers who grow a crop that is regulated as an interstate commerce product unable to grow that crop solely for personal use and not for commerce. *Wickard* meant that these individual citizens no longer were allowed full control over their own labor or over their own labor's output, having had this appropriated by government. *Nebbia* and *Wickard*, together, further asserted the superiority of the government's right to regulate a citizen's production over the citizen's right to regulate his own. By extension, all of us citizens now have lost control of the fruits of our own labor: if it might have an effect on interstate commerce, after *Wickard*, the Federal government may regulate it—and us. The Supreme Court had, in fact, presaged this attitude toward individual rights under the Constitution in *United States v Darby Lumber Co.*.[34] the Court said, appallingly, the 10th Amendment "is but a truism" and not an independent limitation on Congressional power. Obamacare's individual mandate extends this governmental control to all aspects of our behavior.

These distortions in rights have immediate, practical effects on Americans, also—with additional impacts on our moral state. *Wickard* and the other

---

34   Chief Justice Harlan Stone, in 312 U.S. 100 (1941)

CONSERVATISM VS. MODERN LIBERALISM

cases, coupled with the price controls implemented by the government in the form of price supports in 1954,[35] meant American citizens were paying Federally mandated inflated prices and buying less than they wanted, while the farmers' income continued its artificially created downward spiral. And as farmers' debt continued to rise, exacerbated by their falling income, they were increasingly unable even to leave their farms and find other, better paying work.

With the government asserting its right to determine the legitimate purposes of owning weapons (Gun Control Act of 1968), it is asserting its right to determine that there are no legitimate purposes for owning weapons. The only purpose, though, that a government has in disarming (Americans) is to eliminate our power and to assert its own absolute power. This move comes despite the fact that the 2d Amendment is quite clear: "...the right of the people to keep and bear Arms, shall not be infringed." The government wasted no time abusing its newly asserted authority, by the way, immediately beginning a program of illegal prosecutions and harassments of Americans over their firearms. By 1982, fully 75 percent of government prosecutions of Americans over possession of firearms were found to be constitutionally improper.[36]

The trend, clearly, has been for today's Liberals and modern Progressives (of whom Theodore Roosevelt's Progressives were ancestor) to seek to increase the size and power of the Federal government, and today's Progressives are actively seeking to change the very fabric of our government; of our social contract that authorizes and animates that government, bypassing that same contract's defined procedures for achieving such fundamental changes; and of our economy, a major venue within which Americans interact with each other. The damage done to American individual liberties and to the structure of our social contract is no less extensive for all their professed good intentions.

We see, then, that the roles of Liberal and Conservative at our founding have been reversed. The modern Liberal still seeks large, often radical,

---

35   Agricultural Trade Development and Assistance Act, extending the price support efforts of the New Deal.

36   *Report of the Subcommittee on the Constitution of the Committee on the Judiciary, United States Senate, 97th Congress, Second Session* (February 1982)

and rapid, change; while the modern Conservative, while recognizing the need for change, looks for slower, reasoned change, and that only when necessary. However, the Liberal of today—and his successor, the modern Progressive—wants that change to be a hard move away from our founding principles of individual freedom and individual responsibility and hard move toward a large government with greatly increased authority to manage our (individual) freedoms and responsibilities for us. The Progressive, particularly, is in an enormous hurry to bring about these changes as quickly as possible: Obamacare is a 2000-page law that, at critical junctures, was forced to Congressional votes in the dark of night before the vast majority of legislators had had a chance to read it. Dodd-Frank is 1800 pages, most legislators had not read this bill when they voted on it, and it was scraped together in similar secretive hurry. The Tory Conservative of the 18th century has passed through modern liberalism and become outright Progressive.

I have gotten at what a modern Conservative isn't through describing the liberal/progressive move away from our original, uniquely American values. Here, now, is my definition of what a modern Conservative is. Today's Conservative lives by the principles codified in our social contract, written 230 years ago, which has needed modification only a few times, and then only after open national debate of those specific Amendments. A modern Conservative trusts to the wisdom, talent, and strength of the individual American citizen, acting individually or in concert with his fellows, to resolve crises and to make better lives for ourselves and our children, doing so without the hindrance of government welfare. This Conservative recognizes that on those rare occasions where government assistance is warranted, that assistance must be narrowly defined and short-lived. The modern Conservative lives by the tenets provided, at the end of the preceding chapter, as the definition of an 18th Century Liberal.

We have, today, then, the overriding tasks of

- Reversing the damage done by the modern Liberal and his Progressive successors,
- Restoring our society to the safety of our social contract,
- Restoring our government to its original minimalist structure and behavior, and
- Returning government to its sole purpose of protecting our rights

and freedoms—leaving us free to pursue our own Happiness, our own Lives, within our Liberties, bearing responsibility for our own outcomes and enjoying the rewards of our own efforts—rather than usurping these.

Today's Conservative, thus, has the role of restoring and preserving what our 18th Century Liberal forebears produced with blood, toil, and the fire of Rebellion. For the rest of this work, now, I'll use 18th Century Liberal and modern Conservative interchangeably; although I'll use modern Conservative more often, and I'll shorten that to Conservative most often.

At this point, having reviewed the conditions leading to and surrounding the genesis of the American social contract—our Declaration of Independence and our Constitution—and the government created and animated by these documents, and then having reviewed how we've drifted so far from those basic tenets in the last 100 years, I'll pause for a bit and explore other aspects of conservatism: faith, citizenship, nationhood, fairness, the economy, and government; and then I'll briefly contrast these with modern liberalism and progressivism. By then conclusions should be self-evident, but I'll offer some of mine at that point.

CHAPTER 3—FAITH

If there were only one religion in England, we should have to fear despotism; if there were two, they would cut each other's throats; but there are thirty, and they live in peace and happiness.

— **Voltaire**

The fundamental tenets of the American social contract, as I have written before, and I'll repeat again, are that all men are created equal, that we have rights that are inseparable from us by any agency of man because they are gifts from our Creator, and that included in this endowment are the rights to Life, Liberty, and the pursuit of Happiness. These are the American articulation of the natural right of all men: the right to do as any man will so long as that does not interfere with the right of another man to do as he will. The American social contract follows through on this through its existence as an agreement of the members of this contract, American citizens, to accept minimal limits on this right for the purpose of forming a government subordinate and responsive to us for the sole purpose of protecting this right and our freedoms. Thus, we accept minimal limits on our right to free speech: we cannot shout "Fire" in a crowded theater, and we cannot slander another, for instance. We allow this government, our collective employee, to search our private property and our person, under certain narrowly prescribed conditions, in order to facilitate our employee's ability to protect us from the larger loss represented by some preying on others, for instance. Limits such as these in our social contract plainly are applied at the point where the behavior in question impacts the behavior of another.

So it is in the context of this chapter: we demand freedom of religion, and in protecting that freedom, we also demand that no faith—including the faith of atheism—can be allowed to abridge the freedom to practice any other. Further, we enjoin our government from supporting any particular faith; we also enjoin it from interfering with the practice of any particular faith. Thus, religious displays in a private setting, though viewable by the public, are permitted, and they do not interfere with a neighbor's ability to pursue his different faith or to set out his own religious displays. In the same way, religious displays on public property do not automatically represent government support for the faith represented nor an inhibition of faiths not represented. This latter aspect is addressed more explicitly later in this chapter.

Then-Candidate Obama posted on his campaign Web site,[1] "Whatever we once were, we are no longer just a Christian nation; we are also a Jewish nation, a Muslim nation, a Buddhist nation, a Hindu nation, and a nation of nonbelievers." This contrasts with Justice David Josiah Brewer's remarks contained in the unanimous opinion of the Supreme Court on *Church of the Holy Trinity v. United States* (1892), which he authored, that the United States "is a Christian nation." The one remark has been widely interpreted as being a claim that we are not a Christian nation and the other that we are exclusively a Christian nation.

Both are misinterpretations of the men's words. The fact is, simply, we are a Christian nation, founded on Judeo-Christian principles, not those of another faith, nor utilitarian[2] ones, and we were founded by men who were overwhelmingly Christian in their upbringing, education, and outlook. They were church school educated (church schools were, at the time, virtually the sole source of secondary education; this, however, does not alter the fact of the nature of their education), and they included ordained ministers in their number. Recall, though, that these men, also, were recent descendants of refugees from often bloody religious persecution in their respective Old Countries, and they were determined that the new United States would have no such failing. As firm as they were in the underlying Judeo-Christian principles which they used to inform the structure and strictures of our social contract, so then were they that firm in denying to the government being created by this new contract the ability even to conceive of a government-sponsored religion. We are, therefore, a Christian nation that, by design, is both tolerant of the beliefs of others and respectful of their

---

1   http://www.barackobama.com/pdf/ObamaonFaith.pdf , as I write this in the Fall 2011.
2   The moral worth of an action is determined solely by its usefulness in maximizing utility/minimizing negative utility: its worth is determined by its outcome. Also described as, "The ends justify the means."

right to believe differently, and that demands that others respect and accept our Christianity.

To safeguard this principle, this fundamental right of any man to his own faith, our founders built a high "wall of separation between Church & State."[3] They actively advocated religious freedom, with the blood of their own persecuted ancestors in their minds, and they designed our social contract so as to prevent any one religious belief—or a lack of belief— from dominating the government or imposing itself on society as a whole. This is the purpose of the Establishment Clause[4] and of Article VI of the Constitution.[5]

Consistent with this, the judicial branch of government, in the form of the Supreme Court, has deliberately avoided establishing a precise definition of religion, recognizing that religion is dynamic, and so protection of its freedom, and the guarantee and the realization of this protection, must be flexible and responsive over time and across the development of this nation of the United States. The Court, therefore, has interpreted religion to be any sincere and meaningful belief that occupies in the life of its possessor a place parallel to the place held by God in the lives of other persons, and it has held that there is no need for an explicit belief in the existence of God or any type of supreme being in order for one's belief to be protected by the 1st Amendment's Establishment Clause. In fact, a belief does not need even to be stated in traditional terms to be so protected. The other side of this coin applies, also: there is no requirement to follow any religion. In addition to this, Congress has carefully eschewed considering any law that would be contrary to this (and so, of course, the Executive has no thing to enforce regarding faith).

To support this intended timelessness of the guarantee and the protection, the Supreme Court has developed a three-pronged test to determine whether any statute violates the Establishment Clause. A statute is valid under this test so long as:

---

3   Thomas Jefferson, Letter to the Danbury Baptist association [sic], 1802.
4   Contained in the 1st Amendment to the Constitution of the United States of America: "Congress shall make no law respecting an establishment of religion, or prohibiting the free exercise thereof...."
5   "...no religious Test shall ever be required as a Qualification to any Office or public Trust under the United States."

- It has a secular purpose;
- Its primary effect neither advances nor inhibits religion; and
- It is not excessively entangled with religion.

Because this three-pronged test was established in *Lemon v. Kurtzman*,[6] it is known as the *Lemon* test. This test recognizes that government must accommodate religion—the "nor inhibits religion" phrase of the middle prong and the "make no law...prohibiting the free exercise thereof" part of the Establishment Clause—but forbids it from supporting any particular religion. Thus, the Supreme Court has upheld religious displays when accompanied by secular displays consistent with the holiday, religious or otherwise, being celebrated. An example of this is *Lynch v. Donnelly*.[7] The majority opinion in *Lynch* emphasized its historical context: the crèche belonged to a tradition "acknowledged in the Western World for 20 centuries, and in this country by the people, by the Executive Branch, by the Congress, and the courts for two centuries." The display, ruled the Court, passed each prong of the *Lemon* test.

Broadly based as it is on the question of endorsement, however, the court's position on a proper test for violations of the Establishment clause is narrowing, to further limit (and to make the limit more explicit) government's ability to interfere with religious practice, or its lack. In *County of Allegheny v. ACLU*,[8] Justice Anthony Kennedy produced the Coercion Test. In his quasi-dissenting majority opinion,[9] he applied the *Lemon* test with "proper

---

6   403 U.S. 602 (1971). The case that gave its name to the test actually struck down the State of Pennsylvania Superintendent of Public Instruction's attempt to reimburse nonpublic schools (most of which were Catholic) for the salaries of teachers who taught secular material in them. The Supreme Court also has applied this test inconsistently since then; however, the three prongs remain quite clear. Most of the Court's inconsistency has been in their use of the middle prong's "nor inhibits" requirement and their use of the third prong's "excessive" condition.

7   465 U.S. 668 (1984), concerning a Pawtucket, RI, display with both a life-sized nativity scene and secular symbols such as Santa's house, a Christmas tree, striped poles, animals, and lights.

8   *County of Allegheny v. ACLU*, 492 U.S. 573 (1989). The case involved the display of a nativity scene on the grand staircase of the Allegheny County Courthouse in downtown Pittsburgh, PA, and the display of a Hanukah menorah together with a Christmas tree outside the City-County Building, also in downtown Pittsburgh. In a doubly divided set of majority opinions, the Court held, with one opinion, the nativity scene to be unconstitutional and, in a separate majority opinion (whose participants overlapped, but were not the same as, the nativity scene majority), held the Hanukah-Christmas display to be constitutional.

9   Justice Kennedy dissented with the nativity scene ruling and concurred with the Hanukah-Christmas display ruling.

sensitivity to our traditions" in an attempt to improve the primary effect prong by limiting it to prohibiting the government from "coercing anyone to support or participate in any religion or its exercise." In Justice Kennedy's opinion, the *Lemon* test fails adequately to reconcile the pervasiveness of religion, even in today's society, with the pervasiveness of a government sector in the same society: the test cannot identify the border between the accommodation of religion and the establishment (or the preferential treatment) of one. A test of the degree of coercion in the government's behavior comes closer to achieving this.

The Coercion Test is based on the fact that the Establishment clause mandates two fundamental limits: government cannot require—coerce—support of, or participation in, religion, and it cannot give direct benefits to such a degree that it even appears to "establish a state religion or religious faith, or tends to do so."[10] The Coercion Test adds specificity by distinguishing between persuasion and force. If, for instance, a missionary were to proselytize, one might find his actions annoying, but one could not find them coercive. Similarly, as implied even by Justice Sandra Day O'Connor's opinion in Allegheny, a seasonal religious display, placed with a seasonal secular display, can have no coercive effect from the government that allows such a display on public property. Finally, this test adds further specificity by distinguishing between direct and indirect coercion. Direct coercion would include, for instance, government action making following one's own religious tenets (including no religion at all) more, or less, difficult. Indirect coercion, on the other hand, would include such things as the government using tax revenue to support a particular religious ministry. Notice that this leaves room for a broad array of government fund usage, including, for instance, support for an array of nonprofit welfare organizations, generally, both secular and religious. Such even-handed use of the taxpayers' monies would not violate the Establishment clause. (The general legitimacy of such uses will be addressed later in discussions of the legitimacy of Federal government social engineering efforts.)

The intended timelessness of the guarantee is thus further enhanced by the Supreme Court's evolving tests for compliance with the Establishment clause. These tests are moving in the direction of tighter, clearer limits on

---

10   From Justice John Paul Stevens' opinion for the Court in *Santa Fe Independent School Dist. v. Doe*, 530 U.S. 290 (2000).

the government's ability to interfere for, or against, religious faith and its expression.

The members of our social contract were to be free—are, and of Right ought to be Free—to choose for ourselves how we worship, and whether we will worship at all. Indeed, our very Christianity, our Judeo-Christian principle of "love one another," demand no less, and these embrace our endowment of rights. The importance of this to our founders can be understood by the statements in the documents of our American social contract. Our Declaration of Independence acknowledges our Creator's endowments, not our Puritan or Catholic God's endowments, nor even our Christian God's endowments—our Creator's endowments. Our Constitution places the injunction explicitly barring government interference in matters of religion—of faith—in our Bill of Rights, in the first clause of the first amendment.

That matters of faith are woven into the fabric of our society is clear. Our currency carries the official motto of our country: "In God We Trust." Various of our courthouses display the Ten Commandments, the courtroom of the Supreme Court prominently displays Moses holding the Ten Commandments, and the Supreme Court begins each session with a prayer.[11] Our Congress opens its sessions with a prayer. Many of our State legislatures do the same. Our Pledge of Allegiance acknowledges that we are "one nation, under God" (albeit, the pledge is currently under attack by Progressives (for its very existence as well as for the reference)). We elect men of a variety of faiths to Congress; these include Christianity, Judaism, and Islam in the 111th Congress. Our President led a national prayer for guidance and help on the morning of our entry into World War II[12] and he offered another prayer leading into the D-Day invasion;[13] he did not simply, secularly, "Cry 'Havoc!' and let slip the dogs of war."[14] Throughout our neighborhoods, plainly visible to public passersby, and on public property, scenes of the Christian Nativity are displayed during the Christmas holidays, as is the

---

11   The Court's crier calls out, "God save the United States and this honorable court."
12   "With confidence in our armed forces - with the unbounded determination of our people - we will gain the inevitable triumph - so help us God." Lee, Roger A., "The History Guy: Day of Infamy Speech (1941)," http://www.historyguy.com/day_of_infamy.html (1999) as I write this in Fall 2011.
13   "As we rise to each new day, and again when each day is spent, let words of prayer be on our lips, invoking Thy help to our efforts."
14   Marc Antony, in Shakespeare, William, **Julius Caesar**, Act III, scene i.

menorah during Hanukkah.[15] And so it is that the role of faith and the place of faith in our country are well defined. Our Declaration's statement that, "We hold these truths to be self-evident, that all men are created equal, that they are endowed by their Creator with certain unalienable Rights,…" carries the clear implication that we are inherently a Christian nation with an underlying belief that there is a God who watches over us.

That there are conflicts in our nation concerning faith need not concern us; the conflicts are superficial, for all the time spent in court over them. A man's freedom under our social contract, again, is to do, so long as he does not impact another's ability to do. Simple celebrations of faith impact no one, being not impositions of any faith on anyone, nor representing a Federal government's preference for a faith—or for no faith at all—and so this freedom is not impacted. Some will argue that it is a gross imposition on an atheist to force him to walk past a representation of the Ten Commandments or another religious symbol in order to conduct necessary business in a government building. But this "imposition" goes both ways: so it is to force a man of faith to walk through areas shorn of the Ten Commandments or other religious symbols in order to conduct necessary business in a government building. It is no imposition at all. There is no requirement to look or not to look at these displays. There is nothing extant to create an impression that such displays are pressing in on anyone. They could be ignored, as advertisements or bad art are ignored, by those to whom they do not appeal (unless there truly is a Creator's power flowing from these displays, and the atheist feels this power despite himself). There is no requirement to respond at all, in any way, to these displays, since they do not represent any selection or deselection by the Federal government.

In the end, there is no inherent conflict among faiths within this context of the fundamental right of man as articulated in our social contract if we but honor our responsibilities as citizens and respect the rights of our fellow citizens. Further, when we look at the nature of faith, we see an important similarity among them. This critical similarity occurs at the level of First Principles, the things we take to be true and that underlie an entire system of belief—whether that belief be a matter of religion or of hard science. By

---

15   Displays on public property have been the object of law suits; however, with *County of Allegheny v. ACLU*, 492 U.S. 573 (1989), the practice was ruled by the Supreme Court to be generally legitimate and not *ipso facto* a violation of the Establishment Clause.

definition, a First Principle cannot be derived from within the belief; it must be taken solely on faith. A First Principle for people of faith is that there is a Supreme Being, or Beings, Who exercises a measure of responsibility and care for us. (Note that I am not writing a religious or a philosophical tract; I will not address proofs of the existence of God here.)

A more fundamental conflict, though, would appear to be that between faith, generally, and atheism. This conflict, however, also is superficial. For atheists, a First Principle is that there is no Supreme Being. Thus, atheism is itself a matter of faith. This is the critical similarity between men of faith and atheists: both groups' belief systems flow from an article of faith; both groups believe from a form of faith.

Some outcomes are different, though, between a religious faith and a faith in atheism. An atheist's faith is that there is no point to faith, that there is no Being greater than himself; he has faith that there is only the secular world. Flowing from the First Principle of atheistic faith is the concept that we humans are at the pinnacle of life on our planet, and we alone are responsible for our welfare.

The man of atheistic faith has no one on whom to call in the hour of his need; he believes he is alone in the secular world and nonexistent in the spiritual world or the world after death since he believes those worlds do not exist. This man believes in a life that ends with the death of the body. Further, this man necessarily considers that his rights and freedoms are things which we create for ourselves or receive from a government that rules over us, since they cannot come from a Creator, and so the existence of an atheist's rights depends on the continuing good will of his sovereign government or that of his fellows. I have discussed earlier in this book the fate of men and the outcomes of rights and freedoms when these are awarded by superior governments or by other men pretending to superiority.

A religious man's faith, on the other hand, is that the point of faith is the recognition, and the worship, of a Being greater than himself,[16] a Creator to whom the religious man can turn in his hour of need; has he but maintained

---

16   There are religions that do not consider a superior Being, a God, *per se* for instance, Buddhism. This is not a religious tract; I do not treat the various religions in detail. The point of my claim is clear without that treatment.

that faith with his Creator, however imperfectly, then his Creator will keep that faith with him. From the First Principle of religious faith flows the concept that we are endowed with certain attributes, attributes that are an indivisible part of us simply because we exist and they are gifts from our Creator. The man of religious faith is secure in the knowledge that his most fundamental rights are utterly indivisible from his person; although he must, from time to time, defend with his blood that fact and those rights. This need for defense results from an inevitable tendency to slide into subordination. However, it is reversible—it is preventable—because men themselves collectively are Sovereign, not government. Further, each man is endowed with his rights as a gift from his Creator; these are not "granted" by a government, or a powerful few, that presume to define rights and freedoms and to award these, or withhold them, at whim. The man's faith informs, also, his sense of fairness and his sense of charity for those less fortunate than he, as he might be able to receive help from those better off yet than he. And, the life of faith in a Creator is a life that begins anew with the death of the body.

And yet our social contract protects the atheist, also, from his fate of depending on others for his rights and freedoms, as it both protects him from the encroachments of men of faith and protects these men from those of the man of atheism. The Sovereign consists of all of us acting in concert with each other. Our rights already are acknowledged in the documents of our social contract as part of our endowment—including the endowment that is inherent in atheists, for these are men of our Creator, also.

In the end, then, if atheists don't want to feel excluded or threatened by the religious displays of others, then it is important that they recognize that no one is excluding them; they are excluding themselves. While men of atheistic faith passively exclude themselves, though, they actively seek to exclude men of religious faith. Both exclusions need to cease. As Rousseau said, "It is impossible to live at peace with those we regard as damned; to love them would be to hate God who punishes them." This holds in both directions. Tolerance for variations of faith is what lets us live together in a varied, and thereby strong and creative, society.

As Vermont Royster wrote in a 1949 **Wall Street Journal** editorial,[17] "So the

17   *In Hoc Anno Domini*, **Wall Street Journal**, 24 December 2008, http://online.wsj.com/article/ SB123008054671531917.html, as I write this in Fall 2011.

light came into the world and the men who lived in darkness were afraid, and they tried to lower a curtain so that men would still believe salvation lay with the leaders." This is not to say that men of atheistic faith are men of darkness, but it does suggest that no man need fear, it does suggest that no man is bound to a secular leader for his salvation, it does avow that no man need be concerned for his fundamental rights because these are endowed, inalienably, in us by our Creator. If atheists feel left out by any of these principles, they need not, for two reasons. First, our American social contract is, at bottom, a secular contract, for all that we are a Christian nation, and it acknowledges (acknowledges, mind you; it cannot not grant or deny) atheists' right to believe as they will as much as it acknowledges the right of men of religious faith to believe as they will. Second, our social contract holds that all men have these rights: "...**all** men are created equal, that they are endowed by their Creator with certain unalienable Rights..." [emphasis mine], be they atheistic, agnostic, religious, or anywhere else on the spectrum.

It is clear, then, the objections of some to the contrary, faith is not only allowed to play a role in our American society, its usefulness as a stabilizing factor, both personally and in society as a whole, is well recognized. Our government is explicitly enjoined, by the design of our fundamentally Christian social contract, from inhibiting its practice, in whatever guise a citizen might choose, as zealously as it is enjoined from supporting, or seeming to support, any particular faith. These are two sides of the same American coin. It is not possible to inhibit one, or some, faiths, without at least tacitly supporting another, or others. Nor can a government actively support one without inhibiting others.

The practice of religion (or the practice of any form of morality) and the lack of such practice, both are no proper function of government. These are matters for the conscience of the individual and no other. Matters of faith, matters of morality, cannot be legislated, and they cannot be adjudicated. The flexibility of the freedom of a man to practice a faith of his own is a core strength of our society, the way we live under our social contract. To attempt to deny a man access to his faith, whether it be his faith in a Creator, or his faith in his atheism, is to attempt to deny that man the rights with which our Creator has endowed all of us, including the atheist.

CHAPTER 4—CITIZENSHIP

Just because you do not take an interest in politics doesn't mean politics won't take an interest in you.

— *Pericles*

What is citizenship? What does it mean to be a citizen of a nation? What is the difference between being a citizen of a nation and living in a nation as a non-citizen? I intend to address these questions, at the Federal level, in this chapter.

One view of the citizen is the Attic Greek view, described by Aristotle, in the context of the city (with its smaller population) as the nation. Leaving aside for the moment who was allowed to be a citizen (not slaves, for instance; women had restricted rights as members of the community; and freemen had not much more in the way of rights), a Greek citizen was a man who was, by turns, a ruler and a subject. A citizen was an administrator of justice and he shared in the offices of the government. A citizen was one who also could, and would, obey the government's laws, which his fellow citizens created and administered. Thus, the Aristotelian citizen was a leader who could follow when leading was inappropriate.

Greek citizenship necessarily ruled out monarchical forms of government, as a man in a monarchy could be only a subject, never a ruler, and the ruler never could be a subject, thus rendering the very concept of citizenship, in this sense, impossible. This drives a citizen, and the concept of citizenship, into the milieu of a republican form of polity (Aristotle disparaged democracy—mere freemen and women weren't smart enough to administer justice or to govern, but merely to obey, and in any event, decision-making by vote of the general population of citizens was too cumbersome—but that need not concern us here). Civic self-rule, as Rousseau would recognize 2,000 years later, is what legitimizes the government: it is the authoring of their own laws via the general will of citizens acting together, that makes men free and legitimizes their laws. Active participation in processes of deliberation and decision-making are what ensure that men will be citizens, not subjects. It is this republican form that enjoins a rotation of ruler and ruled among the citizen population, thereby facilitating and reinforcing citizenship. To come full circle, Aristotle defined the relationship between citizens and the city in this way: "He who has the power to take part in the deliberative or judicial administration of any state is said by us to be a citizen of that state; and, speaking generally, a state is a body of citizens sufficing for the purposes of life."[1]

But how is a citizen formed in this conceptualization? Where does citizenship originate? One potential source of citizenship is parentage. However, as Aristotle asks, how far back should we go in this determination? Any line drawn is a purely arbitrary one, all the way back to the first generation of a community, who cannot be citizens by parentage, since they will have had no citizen parents. (Rousseau recognized this, as well, 2,000 years later: a government, which cannot predate the people, cannot be the source of the people's rights and freedoms; it can only be the recipient of those authorities the previously existing people choose to grant their government.) Aristotle answers his logic in a circular way: the man who shares in governance is a citizen of the community so governed. Thus, here is the reason for the emphasis of the ancient Greeks on citizenship being founded in political behavior: the man must exist before the government can exist, yet the man cannot be a citizen until he shares in governance. Thus, the men create themselves as citizens by first forming a community of their group and then sharing in that community's governance. Others, who enter the community later, cannot be citizens of that community unless and until the existing citizens accept them into that capacity.

The paternalistic nature of the Greek government, and of the Greek citizen, is revealed by the Greeks' definition of who is fit to be a citizen—who is fit to govern and administer justice (for anyone can obey, as even the citizen must do in his turn). Children, said the Greeks, are not fit to govern. From this initial exclusion, the concept is set, and it is a short step, said they, to exclude slaves (of course) and resident aliens, and also to exclude those who do not govern—the freeman as tradesman (mechanic in Aristotle's words),

---

1   Aristotle, **Politics**, cited in **Ancient Greek Democracy: Readings and Sources**, Robinson, Eric W., 2003

who has other matters on his mind; and women, who have not the emotional capacity for the objectivity required for justice and ruling. As it is the man's job in the family to increase the value of the family's and community's moral and material wellbeing, so it the woman's to maintain these, and if they do not create, they cannot rule.

Thus, the classical Greek view of citizenship was that this was a political status, and a status of obligation toward fellow citizens, both individually and in the community of citizens, but primarily through the community. The Greek citizen actively engaged in the politics of the city's governance, ruling and administering the justice of the time, and by turns being ruled and having justice handed down for them.

The Roman view of citizenship, described by Marcus Tullius Cicero,[2] took a different tack: citizenship is a legal condition. The Roman citizen, while theoretically capable of governing—he [sic] had the mental capacity, and he could be elected to government office—was naturally more concerned with his private interests in the more complex Roman state and had little time, as a practical matter, for governing. The "ordinary" Roman citizen, instead, elected (during the Republic) other citizens to be Senators and to be the magistrates of various types and jurisdictional levels to handle the task of governing, while he went about his business. This was no reduction of position, however, for the rights and obligations of Roman citizens were no less than his Greek conceptual predecessor, and in many ways these gained importance *vis-á-vis* his relationship with the Roman state.

This difference from the Greek concept, and the importance of Roman citizenship to Romans, is illustrated by the manner in which a young Cicero prosecuted a criminal case in Sicily. Gaius Verres was a governor of Sicily and, if Cicero can be believed, a very crooked one. The case centers on the abuse of one Publius Gavius, whom Verres accused, tortured, and executed by crucifixion as part of an extortion scheme during the Third Servile War.[3]

---

2   Roman philosopher, lawyer, and Consul of Rome. During the civil wars following Julius Caesar's murder, Cicero was himself murdered.

3   The Servile Wars were a series of unrelated slave revolts; the Third, or War of Spartacus, was used as the framework of an extortion scheme whereby Roman shipping would be impounded by Verres, the crews and shipping owners accused of supporting the slave rebellion, and payments demanded to make the charges go away. Gavius was one such prisoner; he escaped, denounced Verres, and was caught (again) by Verres, who tortured him and ultimately crucified him on the

In his prosecution, Cicero was less concerned with the actual crime than he was with the abuse of a Roman citizen which the crime included. A Roman was supposed to be immune to such treatment, even if convicted in a fair trial. In the words of Cicero, "To bind a Roman citizen is a crime, to flog him is an abomination, to slay him is almost an act of murder: to crucify him is - what? There is no fitting word that can possibly describe so horrible a deed."[4] Indeed, said Cicero, this violation of the legal status of a Roman citizen threatened the rights and freedoms of all Roman citizens, threatened the power of the Empire, threatened the very fabric of Republican Rome.

Verres' crime regarding Gavius had undermined the rights of all citizens because it was this citizenship that bound all Romans to a common community of people, whether they were Greek-speaking Sicilians or a scion of the oldest family in Rome. A Roman's citizenship responsibilities bound him through a blood kinship to all his fellow citizens. Roman citizenship defined status and rights; it was not defined, in the Greek way, by ethnicity or "worth." A Roman should not—could not—treat his brother in such a way. Further, Verres' crime had undermined the Empire's power: he had made travel to the provinces dangerous for citizens, and worse, his actions had suggested to foreign powers that they could abuse Roman citizens with impunity. Finally, Verres neglected Roman law, treating his provincial population, including his familial citizens, as his slaves, and so Verres had undermined the Republic itself: "A crushed and hopelessly defeated country will often resort to the disastrous expedient of…cancelling the sentences pronounced in its courts of law."

It's entirely plausible that Cicero, in his prosecutorial oratory, was speaking for effect on the particular crime, but he was not exaggerating the importance of the legal meaning of "citizen" in Rome. This status not only set a Roman citizen apart from the rest of the population present in Roman territory. Roman citizenship was central to what it meant to be a Roman and what it meant to the Republic: there could be no punishment without due process of law, and this due process required a court in Rome to hear the case, if the defendant so demanded. The worst punishment possible to a Roman was the social death of exile, a cutting off from fellow citizens—from family—and

---

Italian-facing shore of Sicily, deepening the insult of the crucifixion.

4   **The Verrine Orations**, trans. L. H. G. Greenwood (London: Heinemann, 1928-1935), 2.5.64, par. 170.

from the nation, rather than execution, which was "only" a physical death. Further, this legal status of citizenship was an instrument of Roman foreign policy through its use as a mechanism for power projection beyond its borders: foreign powers knew of the Roman response, backed up by demonstrated capability, to any mistreatment (by Rome's definition) of a Roman.[5]

Thus we have the importance of Paul of Tarsus' words, "*Civis Romanus sum*," "I am a Roman citizen," in his (belated) response to his arrest and detention in Caesarea. This simple assertion, backed by no proof at all, was enough to force his release for travel to Rome for trial. Of course, his responsibility as a Roman citizen was to make that trip; the assertion was not simply "bail," to be jumped at will. And here we have the sum of the primary responsibilities of Roman citizenship: obedience to the laws and the Roman government and the treatment of fellow citizens as equals and as kinsmen, regardless of his—or their—personal station in society. The vertical obligation is reciprocal: the Roman government, made up as it was of Roman citizens acting in an official capacity, was bound to uphold all citizens' rights; to fail was to dissolve the Republic into tyranny. And finally, the citizen had a greater claim, and interest, in justice than in liberty; justice would promote the citizen's obedience to the law, and so preserve the Republic.

The American conceptualization of citizenship began in our colonial period as an active relationship of people working together to solve their community's problems and participating actively in a democratic process for decision-making, such as the New England town hall meetings. This evolved; a major factor was a push for personal economic success and social freedom, which in turn caused people to work more for their own economic interests and to sever ties to a far distant central government, and even to spend less time being involved in local government. This push also created businessmen as politicians, adding to and significantly displacing (although not completely) a citizen aristocratic class whose avocation was governance. Citizenship became less defined by participation in politics and more defined as a legal relation with accompanying rights and privileges, moving in the direction of the Roman conception, but not losing entirely the Greek conception.

---

5   This was a theory of foreign policy and power projection that would be repeated in history—most recently in 1938 by NAZI Germany *vis-à-vis* the Sudetenland region of the Czechoslovakia Republic and again in 2008 by Russia *vis-à-vis* the Georgian provinces of South Ossetia and Abkhazia.

Also occurring during our colonial times and the period surrounding and following our Revolutionary War, were the developments of a national identity and of the concepts of who and what we were as citizens. The Treaty of Westphalia gave impetus to a trend in Europe toward the development of the nation-state: no longer was a man a King's man, or Richelieu's man in that European trend, he was becoming an Englishman, or a Frenchman. That trend was accelerated and crystallized, for Americans, by the conflicts leading into the Revolutionary War and by the War itself. We became not just members of a local community, or citizens (in any sense) of one of the States of the United States, but citizens of our country, also: we developed a national identity; we came to say, with pride, "I am an American." "I'm a Yankee doodle" went beyond a satirical ridicule of an English slur in our colonial times; it bespoke a proud country-ish sense of self.

This sense of self developed further: only American citizens, of all the collections of citizens of nations in the world, explicitly acknowledged the inherent equality of men in our country: class origin meant nothing. "Quality of birth" meant nothing. Position in the social hierarchy meant nothing. The common man was, and is in the United States today, on common ground with, "just as good as," the President of the United States.

This sense of the American-ness of an American citizen, this patriotism, was perhaps most loudly expressed in those early days during negotiations with France during the Quasi-War,[6] when the American delegates, in response to French demands, declared, "Millions for defense, sir, but not one cent for tribute!" Indeed, as we became a nation, rather than a collection of colonies, or a loose confederation of quasi-independent states, it was this very nationhood that enabled our communities of Americans to hang together and maintain our coherence against outside—and internal—forces. This concept of "our nation" has allowed the large numbers of individual American citizens to feel a sense of commonality, to set ourselves apart from others not of our nation while simultaneously creating solidarity among the strangers of us who bring a broad reach of immigrant cultures, and thereby make effective opposition "against a sea of troubles" possible.

---

6   The French response to the Jay Treaty between the United States and Great Britain, which the French viewed as an economic blow against France. The French began seizing American commercial shipping and the US responded with privateers seizing French commercial shipping. The Montefort Treaty, negotiated in 1800, ended this "war."

This American view of citizenship built on the Greek and Roman conceptualizations; it broadened the concept of who is allowed to be, who ought to be, an American citizen beyond the original propertied white adult male to include black men, women, and non-whites, generally. It added the concept of citizen as a common identity and a patriot of a political entity that had hard, physical geographical boundaries that could be seen on a map. An American citizen is a person who is *of* America, not someone merely resident here. A French citizen is a person who is *of* France. And so on.

But what does it mean to be an American citizen? There are, conceptually, three kinds of rights which an American citizen has: Natural Rights, which are the rights of all men and exist inherently in men. These have been identified in our Declaration of Independence: Life, Liberty, and pursuit of Happiness are among them. There are also Legal Rights, which are rights of our nation's customs and laws. These rights gain their legitimacy, not from their having been originated and handed down by government, but through their animation, and their active preservation, of those natural rights. These legal rights, and the laws that give them force, cannot exist as pronouncements by government fiat: they can only exist because the Sovereign—American citizens—have instructed their employee—the government—to enact these laws and to withdraw others found to be no longer useful or wrong outright. An example of a legal right is the right of citizens to vote. Finally, there are Group Rights: these are claims the United States, acting as the community of us citizens, has on us as citizens that supersede our rights as individuals (and one aspect of citizenship is our agreement to allow such supersession—a supersession to which a non-citizen does not have to agree). An example of this is our country's claim on us to report for military duty when a military necessity exists.

Citizenship, though, also entails/implies a duty of the citizen—of us—proactively and affirmatively to act in support of our community and of our nation. This action can be community service or volunteering for national service.

These moral obligations are broad. The complexities of nationhood and of life in a complex nation lend themselves, for instance, to an episodic participation in governance by citizens—by us as members of our social contract. This quasi-periodicity is more than just the rhythms of the biennial election cycle structure of American politics; it's also a generational view of the need and interest to participate actively in politics at all. As the Romans recognized, while citizens can play political roles, we generally do not, as we are caught up in the imperatives of our ordinary personal and economic interests. And yet as the Greeks also understood, it is just as imperative for us to play an active political role, to honor our political obligations, lest our nation descend into the tyranny of the few who are routinely active, and so are able to usurp control for themselves and to reduce or abrogate our rights.

In narrow, legalistic terms, American citizenship means the following non-exhaustive list:

- A U.S. citizen can vote in Federal elections;
- A U.S. citizen can petition to legally bring parents, unmarried minor children, and husband or wife to the United States;
- A U.S. citizen cannot be deported;
- A U.S. citizen must obey all laws of the nation and of the political jurisdictions beneath the national level wherein he is located. (Non-citizen residents must do this, as well, but they can cease to do so simply by leaving.)

But being an American citizen also means the individual has moral obligations to the United States, to the State of which he is a citizen, to his local community, to his neighbors. These include the following—again a non-exhaustive list:

- Actually to vote;
- To stand for office in the government when it becomes clear that a man has better ideas than the incumbent and cannot bend the incumbent to those ideas;
- To volunteer for national service:
  - Military service, including answering a draft and not evading it, if a national emergency forces the enactment of a draft,
  - Civilian national service such as Peace Corps, or NCCC or VISTA;[7]

---

7   Although the Peace Corps involves service overseas, and AmeriCorps NCCC and AmeriCorps VISTA are domestic, service in either helps the nation.

- To answer the call for jury duty in any of the court jurisdictions that call him;
- To volunteer for local service:
  - National, or State, Guard,
  - Neighborhood Watch,
  - Adopt a Highway,
  - Volunteering at a public library,
  - Even the proverbial helping the "little old lady" across the street;
- To know one's neighbors and stand ready to assist them should they need assistance.

Thus the American view of citizenship combines the Greek and Roman political and legal status with the modern nation-state identity to define the American citizen.

What sets an American citizen apart from legally resident aliens? Should there be a distinction? To the second, a resounding yes, I say. To the former, the following is why there should be a distinction and what that distinction is. A good citizen, an active participant in our nation's fabric, has a tight emotional bond with and a sense of patriotism for our nation, an unadorned love of country; a non-citizen does not. This commitment, though, is not simply the emotional bond, and non-citizens often have a similar emotional alliance—the non-citizen who joins the American armed forces, fights in American wars, perhaps dies in those wars, has such an emotional commitment.[8] But the citizen's commitment goes further: the citizen also accepts a legal commitment to his nation, a legal commitment that is far harder to abrogate than an acceptance of an obligation that may, or may not, be broken simply by leaving again. The citizen has accepted the legal binding that attempting to abandon one's country in its hour of need—evading a draft, for instance, or dodging taxes—carries legal sanctions, including loss of freedoms, loss of property, or both. The American citizen, the active citizen, also has, through his bond with America, a willingness to sacrifice for his country, for his community, for his fellows in an hour of need. The immigrant has come to America to improve his life—to seek

---

8   This bond is extremely valuable, and argues for making the path for achieving citizenship easier, but it does not obviate the need to maintain a concrete distinction between the rights and benefits of a citizen of the United States and the rights and benefits of a non-citizen.

fulfillment for himself of the American dream, in which all American citizens share, as well, for our own betterment—but the close alignment does not yet exist and can only be created by learning American culture, participating in American activities and, yes, through American rituals, by becoming American. And this can be demonstrated only through actively participating in the American process and, ultimately, by becoming a citizen. For this citizenship, there must be extra benefit: an exclusive right to participate in our country's governance, for instance, and exclusive access to the nation's benefits/welfare support to which a non-citizen should have no access beyond humanitarian, temporary emergency assistance.

We Americans take in and incorporate (note that verb) immigrants, and gladly so, for they bring fresh ideas as well as fresh approaches to old problems and a renewal of dedication to nation. However, we should not become our immigrants—they need to become Americans, or alternatively to recognize their resident alien status. Those who come to the United States do so for the opportunities here, and they're welcome to share in these opportunities— immigrant and legal alien alike. Immigrants come to America specifically for the economic opportunities, the political freedoms and opportunities, the sociological opportunities—American culture, which they know *a priori* to be different from their own—and which they understand to be the foundation of our American exceptionalism. Those opportunities result from our American culture. Immigrants need to adapt to, and assimilate into, our culture. Some will argue that this implies an imposition of a particular majority culture on minorities, but it is not an imposition. It is a recognition and an acceptance that to benefit from what America has to offer, to benefit from American opportunities, and to preserve these for Americans already present, it is necessary to adapt to that which is America. Parenthetically, this need to preserve these attributes, these fundaments of American exceptionalism, emphasizes, also, the importance of providing civics courses that teach the American social contract and American citizenship in our schools, so as to reach all American citizens.

When the US accepts immigrants (which we have no obligation to do, the benefits to us of immigration notwithstanding: no one has an inherent right to enter a nation of which he is not a citizen without that nation's prior permission, and the receiving nation has no obligation to grant that permission), this acceptance carries no obligation to allow, or much less to facilitate, their declination to assimilate into *American* culture. On the other hand, once immigrants have become citizens, rather than having chosen to remain resident aliens, they can, and should, participate in the discussions concerning the nation's goals and future. What immigrants must do is accept the current political structures, which they knew from the start, and take part in their new community. These new citizens, like the "original" citizens, must speak a common national language and share the commitment to maintaining and defending the nation. And so, having committed to the nation—to America—they will have their impact by engaging as citizens in our common discourse. This need is made explicit by the Oath of Allegiance[9] which all immigrants must take in order to become a citizen. The Pledge of Allegiance[10] which Americans used to recite at the start of every school class is very similar in spirit, and its recitation should be resumed as a reminder of the commitment to citizenship and to the United States that "born citizens" take for granted and too easily neglect.

What if we lose this quintessentially American view of citizenship? One alternative is demonstrated by the long tradition of European societies, with the Portuguese constitution illustrative. Adopted in 1976, this Portuguese social contract defined a Portuguese citizen's rights not in terms of what government could not do to them, with all else reserved to the citizen, but in terms of what government promised to give to the Portuguese citizen.[11] This is an utter reversal of the natural rights of man: no longer is it the case that a man's rights end where the next man's begin; with this constitution, it is a

---

9   I hereby declare, on oath, that I absolutely and entirely renounce and abjure all allegiance and fidelity to any foreign prince, potentate, state, or sovereignty of whom or which I have heretofore been a subject or citizen; that I will support and defend the Constitution and laws of the United States of America against all enemies, foreign and domestic; that I will bear true faith and allegiance to the same; that I will bear arms on behalf of the United States when required by the law; that I will perform noncombatant service in the Armed Forces of the United States when required by the law; that I will perform work of national importance under civilian direction when required by the law; and that I take this obligation freely without any mental reservation or purpose of evasion; so help me God.

10   I pledge allegiance to the flag of the United States of America, and to the republic for which it stands, one nation under God, indivisible, with liberty and justice for all.

11   Its preamble affirmed the necessity of "opening a path to a socialist society," while entrenching nationalizations undertaken after the [1974 Carnation] revolution. Labor was constitutionally empowered, buttressing existing laws that make it extremely onerous to dismiss full-time workers. Citizens were additionally "granted" a multitude of social and economic rights, including the right to work, housing, education, culture, health, and social security. There is no statement of personal liberties or responsibilities.

man's right to demand, through his government as Sovereign (for the men no longer are), his benefits from that next man. Or closer to home, we have the travesty of Franklin D. Roosevelt's "Second Bill of Rights," his "Economic Bill of Rights"[12] of man. This completely ignores the commitment to our inalienable rights already identified in our Declaration of Independence, and it ignores the fact that FDR's manufactured "rights" cannot be achieved by award from any government, which in the end is only an employee of men and so when it gives to one man, which it must do by taking from another, it does so by taking from one of its employers. These "economic rights," and "social rights" that are other than those identified in the American social contract, which a Liberal might assert as belonging to people, are solely the inevitable output of men's efforts when those efforts are carried out within the framework of our inalienable rights. The Liberal, the Progressive, instead asserts that men need expend no effort: government will do for them. As Rousseau has already shown us, though, "the Sovereign,[13] being formed wholly of the individuals who compose it, neither has nor can have any interest contrary to theirs; and consequently the sovereign power need give no guarantee to its subjects."

The sunshine patriot will object to these obligations of citizenship, insisting instead that government is obligated to provide, but the Democrat John Fitzgerald Kennedy had it right: "Ask not what your country can do for you - ask what you can do for your country."[14] The obligation, freedoms, and power of American citizenship results not through the mechanism of socialist Europe's—Portugal's—Government as Giver of Rights, but through minimal government interfering the least amount possible in the endeavors of its citizens as we see to our own ends, we act politically and economically for our own needs, with the aggregated result of greatly increased, and increasing, personal and national economic wealth, personal and national

---

12   * Employment, with a living wage,
* Freedom from unfair competition and monopolies,
* Housing,
* Medical care,
* Education, and,
* Social security

13   Locke and Rousseau have elsewhere, and I have in this book, used "Sovereign" to mean the people as sovereign. In this passage, Rousseau uses the term in its alternative meaning: the government, created by the people and employed by them to act in a sovereign capacity when speaking for the nation as a whole.

14   Inaugural address, 1961. He was quoting Khalil Gibran with this remark.

social wealth, and national power on the global stage. An American citizen is best equipped to decide the proper venue to use his talents, and the American citizen is the sole legitimate decision maker for these. The American citizen, acting on his own determination, or in concert with his fellows, unfettered by a government that pretends to know better, understands best how he should use his resources or how he should spend his money. He is, and they are collectively, the best mechanism for personal and national economic and social prosperity, for it is only through us citizens satisfying our personal imperatives and our own moral obligations that the liberties, the inalienable rights, of American citizens can be preserved.

Finally, the obligation of American citizenship demands that every citizen recognize and accept that America was at its founding, and is today, a Christian nation, with fundamental values that flesh out our inalienable rights, values that are grounded in our Judeo-Christian history and heritage; and he must further accept the basic tenets of American culture. This requires that, even as he practices, for instance, his own religion, or no religion at all, in complete freedom, he respects the right of his neighbor to practice his different religion, or no religion at all. It demands that each citizen practice his own beliefs in the political arena while respecting the right of his neighbor to disagree with those politics and to practice his own, differing politics. It demands that each citizen obey American law, without regard to what the old country might have done in the circumstance.

This is not to say that American culture must be monolithic, or that every citizen must be a cookie cutter counterpart to every other. Quite the opposite; the diversity generated by legal immigration always has been another source of our enduring strength as a nation and as a culture. However, it does require that what is preserved in the United States over time must be American culture, not the individual cultures of the nations left behind by our immigrants. Immigrant heritages have great value, as I've said earlier, but only to the extent they contribute to American culture, rather than seek to supplant it or to remain apart from it while living within our geographic borders.[15] To remain a source of American strength, American

---

15   This is beginning to be recognized in Europe, also. As the German Chancellor, Angela Merkel, said in describing the failure of multiculturalism as a national policy, "[T] the tendency had been to say, 'let's adopt the multicultural concept and live happily side by side, and be happy to be living with each other'. But this concept has failed, and failed utterly[.]" The British Prime Minister, David

citizenship must be seen to retain its value as the protector of our underlying fundamental rights of man and of our uniquely American civil and political rights—those things which make Americanism exceptional. Our citizenship demands, thus, that we honor both our Greek forebears' citizen obligation to take part in politics, and our Roman forebears' legal status of citizenship, and we must act to protect our unique, American sense of national and cultural identity.

There are two broad challenges to this conceptualization of (American) citizenship: one is the asserted need to accept the concepts of contemporary liberal democracies into the American polity, and the second is comprised of the pressures wrought by globalization on the nation state with its fixed geographical borders. However these two challenges argue from false premises. In the first case, the United States is not, was not founded on the principles of, and cannot afford to be, a liberal democracy—a welfare state. The United States is a Federal republic that, by design, preserves the rights of its constituent States, each with its unique and individual approach to life within it, and that limits the power and authority of the federal [*sic*] government. Our republic protects, by design, the individual, inalienable rights of citizens, as well, and limits the power and authority of the central government *vis-à-vis* those individuals, leaving them free to work for their own goals. (This is apart from the fact that our design currently is being honored in the breech by a grasping, overweening Federal government.)

This welfare state that is a liberal democracy is the condition of Europe (see, for example the previously mentioned Portuguese constitution), including Great Britain (Tony Blair, in his memoir, referred more than once to his goal for Britain as being a welfare state). It is the goal of the present Progressives in the United States. But the outcome of government providing "entitlements" to citizens is not only the pecuniary matter of explosion into economic disaster (Greece, Ireland, Portugal, Spain, Italy, on the verge of bankruptcy, Great Britain forced to retrench severely and to recognize government has grown too large and to attempt downsizing). It creates the citizens as dependents of the government, looking to government to provide their benefits and rights of support; it eliminates the government's—this employee of the citizens—role as protector of fundamental rights. It creates a moral collapse

---

Cameron, also decried the failure of multiculturalism, and he said, "Instead of encouraging people to live apart, we need a clear sense of shared national identity, open to everyone."

into a dependency so powerful that when these governments have tried to retrench, even a little, the morally bankrupt, dependent populations, like the addict when his drug is withheld, exploded into riot, often with lethal result, demanding the continuation of their handouts, and never mind the cost.

Just as critically, it destroys the framework within which citizens are free to create their own goals and to work freely to achieve them without government hindrance. In the case of the United States in particular, it usurps the citizen's right to make his own economic decisions and makes the government responsible for everything a citizen might buy, or not buy, in all walks of life, and government responsible for the products a private business might produce and a government-determined price at which it may be sold.[16] It seeks to hook Americans on government handouts even as our budget deficit and national debt explode, in just two years, to levels that both are unsustainable and threaten our independence as a nation. I'll have more to say on this particular subject in the chapter on the Economy. Thus, arguments flowing from the concept of a "liberal democracy" are irrelevant to the United States: we are not designed to be one, and the concept is a failure.

The other challenge, globalization pressures, works from the false premise that a nation has an obligation to let anyone who wants to enter do so. Of course no such obligation exists. Borders have existed since before civilization, and they exist throughout the animal world. Territoriality is a fact of life, and it's a necessary aspect: it's a reflection of the right of a population to protect what belongs to it, a tautologically finite asset, from interlopers. In the case of the nation, it's the right to protect the national population, the national territory and the national and personal resources, both physical and economic, from naked seizure and/or from use by those who are not part of the polity or who do not have permission for such use from the owners. Some will argue that this is selfish. It is, rather, a legitimate protection of ownership and the most efficient allocation of finite resources (I'll have more to say on this subject, also, in the chapters on Fairness and the Economy). A man has no more claim on what I have than I have on

---

16   Patient Protection and Affordable Care Act of 2010, with its individual mandate that every citizen must buy a product of the government's choosing—health insurance, in this case—and its demand that private enterprise provide health insurance that satisfies government imperative, and at premiums satisfactory to that government, rather than business or individual needs or desires.

what he has. Others will argue that we have a duty to our fellow man to help the weakest, the most indigent, the most threatened. This is a stronger argument, but to say the only option is open borders with anyone entering who wishes is a false dichotomy that ignores two facts. It ignores the right of a nation to protect itself by controlling who it will or will not allow in, and in what numbers, should it decide to let in anyone, and the right of a nation to decide these according to its own criteria (just as a private citizen has no obligation to let anyone into his home who knocks—or who simply enters without knocking). The false dichotomy also elides a nation's superior obligation to use its finite resources to protect, first, its own weakest, its own indigent, its own threatened.

This national obligation argument also ignores another solution to the humanity aspect, and a far more efficient one: assisting the home nations, those from which the immigrations/migrations are sourced, better to control their own borders and assisting those nations to correct the internal conditions that drive their own people to emigrate/migrate. This assistance must include, where necessary, the option for imposing controls on those originating nations. The conscious decision of an originating nation not to correct its own internal conditions, or its incompetence in doing so, in no way obligates any other nation to accept within its own borders the costs of such incompetence or irresponsibility. The social contract to which men agree among themselves in no way obligates them to accept others—unless the men, in formulating or maintaining their contract, agree to do so.

I'll close this chapter with this thought: it is critical to the preservation of our distinctly American liberties, to the continued fastening of our inalienable rights to our existence, to the safety and preservation of our exceptionalism, for us to actively execute our duties and obligations as citizens of the United States. As Rousseau put it so plainly those 200 and more years ago, "When the citizens are greedy, cowardly, and pusillanimous, and love ease more than liberty, they do not long hold out against the redoubled efforts of the government." Karl Marx was wrong. It is socialism that is the opium of the people.[17] Recall that the Progressives wish to make us all dependents of government.

---

17   The original remark, "Religion is the opium of the people," was made in the introduction of Marx' 1843 work **Contribution to Critique of Hegel's Philosophy of Right**.

CHAPTER 5—THE NATION

These are the times that try men's souls.
— Thomas Paine

What is a nation? I described in the chapter on Citizenship the meaning of citizenship and the relationship between a citizen and a nation. In this chapter, I will discuss, first, the nature of nationhood: what defines a nation; and the relationship among society (men acting (more or less) collectively), their government, and the social contract that unites men in this entity we view as a nation. This is, as usual, a broad-brushed overview to illustrate the concept, rather than a detailed history. Then I will describe the concept of nationhood in the light of the American social contract.

The territoriality of men is a continuation of our evolution from the territoriality of animals, as I have written elsewhere. This early territoriality was based on a need to preserve what seemed important at the time: scarce resources, valuable hunting grounds, mates, sheltering caves or dens, and so on. As men began to learn agriculture, the need to protect included areas where favored plants grew. As we learned to deliberately cultivate favored plants, and more or less fixed settlements developed for housing those communities that would work these fields, the areas needing protection created a need for yet more explicit boundaries and more explicit protection. Indeed, there is evidence that the Egyptians' development of surveying techniques grew out of a need to reestablish prior years' crop field boundaries and ownership[1] after the annual Nile floods washed away those fields' prior year boundary markings.

The concept of "nation" is described as a cultural and/or ethnic entity, and the concept of "state" is described as a political and geopolitical entity. A nation, in this light, can be thought of as a community of like-minded

---

1   Notice that the relationship between the human concepts of ownership and of boundaries has existed for thousands of years.

people. This like-minded-ness originally was primarily cultural and ethnic; a sharing of values, ethos, a common language, and/or a similarity of race with a tacit assumption that the race held a monolithic world view. Modern communications advances, particularly in networking, allow a broader range of communities to develop. These communities still are identified by a commonality of interests among their members, but only for a very short list of interests for each such community. These groups could rise to the level of "nation" under the broad definition provided, but I will not include them in the present discussion, as these are, in the end, narrow-interest defined groups that otherwise are very diffuse: for instance, they span a broad range of languages rather than sharing a common linguistic set. Beyond a common interest in a specific subject, they do not share, of necessity, a common culture. Multi-ethnic/multi-cultural political entities also have existed, mostly in centrally ruled empires, initially. China, Russia, the Austro-Hungarian Empire, for instance, are—or were—such multi-cultural entities; these do not try overmuch to meld the disparate cultures into one body, though, so much as they try, instead simply to maintain control from the center over the disparate "nations" in the empire.

The state as a secular geopolitical entity[2] (larger than the simpler city-states) began to take shape with the Treaty of Westphalia, described in an earlier chapter. In the context of the present chapter, the salient concept of the Treaty is the acknowledgment that a central government (at the time led by a king or other secular prince) had sovereignty over a geographical region that had fixed, recognized (by other states, if not necessarily clearly marked on the ground) borders. At this point in the development of the state, the Treaty notwithstanding, territorial boundaries were whatever a Feudal lord could enforce, and as states themselves developed, territoriality became whatever boundaries these new countries (née Feudal lands) could enforce. We had, then, secular political entities that were apart from, although they remained in many cases closely entwined with, religious political entities. These secular states also now had focused, fixed-location boundaries, while the religious entities now had a more diffuse placement and were tied together less by geography and more by a commonality of interest—and through their

---

2   By this usage I mean, in addition to ultimate control by non-religious leadership, an entity with a more or less firmly fixed locus, as opposed to peoples (nations) in migration, such as the Lombards and Goths who beset the Roman Empire, or the Huns and Gauls in migration into Central and Western Europe.

physical diffusion, began to lose power to the fixed, centralized secular state. Another effect of this Treaty was to strengthen the nascent states' leaderships enough to facilitate their constitution into central governments capable of bringing their nation and their state to a sufficient level of coincidence that a nation-state began to develop: an entity where "nation" and "state" coincide geographically. This also fed back into the power of the government, and of the nation-state over which it ruled, to manage its own affairs and, at least as importantly, to defy the efforts of others outside the nation-state (including the now more diffuse, and diffusing, religious polities) to influence, if not control, those affairs.

For the most part, though, any allegiance of the population remained to the political leadership as individual men; the population was not loyal to the institution of government, or to the polity of "nation" or of "state," the way either Aristotle's or Cicero's idealized *citizens* were. As a result, the nation-states were little more than geographic areas bounded by lines drawn on a map, and the "citizens" of these states consisted of those who happened to be penned up by those arbitrary lines, regardless of any sense, or lack of sense, of community among these gathered up peoples. To be sure, these groups of people tended toward a measure of homogeneity, but this was as much a fallout of the leadership's border enforcement policies and successes as it was a deliberate policy of inclusion by those institutions.[3] There was very little sense of community, or of mutual allegiance, in such polities beyond the local village; these were merely men who happened to share a common government and geographical boundary.

A nation-state that consists of a territory with geographic boundaries (that are nothing more than what its government can enforce) lacks a critical ingredient in becoming more than a nation-state in name only, in becoming a more complete community of men. For instance, when these boundaries are drawn arbitrarily and with a thick pencil (as for instance by modern colonial powers in the Middle East and in Central Asia—or by the signers

---

3   However, a population of like people *over there* often served as an excuse to expand (usually forcibly) a border from *here* to enclose that group, as the continual conflicts among Poles, Swedes, and the varying Germanic states demonstrated. In those times, groups of people were viewed as resources to be controlled, in the same way a river or an expanse of fertile land were viewed. Hitler did not invent the concept of *anschluss*. This is different from Cicero's Rome, which also used the concept of (Roman) citizenship as an instrument of foreign policy. The use ended with the disappearance of the Roman Empire.

of the Treaty of Westphalia), these boundaries can be a source of conflict between the (artificially created) nations separated by them. They also can be a source of conflict between a people separated from what they consider their territory, their resources, their homeland—or separated from each other—by those artificial boundaries on the one hand and the nation-state now in physical possession via those lines on the map on the other hand.

True nation-states—countries—though, are more than the areas enclosed by map lines; they are the people living there, together with the outcome of the social contract to which they have agreed among themselves and which forms their government (in freedom), or they are the breadth of power and the nature of community which a government, imposed by the strong on the weak, can make stand up (in tyranny). They are polities in which the members—the citizens—feel a loyalty, an allegiance, to the entire polity beyond their individual, local communities, and beyond any personal loyalty to the leadership, and so are willing to sacrifice themselves for that polity.

A mutual agreement among the men greatly facilitates this loyalty, and it creates the framework within which that loyalty can persist across generations. The specific terms of the agreement are less important (within some limits); what matters more to generating loyalty or patriotism is that the agreement is mutual and voluntary. The government that results from this mutual agreement, this social contract, also is widely variable; during the 18th and 19th centuries, when the concept of social contracts was first being articulated in modern terms, the most common form of government to which men voluntarily submitted was a monarchy (thus creating considerable overlap between nations where the king ruled by strength of arms, and those where the king ruled through some form of assent of the subjects).

A tyranny certainly can inspire a similarly powerful loyalty, but usually only in the person of the present leadership. However, if that leadership is broken or key members replaced, or if key members (or the leader) dies, that loyalty usually is lost; it typically does not persist across generations of leadership.

The advantages inherent in voluntary association are what give strength to the nations of social contracts compared to those of tyrannies. It is against the backdrop of the foregoing that I claim that the social contract is, in an important sense, the nation. The development of, and assent to, this mutual agreement gives completeness to the development of a nation.[4] The nation has become a polity that both commands and enjoys the loyalty of its citizens; the nation itself now is a part of their common purpose, even though the individual members may in fact not be overly homogeneous. It is the quality of this social contract that generates—inspires—loyalty across generations. It is the existence of this social contract that enables immigration to occur without dramatically altering the gaining culture (although a natural evolution of culture is as inevitable from immigration, as it is from changing circumstances resulting from the passage of time and changing technologies, attitudes, and capabilities across generations).

Note that none of this reduces in the slightest the importance of national borders. On the contrary, borders are now even more important to a nation's safety and internal unity. These borders form a demarcation line between one country and its neighbors. The border proclaims, irrevocably, that the interior is the nation's property and the aggregation of all of the citizens' property,[5] and they define the limits of national territory. No other entity—nation, organization, or individual—may enter at all, except under carefully delineated conditions of permission. Borders definitively proclaim the demarcation between the precepts of one nation's social contract—its laws and culture, for instance—and those of its neighbors. Even nations like Canada and the United States, who so closely share their Western civilization heritage, have a right and a necessity to draw a line between them and say, "My house. My rules."

It is the social contract which men write, and to which they then agree, that sets society's cultural expectations—in our case of America, this culture centers on the protection of individualism and of individual freedoms

---

4   Having arrived at a complete definition—the people, their social contract, and the government created by them (free country); or the people and an imposed government (a tyranny)—I will begin to use "nation," "state," and "country," interchangeably, rather than attempt a stilted phrasing. I deliberately do not address any further the status of tyrannies as completed nations. These are outside the scope of a book about conservative principles.

5   I refer solely to citizens' rights to property ownership, private property, and so on, only to avoid clumsy phrasing associated with inclusion of the same rights held by non-citizen legal residents in many nations. My use of "citizen" exclusively, in this context, in no way deprecates the rights of these other legal residents, and their rights are included by reference in my use of "citizen" here.

among disparate colonies, while uniting these disparate groups into a single, coherent nation. New Amsterdam descendants; the landed gentry with the plantation worker stratification of the southern colonies; the gentlemen, merchants, and employees of "industrialized" northern colonies; Calvinist vs. Catholic vs. Protestant vs. Quaker religious beliefs of the differing colonies: all of these were, and are with today's newer dissimilarities, united into one nation by our social contract. The inherent exceptionalism of the American nation stems from the uniqueness of this centrality and importance of the individual, and from the explicit articulation of our natural rights as individuals and the equally explicit reservation of national sovereignty to us rather than to our government.

Rousseau wrote 250 years ago, "…the growth of the State giving the trustees of public authority more and means to abuse their power, the more the Government has to have force to contain the people, the more force the Sovereign should have in turn in order to contain the Government…." Here, indeed, is the motivation for a social contract which creates, animates, and constrains government as the subordinate of the Sovereign people who are members of that contract. A carefully constructed contract must place limits on the authorities and powers of a government.

The American social contract was designed and written with a need for vigilance and the likelihood of complacency and drift in mind. The basic documents of our contract are the Declaration of Independence[6] and The Constitution of the United States of America.[7] The Declaration lays out the fundamental, underlying principles of our contract and names some of the fundamental rights of all men (and specifically of the men of this contract), while the Constitution gives structure, authorities and powers, and applies strict limits, to the government We the People hire both to enforce and to protect those rights. I have described the underlying principles before, but it is useful to repeat them here:

- All men are created equal,
- We are endowed by our Creator with certain unalienable Rights; among these are
    - Life,

---

6   Reproduced at Appendix I.
7   Reproduced at Appendix II.

- ◦ Liberty, and
- ◦ the pursuit of Happiness.
- Governments derive their just powers from the consent of the governed and exist solely to enforce and to protect the foregoing.
- Whenever Government becomes destructive of these ends, it is the Right of the People, and it is their duty, to alter or to abolish it, and then
- To institute new Government...in such form as seems most likely to regain, protect, and enforce the foregoing.
- We are, and of Right ought to be Free.

The Constitution structures, empowers, and limits the government hired by Americans to give life to those principles. The basic structure has been described earlier; it is summarized here.

- An assemblage of representatives of the people, elected by the people,
- To counterbalance this assemblage, a national executive officer, also elected (indirectly) by the people, and
- Counterbalancing these two, an independent judiciary (selected by the executive, approved by an arm of the assemblage, and given life tenure) as an equal branch of the government.

The salient powers and limits of our government are summarized thus:

- To collect taxes to fund the government and its activities,
- To conduct foreign policy, including war,
- To regulate commerce among the several States to encourage their mutual cooperation rather than their mutual competition,
- To manage national-level finances,
- To organize and control a national military capability,
- Prevention of writs of *Habeas Corpus* being suspended at the convenience of the government,
- Prevention of bills of attainder or *ex post facto* laws,
- The 10 Amendments of the Bill of Rights; these are known to any schoolchild; they will not be repeated here.

These two documents, together, as our social contract, lay out who we are as a people, what our nation is. Our social contract, in clear terms, describes our collection of inalienable, natural rights, and it creates the structure within which our inalienable duties may be identified and our civil laws giving specificity and animation to those rights and duties enacted. This American social contract is what defines the exceptionalism that is the United States of America. It is useful, now, to discuss our rights and duties in the context of our nation.

Our inalienable rights are inherent in us from no less important a source than our existence as creations of our Creator. We can no more divorce ourselves from them, either directly or through the terms of any social contract—and no government can divorce us from them—then we can be divorced from the precepts of life itself. We can, however, be brought closer to their effect and import, or moved away from these, according to the accuracy of our description of these rights and obligations, and the effectiveness with which the government we hire protects and enforces them.[8] We formed a social contract among ourselves to clearly identify and to protect these inalienable rights and to pledge ourselves to our duties regarding them, not in order to have fewer rights or in order to avoid our obligations, and so we are brought closer.

Other chapters have reminded us (repeatedly) of the partial list of inalienable rights identified in our Declaration of Independence: Life, Liberty, and the pursuit of Happiness; however, these are not all of them. A more extended list, still partial, contains these additional inalienable rights:

- Our right to enter into contracts. This includes the right to enter freely into business contracts. As we are Sovereign over our own persons, and over the fruits of our physical and intellectual labors, we own our own output. Being free men, we are able to arrange conditions of our own choosing to govern the terms by which we exchange our output for that of another man. This contract right also includes our right to enter into moral contracts—marriage, for instance. Again, as free men, we may choose our own associations[9] and our own moral systems. Finally, this right underlies our very

---

8   And the effectiveness with which we keep our government on the straight and narrow.

9   Recall the terms of reference which I laid out in the Preface concerning the meaning of "men."

right to enter into that social contract which is our nation. This social contract is the foundational moral contract which informs, and gives structure to and basis for, all the rest of our contracts.

- Our right to govern ourselves as we see fit. This is the primary purpose of our social contract: we are free to create, and we have created, a government that satisfies our needs. We then animated it with specified powers and authorities, and circumscribed it with limitations, both on the availability to it of powers and authorities and on the specific powers and authorities granted. Finally, we have reserved to ourselves the other side of this coin: the right to alter, even to abolish and replace, this government if it strays too far from our contract to suit us.

- Our right of self-defense, and to bear arms for that purpose.[10] This right includes our right to defend ourselves against a government become destructive of our ends and so is closely related to our right to determine our own means of governance. This right also is closely related to our rights of Life and Liberty. If we cannot defend ourselves, then we are immediately vulnerable to loss of our freedoms, and those of our loved ones, through enslavement by others. We are vulnerable to the loss of our lives and those of our loved ones. If we cannot have the means of defending ourselves and our loved ones—if we cannot bear arms—then we are denied immediately and prejudicially our right of self-defense. The only government that fears an armed, sovereign people is a government with designs on tyranny.

- Our rights to petition, to freedom of speech, to privacy, to assemble. All are necessary to enter into contracts, and most especially to enter into and manage our social contract. These also are closely associated with our right to our private property—our intellectual property, here, our thoughts and the results of our mental labor. If we are limited in our speech, if we may not gather together, if we are not free to conduct our affairs and to think as we will away from the prying eyes of others—including those of government—then we are circumscribed fatally in our ability to speak about, and to exercise our control over, an overweening government, and we are not free to determine for ourselves the disposition of our labor. If we do not

---

10   Or for any other purpose. The 2nd Amendment provides a rationale for our right to bear arms, but it specifies no purpose, leaving that to the individual.

have these rights, we do not have our Liberty, nor are we able to pursue our own Happiness.

- Our right to our own private property. The private nature of our property flows from our existence. We are sovereign over our own persons, and so over our physical and intellectual labors. Therefore, we own the results of those labors. This is a closely allied with our rights to our own Liberty, to our own Life, to pursue our own Happiness. If we cannot be secure in our own property, then we have none of those. With property being private, being ours, we are at liberty to use it as we see fit: for our own benefit, to retain, to exchange with another, or to use in generating other outputs which we might use for our own benefit or for exchange with others.
- Our rights to enjoy the fruits of our own labors, to improve our lot—and perhaps others'—with our inventions and developments. I hold this to be self evident: either we are free men, secure in our property and our persons, or we are not. Either we are free to improve our lives according to our own imperatives and wishes, or we are not free.

Notice how intertwined these inalienable rights are with each other. That they are so often summarized in the three named in our Declaration of Independence can be seen clearly to cause no diminution of them or of the generality, inclusiveness, or universality of the three.

These inalienable rights, though, contain within them associated duties and obligations which their existence in us imposes on us. These duties are as inalienable, as inseparable from our existence, as are the rights just described. These are duties we owe each other not only under our social contract, but because we each exist. We cannot wish these duties off onto the government we have created, dust our hands, and walk away; this would be to try to separate ourselves from our Creator's endowment. We must honor and satisfy them ourselves, and we must maintain a constant supervision over our government to ensure that it helps us satisfy them, rather than presumes to absolve us of them entirely, when we cannot satisfy them by ourselves. I will discuss here only our public duties; our private ones are matters solely between ourselves and our Creator. However, these public duties affect us individually as well as all of us together under our social contract. A partial list of these duties follows:

- Our duty to uphold our laws. If we do not accept this responsibility and act on it constantly, we have no social contract. Failure to honor the laws which we make reaches much farther than simply cheating our fellows; it destroys the fabric of the society we keep; it defeats the very purpose of that contract: to create a mechanism whereby all of our rights are protected and enforced.
- Our duty to accept full, and sole, responsibility for the outcomes of our actions and choices. If we avoid this, then we are laying claim on another man's property and asserting a dominion over that man. If we demand recompense from another for our failure, we are demanding that another give up a measure of his property in order to make us whole, even when that other is not involved in our actions.
- Our duty not to kill except in self defense or in necessary defense of others. At one remove, this is merely a statement of one concrete aspect of the duty to uphold our laws. At another remove, it is a protection of ourselves and our neighbors in our contract by requiring us to respect the inalienable right to Life that each of us has.
- Our duty not to steal, to be honest in our exchanges with our fellows (dishonesty being a form of theft), to honor and to carry out the commitments embodied in any contract into which we enter and the commitments embodied in our underlying social contract. These are simply duties to respect others' rights to be secure in their persons and property, to enjoy their rights to Life, Liberty, and the pursuit of their Happiness. If we lie, cheat, or steal, or dishonor our commitments, we not only directly deprive our victims of their inalienable rights, we indirectly deprive ourselves of our own through the destruction of our own integrity and morality, and the exposure of ourselves to exactly the same sort of plunder. In the end, the only basis men have for interacting with each other is what we know about each other, and what society as a whole knows about us. Dishonesty contaminates that information, gravely harming it, if not destroying it altogether. Dishonesty, thus, is an attack on society and on all of us, not just on the one immediately cheated.
- Our duty to become economically self-sufficient and, conversely, not to seek to apply claims to others' output. If we create ourselves as burdens on others, this is nothing more than a deprecation of their

rights to their own property, to the fruits of their own labor, if only through an undeserved imposition on their moral obligation to aid their fellow man. This also has the same effect as claiming dominion over those others. Failure to honor this duty also denigrates our own morality, and it subordinates us to those others, for claiming dominion over them ties us irrevocably to them as we make ourselves dependent on their output.

- Our duty to provide for the needs of the less fortunate who cannot do this for themselves. This is no contradiction of the foregoing. There are those among us who cannot see to their own welfare. We have the obligation a man has to his fellows to assist these. There are those among us who are, in the vernacular, down on their luck. We have the same obligation to help these to get back on their feet so that they can resume their own responsibilities, and so we can resume enjoying their society and the outcomes of their labor through resumed free exchange. Note that their acceptance of this hand up is no violation of that prior duty, either.

These are partial lists of our natural, inalienable rights, and the natural, inalienable duties associated with them. Now it's useful to turn to a brief discussion of civil law,[11] and its relationship with these inalienable rights. As Blackstone wrote, just before the construction of our American social contract, "…if he makes his vices public, though they seem such as seem principally to affect himself…, then they become, by the bad example they set, of pernicious effects to society; and therefore it is then the business of human laws to correct them."[12]

Civil rights inhere in a man simply as a result of his membership—not his station—in society. Each civil right originates in an inalienable right, but it consists of a thing which an individual is less able to do for himself, or to enforce alone: his security and protection, for instance, and the judicial enforcement rights necessary to obtain redress for wrongs done. Notice, though, that even with civil rights, government does not grant anything;

---

11   In this usage, I make no distinction between civil and criminal law; my distinction here is solely between the natural law that underlies our inalienable rights and obligations and the civil law, generally, that protects and enforces them. This civil law can subsequently be parsed into modern civil and criminal law, but this adds nothing to a discussion of the relationship between natural law and civil law.

12   Blackstone, Sir William, **Commentaries on the Laws of England**.

it merely acknowledges existing rights: men, through their government, describe salient aspects of inalienable rights—civil rights thus derived from the inalienable rights—and then enact civil law(s) for the purpose of protecting and enforcing that aspect of the inalienable right—the derived civil right. Notice, further, that civil rights, being formed of inalienable rights, cannot individually or in their aggregation be used to counter, to change, or in any way to deprecate our inalienable rights. In any conflict between an articulation of a civil right or collection of civil rights and inalienable rights, the error is in the articulation of the civil right and the conflict must be resolved in favor of the inalienable right. A civil law that implements this erroneous articulation is, itself, invalid.

Civil rights flow from inalienable rights, as I have said, and they have no other source than those. They are, however, inherent in the nation created by the social contract, as they are that animation of our inalienable rights. Civil rights, further, recognize some transfer of responsibility for a fraction of a natural right to the government so that the government can better protect the whole for all men together. This is accomplished through enactment of civil laws as the implementation of these civil rights. Some examples can illustrate the concept.

- We have an inalienable right to Life, and an inalienable duty to preserve life except in self-defense or the defense of others (where we actually are not only seeking to live but acting on our duty to preserve our life). To facilitate this, we enact, through the mechanism of our government, civil laws that outlaw various forms of non-self defense killing: murder, negligent homicide, and the like. To give these civil laws credence and effect, we also enact associated laws prescribing the punishments to be meted out in response to these crimes, or we include these sanctions in the original civil law(s).
- We have an inalienable right to our property, and an inalienable duty to protect both our own property and that of our neighbors. To facilitate this, we enact civil laws that outlaw theft in its various forms, trespass, and so on, together with punishments to be meted out.
- We have an inalienable right to be secure in our persons and our homes. To facilitate this, we enact civil laws governing the way in which governmental searches and seizures may be carried out (for

instance in enforcement of the above civil laws), and the recompense to be provided if these are done improperly. We enact other civil laws governing the methods for appropriating private property, for the compensation to be provided for the appropriation, and for objecting to and blocking the appropriation when government asserts a need for the property.[13]

- We have an interest in pursuing and bringing to justice men who violate our laws (or our inalienable rights). To facilitate this, we enact civil laws creating and empowering police forces to conduct the necessary investigations, pursuits, and arrests. In conjunction with this, we grant the police, under carefully described circumstances, authorities to enter our homes to conduct reasonable searches and seizures of our property, and to seize our persons (arrest us). Here is an example of transferring responsibility for a smaller part of an inalienable right to government in order to facilitate the preservation of the rest of that right.

- We have an interest in preserving ourselves and our neighbors from harms that can be done from irresponsible speech (for want of a better term). To facilitate this, we transfer responsibility for a small aspect of our freedom of speech to government for civil laws to be enacted to bar slander, incitement to riot, "shouting fire in a crowded theater," and the like.

Though we can transfer to government responsibility for a small part of each right and duty, such transfer can be only for the purpose of increasing the ability of all of us as a whole to protect that right for each of us individually, and for the purpose of facilitating our own discharge of our collective duty. Thus an individual may transfer a small part of responsibility but this can only be so that all of us collectively can preserve, in its entirety, that right

---

13   *Kelo v. City of New London* (545 U.S. 469), however, is a coarse distortion of this power of eminent domain. The 5th Amendment says, explicitly, "… nor shall private property be taken for public use, without just compensation." The Supreme Court authorized the City of New London, CT to seize private property for the purpose of transferring it to another private person, rather than for "public use," under the fiction that the city would be able to collect more tax revenue from the gaining private person than it had been from the property's original owner. The ruling creates a gaping breach in a citizen's right to his own private property, and it does so by asserting the fiction that private property may be seized by government for the sole purpose of increasing government's tax collections.

and its responsibility—thereby preserving that right and duty, undivided, for each individual.

In this way, our body of civil law is intended to enact in a concrete fashion our inalienable, natural rights and duties; it can neither create new rights nor disparage our existing endowment of rights. Our civil law can only flow from natural law—it can never be separate from that source. Where we draw the line between retention of our freedoms, our liberty, and our rights as individuals and the necessary authorities and powers of the government we create to protect and enforce these—both our inalienable rights, which cannot be ceded to a government, and the civil rights which give concrete force to our inalienable rights, which can be authorized, in part, to a government in our name—is the subject of considerable discussion. Indeed, it is a major factor in the need we have to remain active in the politics of our nation, to remain active in the oversight of and control over that government.

This line must be able to move according to the exigencies and the emergencies of the day, and the greatest care must be taken to ensure that wherever that line is drawn, it cannot be made immutable; we must be able to bring that line back toward us at will. This is best done by keeping firmly in mind that no civil right exists alone: it must have as its antecedent an inalienable right, or it is no right, civil or other. The law which effects that civil right—or which animates directly an inalienable right—must be traceable directly and briefly back to that inalienable right, or that law is invalid.

There is one more aspect of nationhood that needs discussion, and this is loyalty to the nation and how our nation earns (not demands) that loyalty. How does a nation go about inspiring loyalty not just to itself, but also to its creating and governing social contract? How does a nation continue inspiring loyalty from all the generations beyond the initial, founding generation? How does a nation go about inspiring this loyalty in repeated waves of immigration, as more seek to move here from their original country, which might be seen as having a preceding claim to these men's loyalty?

One way, and an aspect that contributes to the exceptionalism of the United States, is that people are here because they want to be. Our borders are not closed against those who wish to leave. Immigration into the United States is higher than for any other country on Earth—and this includes immigrants from nations that used to be plundered, including by us, for slaves. Our culture—the freedoms and rights acknowledged and enforced by our social contract—provides enormous opportunities both for Americans and for all who wish to join us to reach goals determined by each of us, not determined by any government, and to enrich our lives in ways important to and defined by us, not by any government. American culture and opportunities draw men to us. People come to the United States voluntarily, at great personal cost, and often at great risk to themselves.

We retain the loyalty that generations of men offer, and have offered, through a number of mechanisms. Our culture retains its respect for the individuality of men and their goals. Our nation, when our government and we already present are functioning properly, goes beyond simple preservation of existing opportunities and develops and fosters new ways for men to devise their own goals and then to achieve them. Our education system, when it is working correctly through local community control, educates all members of our society to our common American history, to our common American legal system, to our common American dialect of the English language, to our common American culture, to our common American ethos. Our education system does this without deprecating (rather, by making use of the best aspects of) the heritage that all of us bring, or brought generations ago, to our country. Our culture thus remains attractive to all, and it assists everyone to understand and to appreciate our American nation. Our culture is open to new ideas, so long as those suggesting them respect the primacy of our founding principles. However, it is our fundamental American culture that draws men to us, and so it is this foundational American culture that must be preserved by our educational system and by our laws.

The members of our American nation share our successes and our tribulations: no individual group is shielded from either, yet the fruits of individual success remain those of the individual who earned that success, and the individual also retains his freedom to fail—and so to recover. It is these freedoms and rights (and duties) and opportunities that attract men and inspire loyalty.

A free nation, then, is a combination of a people, the social contract to which they agree among themselves, and the government which, with their contract, they create to be subordinate to them and to protect their rights and freedoms. A nation is imbued with the culture that develops in it within the structure and form of that social contract and its imperatives. A nation might also be a combination of a people and a government that has usurped these freedoms and rights to itself and assumed power over the people, whether with their acquiescence or not, together with the subservient culture that develops in such an environment. The United States is a nation of the first sort, with the most effective social contract, but one in which we, the people, must reassert ourselves to regain control over our government, and bring it to heel, and restore it to its proper function, and so our nation to its greatness.

The inalienable rights and duties of our American nation, as given voice by our social contract, have created a uniquely American culture. This is a culture of individualism, of respect for the primacy of the individuals collectively over the government, of recognition of the broad freedom that any man has to do as he will, and to own and dispose of his own private property, limited only by the requirement that one man's actions not interfere with another man's broad freedom to do the same.

But we must always be actively careful. Rousseau warned of "…the growth of the State…." Mill wrote not so long ago, "The worth of a state, in the long run, is the worth of the individuals composing it;…a state which dwarfs its men, in order that they may be more docile instruments in its hands even for beneficial purposes—will find that with small men no great thing can really be accomplished; and that the perfection of machinery to which it has sacrificed everything will in the end avail it nothing…." Government, being populated with humans, and the members of the social contract being themselves humans, can be victims of the drift of which Rousseau warned. The members can let their force dissipate and their subordinate government's grow, if the members are not always vigilant. Eternal vigilance is, indeed, the price of liberty.[14]

---

14   The admonition most often is attributed to Thomas Jefferson; however, it also is occasionally attributed to Patrick Henry.

CHAPTER 6—FAIRNESS

2+2 must always equal 4.
*— **Polish Freedom Slogan***

There are a number of views of what constitutes "fair," what it means, how it is achieved. One such meaning has fair being defined solely by the powerful. Fairness is what they say it is, what they are capable of enforcing. This is the hoary concept of might making right. Since Hammurabi[1], though, civilization has been moving away from this, for it leaves the weak, the less fortunate, the less capable at the mercy of the strong. It is this exclusion of, if not outright preying on, these less well off (to whom I shall refer in this chapter, without coloration of any sort, as the unfortunates), that forms the motivation for men to delineate the natural, inalienable rights inherent in every man and the subsequent formation of social contracts, including our uniquely American one. Indeed, our contract explicitly acknowledges these rights and protects them for all members, perhaps most especially for those of our citizens who are among the unfortunates.

A second meaning of fair is the theoretical economist's. According to this definition, useful for analysis of some things under idealized conditions in the same way that an engineer will ignore air friction when preliminarily investigating a ballistics question, all outcomes are equally likely to occur. This is the fair die, for instance, where all sides of the cube, each of the values from 1 to 6, have the same probability of being thrown. There is nothing a player can do, no level of effort or variation of action, no skill in the wrist, that can influence the outcome. The result of a participant's throw is purely random; it requires only that he play at all, according to his own choice.

---

1   There were several older written codes of law, including those of Lipit-Ishtar, Eshnunna, and Ur-Nammu. Hammurabi's Code is better known for two reasons: his Code was discovered first by some 30 years. The second reason stems from fact that the Hammurabi Code seems to be the first that has at least the beginnings of a concept of "innocent until proven guilty."

A third meaning of fair flows from that second meaning, that of the fair die. When a fair die is used outside the theorist's laboratory, it is not used in isolation; the outcomes of several die throws are aggregated into what turns out to be a variety of likelihoods for the outcomes. Simplistically, for instance, at a Las Vegas casino craps table, the dice are used in pairs, and the outcomes are not equally likely: there are more ways to throw a 7—or a 6—than a 12, and it is impossible to throw a 1. Crucially, though, the likelihoods of these combinations are known in advance, even though each outcome of a given throw remains completely independent of a participant's action, still requiring only that he participate. So it is away from the craps table, with some of the friction of life added. A man contemplates a decision, and from this potential decision, a range of outcomes is known, including that there exist outcomes about which little is known other than simply that they exist. Further, the participant knows, or can estimate, the range of likelihoods of all of these potential outcomes, together with the fact that each of these has a different range of possibilities flowing from it. Finally, the players are free to make their own decisions on whether or not to play; no one can force them to do so. Note that learned skill or innate talent are not factors in this construction; the actual outcome remains independent of the participants' action beyond a need actually to participate to receive an outcome.

A fourth meaning of fairness is a variant on the third meaning above. In this concept, there may more than one path to higher levels of achievement, or of success, or to some desired goal. As before, most these paths are well known, but we now include the added friction that many, if not all, the paths have uncertain outcomes, i.e., a given path might have a variety of possible results. We add further the factors that the level of effort, skill, and talent required to follow each path can be reasonably estimated. Included now is the friction that it is known that there may be whole paths that are unknown to the participants. This concept adds as a final attribute a direct influence on success or failure from the individual's level of effort, his learned skill level, and his inherent talent, levels that are unique to each participant. Thus, each man has the opportunity to achieve the fullest of his own potential and capability, his own talent; and the decisions to make the effort at all, and if so, the amount of effort, are the individual's alone. As before, knowledge of all of this is available to any who wish to participate, and the paths are available to be attempted by all who wish to try. In this manner, the level of success is determined primarily by the individual and his own choices.

A fifth definition of fairness is a close variant on the economist's idealized conditions with the fair die: equal outcomes for all participants: not just equal likelihoods of a collection of outcomes, every participant receives the same value, according to some metric, as everyone else. This concept, though, renders the degree of effort and skill put into achievement, or the degree of talent that underlies any effort or skill, irrelevant; all receive the same outcome regardless of effort or input. To achieve this, either the more successful—those who tried harder, had more skill, and/or had more talent—must be held back to the level of the less successful, or the less successful must be subsidized in some way so as to receive the same value of outcome as the more successful.

In the end, though, fair is what men decide it shall be when they create, and then maintain, their social contract among each other. But any contract that does not recognize, protect, and implement our Creator-given inalienable rights[2] is an invalid contract because it functionally attempts to separate those inherent liberties from each member. Fair must be, in our social contract, a concrete animation of these inherent liberties. When it is, fairness results in justice. In this manner, fairness preserves the weak or less fortunate—the unfortunates—from the ravages of the stronger or more fortunate, for the unfortunates have the same suite of inalienable rights as the strong and fortunate. Fairness also allows each individual to work to the level of effort he decides; to use the tools he has available to him, or chooses to acquire, to fulfill his own potential; to use his own capabilities to the extent he wishes, without limits imposed on him by others; while receiving only the results—success or failure—of his own decisions and work.

Restraining the more successful, or subsidizing the less successful (that fifth definition of fairness), are the same thing: the more successful are denied full value for their work, their talent, and their skills. In the first instance, the more successful are held back directly, with the full measure of their success denied them. In the second, the more successful are denied the same extra return to their performance that is awarded the less successful through

---

2   The dual nature of rights and duties are discussed in the chapter on Citizenship and more fully in the chapter on the Nation.

subsidy. Here, for instance, is every child receiving a prize, independent of the outcome from his effort or skill or talent, and so both the self-esteem of the child who did not do well and that of the child who won the competition are damaged by not being able to reap a reward consistent with actual effort or reap the consequences of failure and the opportunity to learn from that—with its own concomitant return to self-esteem. Each child functionally receives only a participation award. Here, too, is the high school orchestra, having won a state-wide competition in one year denied by rule the opportunity to compete at all in the following year. This punishment for success denies the successful orchestra the opportunity for further success, and it denies the newly "winning" orchestra the opportunity to show that it is truly the best in the current year by outperforming last year's winner. Here, too, is the man who worked hard, both at the particular endeavor and at acquiring the skills necessary for success in the endeavor, and who was able to bring his talent to bear, being forced to give up some portion of the results of his more successful effort to another who did not do as well. This concept of equal outcomes punishes the successful for their success, and it denies the unsuccessful the opportunity to do better and to become successful in their own right.

The American social contract implements the fourth meaning of fair that I described above; although the current Progressives are trying to push us into the fifth meaning. Each American has an equal opportunity to achieve his version of the American dream, to achieve the full potential of his own capabilities. This necessarily produces unequal outcomes when measured merely by fiscal wealth or material possession. However, this equal opportunity is a grand implementation of American rights and liberties, as it provides the greatest equality for Americans in national-level protections of each individual's existence, rights, freedoms, and social well-being. This also produces the greatest moral strength and the most national wealth and greatest national power. As Rousseau has said, "Equality of rights and the idea of justice which such equality creates originate in the preference each man gives to himself, and accordingly in the very nature of man." And further, "The Sovereign never has a right to lay more charges on one subject than on another."[3] Mill addresses the matter, also: "There is no room for entertaining any such question [of a person's conduct affecting prejudicially

---

3   See footnote 13 in the chapter on Citizenship for a clarification of Rousseau's use of the term Sovereign.

the interests of others] when a person's conduct affects the interests of no person besides himself, or needs not affect them unless they like."

And so we have a description of the unfairness, of the injustice, of a government-mandated forced redistribution of wealth from one man to another, however sympathetically the idea may be couched in terms of the successful "sharing" with unfortunates. Nor does an unfortunate have a legitimate claim on the resources or rewards accruing to the successful from their efforts, as this is a precise example of Mill's prejudicial conduct.

Note that this also guarantees each actor against receipt of any compensation or repayment in the event his endeavor fails for any reason other than himself being a victim of some criminal or civil wrong. Whether the failure is a result of lack of effort, or of the skills employed being insufficient, or of the talent available being deficient, or of plain bad luck, that man must accept the result without claim on any other to make him whole again. Freedom to gain freely from one's own actions carries with it the other side of that coin: the freedom to fail and to absorb alone the consequences of that failure. This freedom to fail carries with it this addition: the increase in moral strength from trying again, and this time succeeding, without recourse to claiming a portion of another man's success; and the increase in self-confidence from that recovery and subsequent success.

Therefore we see that our concept of fair as thus far developed is simply stated, if profound in its effects. It is fair if all citizens under our American social contract have the same, or access to the same, knowledge of potential outcomes and of the varying ways of achieving them. It is fair, also, if all are free to choose to pursue or not pursue a particular outcome or collection of outcomes. It is fair, further, if all who choose to engage in the pursuit are free to do so with however much or little effort, skill, and/or talent they decide for themselves to bring to bear on the endeavor. It is fair, finally, if the results of these efforts, whether representative of success or failure, accrue to that individual and to no one else. If these four conditions are met, then the situation, as thus far developed, is fair.

Parenthetically, here is fairness as what I refer to as positive justice. Each man gets what is justly his because he has earned it through the fruit of his own labor, using his own suite of acquired skills and talents, and each man suffers the consequences of his own lack of success, without consequence imposed on him by any other(s). A citizen's degree of success or failure must be driven, nearly entirely (to be sure, random chance plays a role), by his own decisions and by his own talent. I contrast this with negative justice, which results in an individual being justly punished for a transgression which he commits, an act injurious to another done by him, whether this be criminal or civil, coupled with the victim being fairly compensated for the civil wrong.

Given this concept of fairness as developed thus far, what then of the unfortunates? Are they to be left to fend for themselves, and the Devil take the hindmost? No, for our concept of fairness is incomplete: remaining is one more facet of American fairness. Our Judeo-Christian heritage, and our social contract all enjoin us to help the least among us to a degree that enables their survival in our world, if not to share fully in the material well-being that our efforts provide for ourselves. There is a purely practical aspect to this, as well as the moral. If we do nothing to help the least, if we simply let them fall by the wayside, then the threshold for who is least will steadily rise. Ultimately, we will be the hindmost.

"Fair" requires justice, and it requires contribution by everyone, including the strong, to the protection of the inalienable rights of everyone, including the weak, for all men—strong and weak—possess these rights. Just social contracts—including our own—are formed specifically to protect these rights for all members of the resulting polity. Through our social contract, we create and employ a government for the purpose of protecting these rights for all of us, but our government is not a wind-up device to be set in motion and forgotten about. Our government—all governments—require constant oversight by us citizens, but more to the present point, each of us must directly see to the welfare of the less fortunate around us. Government—our employee—cannot be the sole, or the first, recourse; nor can it be allowed simply to take from some of us in order to give to some others of us, for government does this impersonally, inefficiently, and cookie-cutter style.

We can see, if we look, the less fortunate around us, and we can provide assistance according to our own measure of our available resources and our own choices of where that assistance is both legitimate and most needed. Then who are these people, if we can see them so easily? Luke 10:29-37, in the Christian Bible, is instructive.[4] Notice that the need to help the unfortunates is not a requirement to give them equal shares, but to share to the point of survival with a measure of comfort. Indeed, Proverbs 22:9 says, "He that hath a bountiful eye shall be blessed; for he giveth of his bread to the poor." The verses concerning Ruth and Boaz also address this. The other part of our Judeo-Christian heritage contains similar injunctions about succor for the least among us. The Talmudic teachings of Rabbi Yitzhak with commentary by the Marasha, in the passages concerning giving a coin and/or consolation to a poor person contain, in addition to other wisdom, an injunction to share a portion of our greater good fortune with the man who is in need. The Torah contains similar injunctions. We are enjoined, then, to share, while we are legitimately entitled to retain the greater portion for our greater success.

It is clear, then, that the injunction to aid unfortunates, whether explicitly Judeo-Christian or from the morality that the unfortunates possess the same inalienable rights as all of us, and the American social contract's injunction to guarantee these rights, is a personal injunction; it is not mandate from government. And so our completed concept of fair and of the justice that results from fairness includes the need to give comfort and aid to the least among us rather than simply abandoning them to an otherwise Hobbesian fate or to a grasping, ill-controlled government. Our concept preserves

---

4   The full passage is:

29 But he, willing to justify himself, said unto Jesus, And who is my neighbour?

30 And Jesus answering said, A certain man went down from Jerusalem to Jericho, and fell among thieves, which stripped him of his raiment, and wounded him, and departed, leaving him half dead.

31 And by chance there came down a certain priest that way: and when he saw him, he passed by on the other side.

32 And likewise a Levite, when he was at the place, came and looked on him, and passed by on the other side.

33 But a certain Samaritan, as he journeyed, came where he was: and when he saw him, he had compassion on him,

34 And went to him, and bound up his wounds, pouring on oil and wine, and set him on his own beast, and brought him to an inn, and took care of him.

35 And on the morrow when he departed, he took out two pence, and gave them to the host, and said unto him, Take care of him; and whatsoever thou spendest more, when I come again, I will repay thee.

36 Which now of these three, thinkest thou, was neighbour unto him that fell among the thieves?

37 And he said, He that shewed mercy on him. Then said Jesus unto him, Go, and do thou likewise.

fairness and justice for all concerned, for an act or an outcome cannot be fair for a recipient if it is not also fair for the giver and fair for all others who may be affected by the exchange. It cannot be fair for one if it is not fair for all.

But how does this actually work under our American social contract? We, individually and as a people, help sustain our fellow citizens who cannot sustain themselves, although this is not a mandate for an equal share for unequal input. We are obligated, by duty to fellow man, to help our fellow citizens to reach a sustainable level of living. We are obligated to help them maintain and live within their own inalienable rights—as all have this same suite of rights. Since, though, this is a moral obligation as well as a legal one, where does the primary responsibility lie? Our Declaration of Independence acknowledges the inherent moral and fundamental equality of all men[5], and the 14th Amendment guarantees that all men—rich or poor, successful or unsuccessful—are equal under the law.[6] The nature of our social contract, that we are Sovereign and the government works for us, means that our government cannot take from one of its employers in order to give to another of its employers, unless we allow that through our elected representatives in our employee government. In particular, our government cannot mandate what our morality shall be, beyond the basic morality of defining crimes and their suitable punishments (to which definitions we agreed by our elections of our representatives and our authorization of them to pass such laws).

The answers, then, are contained in the existence of our Social Contract, wherein we agree to give up (limited) rights to a government for the greater protection and preservation of our inalienable rights and liberties. We band together so that we can more efficiently and more effectively see to the needs of all of us far better than can we individually see to each of our individual needs. And in this agreement to cooperate for our common good is the seed, further, of seeing to the needs and welfare of the less fortunate.

Our aid to unfortunates, our charity, and the recipients of our charity, are moral choices, nothing else and nothing less. We provide our charity because

---

5   " We hold these truths to be self-evident, that all men are created equal, that they are endowed by their Creator with certain unalienable Rights...."
6   "...nor shall any State...deny to any person within its jurisdiction the equal protection of the laws."

it is our moral obligation to our fellow citizens (our fellow man generally, but I am speaking of America in this book), our duty, to do so. Merely to remain indifferent, to do nothing in the face of need, is not a passive act; it is actively malevolent. An admittedly extreme example illustrates. A man walking, passes by a baby being brutally abused and says, "I don't care. It's not my baby." Here is the malevolence of indifference. This passivity is self-evidently immoral. As the parent is responsible for the welfare of the child, so are we responsible for the welfare of the unfortunate. This does not create a parent-child relationship between the benefactor and benefited, however; I offer the coarse analogy solely to the extent that, in both cases, one cannot take care of himself, and so another must satisfy the need. The assistance an individual chooses to provide, and to whom, are strictly individual moral choices, and so are the sole province of that individual. No outside agency or government can usurp that choice or appropriate an individual's resources to that entity's ends. Doing so creates an unfair burden on all parties directly involved by dint of that involuntary appropriation. Further, it prevents those resources from being used for other ends which the resource owners might have selected, imposing a separate unfair burden on both the owner and his preferred recipients. In the end, primary responsibility for satisfaction of this individual moral imperative lies with the individual citizen. The government, as mediator of some assistance, at some time, both is a last resort only and a recipient from us citizens of the limited resources it must have for this welfare.

But what is help? How do we, in fact, help the less fortunate? Is it by redressing his shortfall and giving him that which he lacks for his sustenance? Is it by satisfying every need for which this unfortunate asks assistance? I say a resounding no. Doing this, giving the man the fish, as the aphorism has it, is no help at all. Indeed, it is the opposite: it develops and maintains that man's dependence on us, and it destroys his ability to become his own man and to be free and self-reliant. That dependency harms us, as well, since quite aside from the material drain on our resources such a dependency represents, it becomes, also, an enervating, addictive balm for our own egos. It creates and maintains a dependency in us on that very dependency of our now permanently destitute unfortunate.

On the contrary, we must, to finish the aphorism, teach the man to fish. We must provide our assistance in a form that enables that unfortunate to redress his own shortfall, to satisfy for himself his need. Only in this way can that man gain and maintain his freedom: his freedom to do as he will, as the rest of us can; to think and say as he will, as the rest of us can; to seek his own way through life without needing to ask leave of his "benefactor," lest that one threaten further benefit against the unfortunate's "proper" behavior. Even Terry Malloy "coulda been a contender, coulda been somebody"[7] with only a little help and none of the dependency into which he had been dragged. Further, only in this way can that unfortunate develop his own moral competence and the self-respect and self-confidence that come from his freedom and independence (including not depending on another for his sustenance). And from this freedom and independence comes the free and developing thinking, ideas, contributions that yet another creative individual now can provide for himself and for the surrounding community. And from this independence, and from this lack of dependence, comes benefit to us as a true benefactor: we do not suffer addiction to that dependence—and so we can continue as fully contributing, clearly thinking generators of ideas and contributions that benefit not only ourselves, but that same community. We are not seduced by our own benevolence into believing we are anything other than the unfortunate's equal.

It's necessary to keep in mind, further, that our resources are our own; we do not cede any significant portion of our rights in our property to any government, beyond such money taxes we authorize that government to collect for our common welfare. This makes personal the assistance that is rendered the less fortunate. We must provide that aid; we cannot wait upon others or government to do it in our stead.

I submit that charity must flow in the following way. As another aphorism puts it, charity begins at home. First is that person's, or group of persons', family or families; they must provide the help. Where these cannot, then we as individuals and the churches and religious and secular charitable organizations in our society must step in. Note, though, that the organizations depend on us for the assets that make possible the charity they provide. Even though these organizations are professionally staffed, they need our volunteered time and effort with their organization, as well

---

7   **On the Waterfront**, 1954, directed by Elia Kazan, written by Budd Schulberg

as our financial donations. These organizations' needs are not very different from the unfortunates'.

Where we provide assistance to an unfortunate, though, it must be anonymous whenever possible: if the recipient knows who is his benefactor, then the aid is not charity; it is obligation, and there can be no creation of obligation stemming from our assistance—this is simply mutual dependence again—nor can any of us have, or gain, dominion over another (which is another aspect of this kind of obligation) as a result of events that are no fault of either. Where the benefactor is the individual's family, identities are of course known, as this is nothing more than the obligation of family to family member. Where the benefactor is a charity or similar organization, anonymity is impossible. However, the recipient knowing the identity of the organization, and so incurring a sense of obligation to that organization, does not surrender dominion over himself to that organization for that sense of obligation can be satisfied according to the nature of the agreement the recipient voluntarily enters into in return for the assistance.

How, if the recipient does not know his benefactor, might he express his legitimate gratitude for the aid which he receives? For us as individual benefactors, through the best way appropriate: by himself assisting another who needs help, in any way our recipient can provide that help. We are fully repaid by our aid being passed along. Further, the recipient of our aid, by repaying in this way, by paying the aid forward, joins us in the morality not only of self-sufficiency, but also in the morality of aiding those less fortunate than him. And as a purely practical matter, his contribution reduces the burden on all. For the non-government-mediated charity, the assistance is repaid either in accordance with the agreement the unfortunate entered into or by passing the aid on to another unfortunate if the organization's aid was freely given.

Even if these two layers of charity are provided diligently, there will still remain, though, some few who yet need assistance, whether there are not enough private resources to go around in a locale; whether the aid is a long-term need, with an associated long-term monetary and/or facility cost that is beyond the capability of the first two layers; or for any other reason. Here, and here alone, government-mediated welfare—that is, our collective assistance in the form of some portion of our tax payments—will be appropriate.

Where the benefactor is the government, however, anonymity also is not possible. The relationship here between benefactor and benefitted involves resources commandeered by the government, and so a careful accounting of the resources so committed is necessary, not the least to ensure those resources are being used efficiently and for the intended purpose only. Charity—welfare—from the government, though, must be paid back to the government or earned in some way; it cannot be paid forward. The distinction is this: private charity is a voluntary act, with the donor knowing to whom or to what charitable organization the donation is made, but charity from the government is both a forced donation (albeit agreed to at some time prior in the form of a law having been passed by the representatives of the citizens) and the donation goes to a person or an entity necessarily unknown to any specific donor. Thus, the recipient of this welfare payment, appropriated as it is from the general population of fellow citizens, must repay or earn the charity. The earning/payback can be in the form of a pay forward, but the terms must be set by the government agency involved.

I have been writing, so far, primarily of unfortunates who are, in some sense and for a short or long duration, down on their luck; their situation is inherently temporary and reparable. But there are two other groups of unfortunates: those who are simply incapable, and so have a permanent true need, and those who are lazy, *i.e.*, amoral, a condition that may or may not be permanent. These two groups must be handled also.

How are we to handle the incapable? The chain is the same: charity from private sources first, the government last. The incapable, however, generally are not able to repay the private sources or to earn or to repay the government's—our collective—charity. These few only must receive uncompensated support—grants.

How are we to handle the lazy, though, as opposed to the incapable? As Mill has pointed out, no one is required to associate with those who misbehave (although his remarks were in the context of those who actively misbehave through antisocial behavior, criminal behavior, etc). The lazy are misbehaving passively; still, no one of us is obligated by duty or any other imperative to help the lazy, those who abuse our aid, these amoral ones. However, we citizens as a group are obligated to help the least among us, including these lazy—all of us have the same inalienable rights which, Creator-endowed, are indivisible from us by any man-made agency, including one's own amorality. Further, all men are equal under the law, and this equality is not in any place in our social contract caveated on degree of effort. Thus, even the lazy man, if he cannot find succor from private charity, has a claim on our collective charity—government-mediated welfare. The lazy, though, especially must be required to earn that welfare. For these, the only appropriate program is a work-for-welfare program. To be clear, in such a case there can be no question of the work available being "beneath the station" of the recipient. The Doctor of Philosophy whose position has reached the point of needing government-mediated welfare is in no position to eschew the work of a common laborer to earn that welfare. Finally, note that the mechanics of distinguishing the lazy from the incapable from the temporarily down, or of assigning work for government-mediated assistance is beyond the scope of a book discussing principles.

In the end, charity is an obligation each of us, including the charity recipient who is capable, has toward our fellows. The recipients and methods of our charity, though, are personal moral choices. The intrusion of government into these is an overextension of government's legitimate authority. An assertion might be made by a government (or by a government official, which is the same thing) that this thing is a moral matter; you must give Us from your resources, from your property, from your money so that We can do this moral thing for you. A statement might be made by a government official that this is patriotic, so give Us from your money so that We can do this patriotic thing for you. These are merely self-serving attempts of that government person to define for you what your morality is, what your patriotism is. It is merely the arrogance of a Progressive who uses these claims to say, "We Know Better. You should listen to Us and do as We instruct." Such arrogance is not far removed from tyranny: "Give Us your property, your resources, your money. We Know Better than you how these should be used. You misunderstand, you are misinformed, you are wrong. Just do as We instruct." There are two responses to this arrogance. The first response is to demand that the government official make public his personal contributions to the cause espoused, and the relationship of those contributions to his income and total resources. The government official who says that it is patriotic to (for instance) pay taxes should be required to say how much money he has donated to the Treasury beyond the taxes he already pays, as well as the amount of those taxes he pays, and that sum compared to his total income and resources. The second response is to recognize that such arrogance renders the speaker unfit for office and to vote that person out of office at the next election.

And so we arrive at my conception of American fairness and its place as part of the foundation of justice. If the following conditions are met, we have a fair and just society within our social contract:

- All members of our social contract have the same knowledge, or access to the same knowledge, of potential outcomes and of the varying ways of achieving them.
- All members are free to choose to pursue or not to pursue a particular outcome or collection of outcomes.
- All members who choose to engage in the pursuit are free to do so with however much or little effort, skill, and/or talent they decide for themselves to bring to the endeavor.
- The results of each member's efforts, whether representative of success or failure, accrue to that member and to no one else.
- We share a measure of our good fortune to the sustenance of unfortunates: those who cannot see to their own care and existence; those who need some momentary assistance, a hand up; even those who will not see to their own affairs.

CHAPTER 7—THE ECONOMY

Egalitarians create the most dangerous inequality of all -- inequality of power. Allowing politicians to determine what all other human beings will be allowed to earn is one of the most reckless gambles imaginable.

— *Thomas Sowell*

Economies that have been managed by governments have failed all over the world. The Union of Soviet Socialist Republics has ceased to exist, and its destruction was an economic one: no shot was fired, and the USSR never was conquered. Without the external prop of the USSR, eastern Germany collapsed economically and sought reintegration into, and bailout by, the Federal Republic of Germany. The managed economy of The People's Republic of China is incorporating capitalist, free market principles, and its economy began growing rapidly from the depressed base of completely centralized management as soon as this incorporation began. The socialist economies of last century's Europe, generally, gave way to more free market-oriented principles with markedly decreased government intervention, and Europe saw a period of prosperity unequalled at any other time in that century. Even the strongly socialist-leaning government of Great Britain's Tony Blair was forced to reduce the level of government control over, and to allow competition to enter into, its National Health Service as the only means to save the British health care system; this reduction in government management is being continued and extended by the current Cameron government. The ongoing economic crises of the 21st century European Union all are the result of national and European Union government controls having been reimposed on their respective economies as these governments resumed relieving their populations of responsibility and promising, instead, that government would provide for them.

In this chapter, we'll look at the failed government interventions into our own free market economy, as first modern Liberals, and then Progressives, enacted government controls and government-driven wealth redistribution programs. Then we'll look at what might have happened had the government not intervened. We'll see some results that might have occurred from the far more efficient wealth redistribution that comes from letting market forces guide responses to the dislocations and from leaving the wealth of citizens in the hands of the owners of that wealth. Then we'll look at other advantages of free market economies, with their built-in emphasis on individual freedom and responsibility, concepts that are central to conservative principles. We'll close with a look at a few ways of recovering these advantages.

Even necessary entries by government into an economy, simply to buy goods and services necessary for the government to function or to satisfy its legitimate purposes (*vis.*, equipment, supplies, and training for our national defense), are fraught with inefficiencies. There are extra layers of middlemen in the government's transactions, for instance. These layers of middlemen (this is far from an exhaustive list) include the government's tax office which collects the money, the government's contracting office which arranges the purchase, the receiving office which accepts delivery, and the layers of bureaucrats who must report to the Congress' and the Executive's overseers, describing and certifying the expenditures. Here is a summary of the Contracting Office's procedures, and the requirements which private enterprise must satisfy in order to participate.[1]

> [A]cquisition personnel, after determining their agency's requirements (that is, the goods and services the agency needs), post a solicitation on the Federal Business Opportunities (FedBizOpps) website. Interested companies prepare their offers in response to the solicitation, and, in accordance with applicable provisions of the *Federal Acquisition Regulation* (FAR), agency personnel evaluate the offers. Another type of procurement opportunity for a company is to serve as a subcontractor for a government contractor. To be eligible to compete for government contracts, a company must obtain a Data Universal Numbering System (DUNS) number, register with the Central Contractor Registry (CCR), and complete an Online Representations

---

1   Halchin, L. Elaine, "Overview of the Federal Procurement Process and Resources," **CRS Report for Congress**, Order Code RS22536, November 20, 2006. Note carefully that title. The entire document is a summary of Federal procurement procedures, yet it runs to six pages

THE ECONOMY

and Certifications Application (ORCA). Several agencies, such as the General Services Administration (GSA), provide assistance and services to existing and potential government contractors. Research and development (R&D) procurement opportunities may involve traditional contracting methods, such as solicitations and contracts, as well as nontraditional methods, which include agency sponsored contests and venture capital funds.

There is a similarly extensive chain of middleman bureaucrats supporting the government's borrowing efforts. Thus, significantly more money over and above the cost of the goods themselves must be taxed and/or borrowed so that these middleman costs, also, can be paid for.

The costs of these government middleman layers are imposed on the entities selling to the government, too: the sellers must report in detail the receipt and use of the money which the government paid them. This reporting and associated paperwork add significantly to the sellers' cost of doing business with the government without adding value to the goods sold.

Finally, the sheer size of the government creates a volume of demand that unavoidably competes with the demand of private enterprise and of individuals for the same goods and services. This increased demand creates an upward pressure on the prices we all pay. This effect is not limited to the particular product: when the government puts money into the economy at all with its buying, it increases the amount of money available in that economy generally,[2] which raises prices generally; this is the definition of inflation.

I'll leave aside, now, the negative effects of simple government purchases of its necessities. These are unavoidable, and their effects are, in the end, relatively benign compared to attempts to manipulate the economy through intervention. Instead, I'll explore here the nature and effects of deliberate government interventions.

---

2   To be sure, there are other, stronger mechanisms for adding money to the economy, such as the Federal Reserve Bank lowering the fractional reserves banks must maintain, or simply printing money. Nevertheless, the cash added via government purchases is significant.

Government interventions—acts of manipulating the economy (*vis.*, deductions for home mortgages, "green" energy subsidies, government bailouts, and so on) for specific social or claimed economic purposes—are not just bad economics, leading to inefficient and destructive allocations of resources and of wealth. They are also an intrusion into, and a reduction of, the freedoms of men, and they amount to an assault on the morality of men, all regardless of the good intentions that may underlie these interventions. They are contrary to our American social contract. Following are some examples which, as before, are selected more or less at random and with no attempt to provide a comprehensive history. They illustrate, though, the deleterious effects that result from attempts to intervene in, or to control outright, even apparently isolated segments of our free market economy.

The Theodore Roosevelt administration, in its response to the railroad shipping rate collusion matter described earlier, intervened in a segment of the transportation market with government-mandated price controls. Despite the availability of existing law to eliminate this pricing abuse, Roosevelt instead used the problem to further his larger goal of bringing the railroads under government regulatory control. This intervention, though, ignored the trucking industry, then nascent but growing rapidly. With the railroads hamstrung by government controls, but trucking free to operate without constraint, trucking gained business and revenue at the railroads' direct expense. The Hepburn Act provided additional government intrusion, giving the Interstate Commerce Commission authority to inspect the railroads' accounting books on demand, facilitating increased government constraints on the railroads. The cascade of results from this government distortion flowed: trucking gains combined with railroad rate regulation to sharply depress the value of railroad securities, and this deep fall in railroad value was a major factor in the Panic of 1907[3].

The Franklin Roosevelt administration's agriculture interventions (*vis.*, the Agricultural Adjustment Acts of 1933[4] and 1938) led to artificially inflated prices through government funded price supports. These supports,

---

3   The Panic proximately was caused by a failed attempt to manipulate the copper market. However, at the time, railroad securities were key collateral used by banks throughout the economy; with the rapid depression of railroad security values, the collateral collapsed and so did many banks nationwide.

4   The 1933 Act ultimately was ruled unconstitutional by the Supreme Court; the 1938 Act was its replacement.

though, created artificially inflated prices for those farm goods at a time when Americans were at historic levels of unemployment (17-24%) and so could ill afford the higher prices.

During this same period, the Roosevelt administration seized citizens' wealth by executive fiat,[5] confiscating privately held gold for redistribution into government purposes[6] and to attempt to control the value of the dollar internationally. The gold, when held privately, was almost never held as bullion; it was in the form of gold dollar currency. The private owner, who certainly often stored the gold himself, viewed such holdings as savings, though, and would have been able to spend it at need or desire—adding cash flow to the existing economy. The high prices, generally, and the loss of wealth from confiscation were followed by reduced demand, and this prolonged the Great Depression for years.

The Roosevelt administration further circumscribed the economy by intervening in the labor segment. Here, the government acted[7] to set floors for both wages, and it encouraged unions to strike for increased wages. These provisions drove up the cost of goods and services to consumers, through the higher labor costs—at those historic unemployment levels mentioned just above. These potential consumers also were laborers, though, and now they were being priced out of the labor market by those wage controls (while businesses were being struck for yet higher wages). Faced with little demand for their output, these businesses could not afford to hire at any wage, much less at the government-mandated floor wage. These additional price controls and wage floors also contributed to prolonging the Great Depression.

With prices now inflated to the extremities of the reach (and, too often, beyond it) of an unemployed population, the Roosevelt Administration, in 1939, created the first Food Stamp Program, intending to help individuals pay for food. The program's first administrator, Milo Perkins, justified the

---

5   **Executive Order** 6102, signed in April 1933.

6   The government kept the gold primarily simply to store, as a prop for the dollar.

7   The National Industrial Recovery Act of 1933 (NIRA), with its National Recovery Administration NRA), and the National Labor Relations Act of 1935 (NLRA). Although the NIRA, which also attempted to set floors on prices beyond agriculture, was declared unconstitutional (*Schechter Poultry Corp. v. United States* 295 U.S. 495 (1935)), the NLRA was able to do its damage. Further, the Supreme Court's "uncooperativeness" with both the AAA and the NIRA of 1933 led FDR to begin his assault on the Court.

need for the program by saying, without a trace of irony, "We got a picture of a gorge, with farm surpluses on one cliff and under-nourished city folks with outstretched hands on the other. We set out to find a practical way to build a bridge across that chasm."

The Eisenhower administration continued these government interventions with grants-in-aid and, especially, matching funds programs for the states. These interventions, though, did little more than trap the States into programs they couldn't afford (and in many of which they're still trapped) but still were required to provide even if the Federal government were later to decide to cease making the funds transfers (which State governments subsequently would claim as justification for raising taxes). As President Eisenhower recognized (but in the end, did little about), "While [the programs and transfers] have stimulated the development of certain [Federally "encouraged"] State activities, they have complicated State finances and... made it difficult for States to provide funds for other important services"[8] of their own selection. These State-preferred programs suffered because the States had to provide their own monies for the "encouraged," if not outright mandated, programs in order to receive the grants or matching funds, and so the States' own programs were forced to compete with each other for a reduced pool of State monies.

Under the Johnson administration, Medicare and Medicaid programs were created as interventions into the market for medical services. However, rather than alleviating costs, these new programs made the situation worse. In the year before Medicare was passed, the cost of a hospital bed was rising at 5% per year—three percentage points higher than the overall rate of inflation for that year. By the fifth year following Medicare's enactment, the cost of that same hospital bed was rising at 8% per year, a 60% increase in the rate of inflation for the bed, against a baseline, still, of just 4% overall inflation. Further, the combined "advantage" of Medicare and Medicaid, through 2001, accounted for fully 25% of the inflation in the overall cost of medical care. The tax exempt status of employer-provided medical coverage

---

8   "Special Message to the Congress Recommending the Establishment of a Commission To Study Federal, State, and Local Relations," March 30, 1953. President Eisenhower added, "...especially within the past twenty years, the Federal Government has entered fields which...are the primary responsibilities of state and local governments. This has tended to blur the responsibilities of local government.... It is time to relieve the people of the need to pay taxes on taxes."

(another "boon" for the individual), accounted for another 33% of the inflation in total medical services cost: these two government interventions in the health care market are responsible for nearly 60% of the inflation in the cost of medical care.[9]

Basic principles of economics make the reason for this failure clear: Medicare is a mandatory program; participation is required, whether the individual wants any part of it or not. This mandatory participation artificially increases demand for medical services, although the amount of medical services available—hospital beds, doctors, and so on—did not, and still is not, rising nearly as quickly. Participation in Medicaid is very strongly encouraged by the government, further exacerbating demand compared with the supply of services. On the consumer side, the tax status of employer-provided medical insurance coverage also heavily accelerated demand for medical services. The price must rise. This government intervention has led to medical care costing far more than it would without that intervention, whether it's the individual, the employer, or the government (*i.e.*, all of us) paying the costs.

Yet another government intervention is Federal interference with the housing market. With the Community Reinvestment Act (CRA) of 1977, the Federal government began pressuring banks and savings and loan institutions—and the finance industry generally—to lend money on relaxed credit standards in order to encourage home buying. With the legislative adjustments to the CRA of the 1990s, the pressure on banks to lend increased, now including a push specifically for higher risk individuals to be granted lower interest rates: the institutions simply were to lend more money and not concern themselves so much with credit worthiness. This artificially elevated demand led to rapidly increasing housing prices and to correspondingly larger loans, to higher risk borrowers. The resulting housing mortgage crisis, precipitated in part when the resulting housing bubble burst and housing prices collapsed and in part when all those high-risk borrowers began defaulting, led directly to the Panic of 2008, in which we remain mired as I write this.

There ensued government intervention from simply flooding the economy with taxpayers' money. When the Panic of 2008 became manifest, the Bush

---

9   Friedman, Milton, "gammon's Law Points to Health-Care Solution," **The Wall Street Journal**, 12 November 1991, and Friedman, Milton, "How to Cure Health Care," **Hoover Digest**, 2001

and Obama administrations together spent nearly $700 billion of "rescue" funds via the Troubled Asset Relief Program (TARP),[10] and the Obama administration immediately followed this with an additional $787 billion in spending via the American Recovery and Reinvestment Act of 2009 (the Stimulus bill).[11] At a stroke, these two bills added nearly $1.5 trillion to the national debt.

At the start of the Panic, lenders had on their books a vast volume of bad loans, along with secondary debt instruments that used these loans as collateral or as other forms of security. TARP was passed to allow the Federal government buy these bad loans from their holders,[12] but the program was changed quickly by the Obama administration to facilitate bailouts of auto unions and to nationalize large banks and other financial institutions, rather than letting these failing companies and unions complete their failures through the existing bankruptcy court system and the financial crisis to work its way through resolution normally.

The Stimulus bill was passed on the promise of putting Americans back to work by funding so-called "shovel ready" jobs,[13] but national unemployment continued to rise from the 8+% unemployment rate at the start of 2009 to over 10% in 2010, and it has remained above 9% since.[14]

The normal business cycle recovery that has been showing signs of appearing for the last 24 months (indeed, the "recession" officially ended

---

10   The Bush the Younger administration pushed TARP through Congress in October 2008 and spent the initial allotment. At President-elect Obama's request, Bush persuaded Congress to release the remaining TARP funds so that the Obama administration would have them available immediately on his accession to office.

11   Enacted February 2009

12   TARP was passed over the objections of American citizens, an objection so vociferous that the House of Representatives rejected TARP the first time it came to a vote. The Federal government's employers recognized better than the Federal government the moral and economic bankruptcy of a bailout plan that kept failing companies propped up—and at taxpayer expense—rather than letting the bad companies fail and recover through the existing bankruptcy system.

13   18 months later, Obama finally acknowledged, "there's no such thing as shovel-ready projects" in an October 2010 interview with **The New York Times Magazine**. He joked about his lack of understanding of "shovel-ready" during a June 2011 public meeting of his Jobs and Competitiveness Council in Durham, NC.

14   In the winter of 2011, the unemployment rate fell to 9% as more and more Americans gave up looking for work and left the work force altogether, thereby shrinking the numerator of the unemployment ratio.

THE ECONOMY

in June 2009) remains inhibited by the ongoing interventions of TARP (officially "expiring" in December 2010, but many banks and other financial institutions remain effectively nationalized, and the Federal Reserve Bank continues to guarantee many loans made by these and other, not yet formally nationalized, banks) and the Stimulus bill. The massive debt explosion from this intervention, coupled with exploding business and personal costs from the Patient Protection and Affordable Care Act, discussed below, and the Obama administration's constant calls for raising taxes have inhibited investment in business, hiring by business, and spending by individuals—and so prolonged the Panic.

The just-passed (in the depths of this Panic) Patient Protection and Affordable Care Act (PPACA) is the latest example of the failure of government intervention in the economy. We've seen insurance companies already raising their premiums to cover the costs of mandated additions to coverage, and we've seen the government's response: threatening to bar those insurance companies from the government's market if they persist in seeking these premium increases. I describe this in Chapters 2 and 9. We've seen insurance companies in a number of states withdraw from those states' health insurance market altogether,[15] because they no longer can afford to offer the mandated coverage at the allowed premiums. We've seen doctors stop taking Medicare patients because they no longer can afford to provide their services at the Medicare-mandated reimbursement rates, and we've seen a significant percentage of remaining doctors announce their impending retirement or other departures from medical services,[16] because they anticipate conditions to be even worse as the various programs of the PPACA begin to take effect. We've seen employers take significant charges to their revenues in anticipation of the increased costs imposed by PPACA.[17] We've seen other employers, and unions, request waivers to various aspects

15   WellPoint and CoventryOne, for instance, announced in September 2010 that they would stop selling child health care insurance in California, Colorado, Ohio and Missouri due to PPACA-caused increases in cost of such coverage.

16   A survey conducted by Medicus Firm, "Physician Survey: Health Reform's Impact on Physician Supply and Quality of Medical Care," found that 29% of 1,200 doctors who responded said they would quit the profession or retire early.

17   AT&T took a $1B charge, Caterpillar Inc. took a $100M, 3M Company took a $85-90M charge, AK Steel Holding Corp. took a $31M charge, to name a few. This prompted the attempt by Congressman Henry Waxman (Dem, CA) to conduct a Congressional Inquisition against the executives of several of these companies, as described in the chapter on Conservatism vs. Modern Liberalism.

of PPACA in response to anticipated PPACA-caused cost increases.[18] This is a medical services market intervention that is succeeding only in reducing the supply of medical services while simultaneously increasing demand and cost. (Some have suggested that this is, in fact, a long-term goal of the Obama administration when it passed PPACA in its strictly partisan manner: to drive out all private/commercial players so that the government can institute its own single-player [sic] health provision program.)

The government's tax policies are another, more subtle, form of intervention into our economy. What are the purposes of taxes and of taxation? This question can be answered with finality only in a discussion of the purpose of government, the subject of another chapter. The question is important within this chapter, however, as taxation takes money from individuals and their businesses in order to be used for the government's purposes.

The government's seeming purpose for levying taxes is revealed by its behavior these last 80 years: redistribution of the monies collected. Nearly 40%—$1.5 trillion—of President Obama's proposed 2011 Federal budget, for instance, was intended to be spent solely on transfers from one man to another: Social Security, Medicare, and Medicaid. Another 6.5% was intended for interest on the national debt—not to pay down the debt, just to pay its interest. Note that this is in addition to those $1.5 trillion spent on transfers to failing businesses and unions in order to bail them out of the consequences of their own decisions and on transfers to other unions and to states via failed jobs creation programs. Further, these redistribution payments are subject to the same middleman layers of expenses as the product purchase described earlier, and substantially more than those $1.5 trillion must be collected (or borrowed) in order to pay out that much, or as was the case with the actual payouts from the TARP and Stimulus bill, the actual transfers were greatly reduced by those middleman layers.[19] Note

---

18   Bricklayers Local 1 of MD, VA and DC, with nearly 1200 members; Local 1102 Health & Benefit Fund, with over 4600 members; Local 338 Affiliated Benefit Funds, with over 18,200 members; The Mentor Network, with over 6800 employees. The requested number of waivers was over 770 by January 2011 the number granted was over 1400 by May 2011.

19   Some project that TARP actually will make money for the Federal government when the dust has settled. This elides a number of factors, though: the government is not intended to be a profit-making concern. The TARP funds transferred to the auto unions via their use, nominally, to bail out General Motors Co. and Chrysler, LLC, will never be repaid, according to those same projections. The opportunity cost of potentially greater returns had the money been left in the hands of its owners is unconsidered—indeed, opportunity costs, generally, are usually overlooked. The cost of the moral

that these do not include other transfers such as farm subsidies, transfer payments to the poor (beyond Medicaid), low income tax credits, and the like—all of which are paid for by taxes collected from the rest of the American citizens, or borrowed from our children's future (because it'll be their tax payments that will repay our current borrowings).

In looking at the degree of usefulness of taxation in fostering economic growth, and so increasing the wealth of American citizens and improving the quality of our lives, we see stark examples. When Franklin Roosevelt raised taxes to the levels he did—up to 74% of business' retained earnings (Roosevelt objected to businesses retaining earnings for savings or for reinvestment; instead, the monies needed to be paid to labor), and personal income tax rates to as high as 79% in 1935 (and to 94% by 1944)—he withdrew money from an already depressed economy and prolonged the Depression. President John Kennedy, after Eisenhower refused to reduce income taxes and against the advice of his own advisors, proposed a tax cut lowering the top marginal rate by 20 percentage points (from the then 91% to 71%), and this was enacted in early 1964 (shortly after his murder) in President Lyndon Johnson's administration. Gross National Product rose 10% in the first year of the tax cut, and economic growth averaged 4.5% per year over the next eight years. Disposable personal income rose 15% in 1966 alone. Federal revenues increased at these lowered tax rates—due to the resulting increase in economic activity—by nearly two-thirds over the next several years, from $94 billion in 1961 to $150 billion in 1967 as economic lags in money, savings, and investment flows were worked through. The Reagan tax cuts[20] produced similar economic growth, pulling the country out of an ongoing recession.

Some might call such tax reductions interventions in the market. However, they are not interventions. They are removals of the prior interventions of confiscatory tax rates; they return to an environment where Americans retained more of what was theirs—their own money, in this case—rather than the government appropriating more than actually needed, and then using this excess for government's purposes rather than those of the erstwhile owners.

---

hazard of telling businesses that they need have no concern about failure because the government will bail them out is immeasurable.

20   Which extended the supply-side economics concept of that Democratic predecessor.

Beyond these utilitarian and monetary concerns, government intervention into the economy also leads inexorably to a reduction of individual freedom and choices. Whenever the government intervenes in the economy, whether explicitly to redistribute wealth as is President Obama's plainly stated purpose[21] or to engage in social engineering in order to achieve government-determined social purposes[22] (which is just wealth redistribution by another name), it reduces the choices available to American citizens.

Our choices are reduced directly by taking money away from us—money that we now cannot spend on our own goals—and our choices are reduced by the distortions such wealth redistribution causes in our commerce. The mortgage interest deduction, for instance, actually drives up the price of housing by apparently making home buying cheaper: if we can deduct the interest portion of our mortgage payment, it must, so the thinking goes, lower the total cost of the home. However, this actually results in our being able to "afford" a more expensive home, driving up demand—and therefore the prices—of those homes. It also drives up the price of the originally considered home, since the deduction makes more money available with which to pay for that home. Even if we prefer to rent, and so are not in the house-buying market, this wealth redistributing deduction hurts our choices: with home purchase costs going up, so do rents on houses and apartments that are competing for the overall housing dollar.

When government inhibits business reinvestment, whether deliberately or as an unintended consequence of a well-intentioned policy, it harms both business and individuals. It harms business by lowering its capital improvement capability (at the expense of productivity, and so cost to customers) and reducing its capacity for research and development (at the expense of long-term productivity and product development and so the business' ability to compete). This harm reduces the range of products in the market and so limits the choices available to Americans. Existing products are also sold at higher prices than would have been the case, further limiting individual choices. These artificial strains then inhibit business expansion

---

21   "I think when you spread the wealth around, it's good for everybody" and "I think at a certain point, you've made enough money," cited in an earlier chapter.

22   *Vis.,* mortgage interest deductions and lowered lending standards to encourage home ownership, or retained-earnings taxes to discourage business reinvestment.

and hiring—at the direct expense of individuals' abilities to see to their own Happinesses.

When a government presses on us, with tax policy for instance, to do one thing, or not to do another—even if it does not outright mandate these—it inhibits us from doing their opposite. Freedom to do cannot exist unless we are free, also, not to do.

Beyond that reduction in choice, there is a stark reduction in individual liberty. It's necessary to revisit *Wickard v Filburn*, which is not an Executive or Legislative branch intervention, but a judicial branch one. I described this case in Chapter 2, and I wrote that it is a distortion of our Constitution. It is, though, also an assault on the foundation of American freedoms. *Wickard* completed the circle drawn around our freedoms and our economy begun in the early and mid-1930s with FDR's New Deal. It brings men's labor directly under government control, and it reversed, for instance, *Kidd v Pearson* and *United States v E. C. Knight Co.* as well as 100 years of precedent (also described in that earlier chapter). This is the government asserting its power to control merchants, once they've become merchants: a farmer, for instance, who sells his crops on the market can no longer produce extra to feed his private animal stock, or his own family. Beyond this, it asserts that a man who is just starting to farm may not grow exclusively for his own consumption, except under government control. As businesses are agencies of men, this extends directly to government control over both individual behavior (that small farmer is a direct example) and over businesses.

We must keep firmly in mind that the primary means of production is the man himself: his body and his mind. When *Wickard* reversed *Kidd* and *E. C. Knight* by saying that the government can control the means of production as a part of controlling "interstate commerce," it said that government can control the man himself by controlling the labor of his body or his mind. We see plainly, then, that *Wickard* set the stage for the next logical step in the erosion of our freedom: control of what we do with what we earn by our labor—the Individual Mandate of PPACA. Here we have the government demanding—coercing—that a man expend the results of his labor on things of the government's choosing. The government now asserts an additional right, s right to control an output of our labor, our income from it. Beyond this, we have a Federal judge, in upholding this "right of government," issuing with an absolutely straight face the most odious opinion that a judge in a free nation can possibly issue: a man's simple decision to engage, or not, in an activity—a man's very thoughts—are subject to Federal control. In *Mead v Holder*,[23] Judge Gladys Kessler held "...mental activity, i.e. decision-making.... [T]his Court finds the distinction [between mental activity and physical activity], which Plaintiffs rely on heavily, to be of little significance. It is pure semantics to argue that an individual who makes a choice...is not 'acting....'"

We can see, now, that government mandated wealth (re)distribution is simply government-driven welfare (as opposed to the citizen-driven welfare described in an earlier chapter), and we can see the effect of this on an individual's morals. Government welfare hooks Americans on the drug of government handouts. Social liberalism—Progressive ideology—holds that individuals can expect—indeed have a right—to be provided for by government, with the government claiming wealth from others in order to provide these "benefits." This denigrates the inalienable right of the individual being thus taxed to own without fetters his own body and mind and the produce of his labor. It also deprecates the morality of the recipient by reducing, if not outright eliminating, his obligation to work for his own well-being,[24] together with the other side of that coin, denying the recipient the returns to his own success by denying him the very opportunity to earn that success.

This is made manifest by "liberal," and then "progressive," government redistribution policies. The FDR administration's economic policy was clear: no longer should a man be responsible for his own outcomes and for his own

---

23   Case 1:10-cv-00950-GK Document 39. Judge Kessler upheld the constitutionality of the Individual Mandate portion of PPACA on the basis that a man's decisions—his thoughts—are subject to Federal control under the Commerce Clause.

24   A man was cited in a December 29, 2010 **Wall Street Journal** article on home foreclosures: For two years, [a man] and his wife received $1,200 a month in unemployment payments, in addition to their $3,200 social-security checks. The unemployment payments have now run out, so [the man] said he was going back to work—not that he now had to, but that he now was willing to. Another man was quoted in a January 8, 2010 **Wall Street Journal** article on weak hiring as saying, "There are jobs around if I want to make less than what I'm making on unemployment, but that would put me in a worse spot." Social liberalism saps the morality of men who are not in dire straits, when they see the lack of morality around them. A 27-year-old real-estate investor was cited in the same December article: "He said he had no difficulty paying [his] monthly mortgage.... Concluding that the home, now worth about half of what he paid, won't recover..., [the owner] decided to walk away [and default on his mortgage]." "It's a no-brainer once you do the math," the owner said.

THE ECONOMY

welfare; government should do for him those duties, those responsibilities, those rewards of his own efforts that used to be his. Government should guarantee jobs for everyone, government should guarantee a house for everyone, government should provide pensions for everyone. Never mind that this eliminates a man's moral obligation to be the first to see to his own welfare, or that it reduces the man to government dependent. Never mind that a truly free and open market produces these very opportunities and the capabilities for every man to answer them, and better, through his own labor. Never mind the immorality of the dominion that government asserts over some by claiming a portion of their assets for the explicit purpose of transferring them to others—or the dominion over those others that the government gains from their resulting dependency.

The Obama administration has acted on this ideology through the claim that "you've made enough money," and the demand that free individuals buy products selected by his government, in order to "spread the wealth around." For example, the Obama administration demands that every man buy health "insurance" (at prices that are set by government fiat independently of the risk being assumed by the captive insurance companies), solely in order to fund the "benefits" of some at the expense of others.[25] It also pressures lenders to alter the terms of existing mortgage loan contracts again only to transfer wealth from one group to another.

This immorality goes further: there are confiscatory taxes on families' Estates—death taxes. Here the heirs are punished for the success of their antecedents; families are not allowed to retain the fruits of their ancestors' labors. We even have Congressman Anthony Weiner (Dem, 9th District, NY) insisting that it's legitimate for government to take a man's estate: "You aren't paying anything [in terms of taxes] in that case because you'll be dead.... Do you know how much this adds to our debt? It adds an enormous amount."[26] Finally, the government's PPACA openly seeks to debase the morality of Americans by actively encouraging adult Americans to remain on their parents' insurance card at their parents' expense, if not the expense of the health insurance company required to act as the government's agent.

---

25   Those others, by the way, aren't seeing lower costs. They're paying for two coverages: their own, whether they want it, or not, and the coverages of those who are not paying for themselves.
26   Interview with Megyn Kelly, "America Live," Fox News Channel, 8 December 2010.

The judicial branch of our government has intervened beyond deprecating our right to control our bodies and minds. It also has been reducing our rights to our external properties. This is illustrated with two Supreme Court decisions that deprecate our ownership of real private property through a significant expansion of the government's powers of eminent domain: *Hawaii Housing Authority v. Midkiff*[27] and *Kelo v. City of New London*[28]. The concept of eminent domain allows government to seize private property for legitimate public use, with the losing owner given just compensation for the seizure.[29] With *Midkiff*, the State of Hawaii was granted the power to seize land owned by a private citizen who had leased that land to several other private citizens, with the latter building homes (which they then owned) on that leased land. The seized land was then given to these private citizen homeowners. Using the Hawaii Housing Authority as its example, the government's rationale was that original landowners, as oligopolists, were "skewing the State's residential fee simple market, inflating land prices, and injuring the public tranquility and welfare." By seizing the land and giving it different private ownership, the government claimed a useful public purpose in correcting this situation. Of course, this seizure and transfer to other owners did nothing to increase the supply of land or of homes. By combining land and home ownership in the same person, however, the property became more attractive to other market forces, and the cost of housing in the area doubled over the next six years. This redistribution of private wealth resulted in hurting both the original and the "new" owners.

Kelo is an even more egregious example. This case allowed the City of New London to condemn and seize a number of private homes that stood in the way of a private commercial developer's project. With this case, the government asserted an even broader right to seize private property for transfer to another private owner, now for the dual purposes of allowing the new owner to profit from resulting business opportunities (governments, with this ruling, now can subsidize preferred businesses with private property seizures) and increasing tax income for the political entity engaging in the seizure. In this case, the developer expected to erect a hotel/retail/condominium complex, and the City expected to collect an additional $1.2 million per year in taxes (taking the money from citizens' use and applying

---

27   467 U.S. 229 (1984)

28   545 U.S. 469 (2005)

29   This is the Takings clause of the 5th Amendment.

it to the city's chosen purposes). As with *Midkiff*, though, the goals were not realized. The seized property is now vacant, and the expected tax revenues cannot be collected: the developer was unable to obtain sufficient financing, and the project failed. New London and the state of Connecticut did gain, however, a $78 million dollar bill for the condemnation proceedings, which can only be paid by taking tax money from the wallets of private citizens, and/or borrowing the money—which loans can only be repaid with tax money.

Forcing equal outcomes—which is all that government interventions (social engineering, wealth redistribution) are intended to achieve—is nothing more than denial of the first man's right to Liberty and to Life by denying him the right to the fruits of his greater success, his right to live his life to its maximum liberty or to achieve his fullest potential, and it holds him back for no other reason than that others have not kept up. This also subsidizes the less successful so they have the same outcomes as the more successful independently of the result of their own labors. This subsidy then denies the recipient the opportunity to earn his own way and to live his life in liberty: it reduces him to government dependent, as I have written before. As discussed in the Chapter 6, the welfare state, government welfare, usurps the citizen's right to make his own economic decisions and makes the government responsible for each individual's welfare, eliminating that individual's own responsibilities and obligations.

We see, then, that government interventions of any kind make men dependent on that government, and this is an addiction that is very hard to break. The danger is clear in the welfare state crisis in Europe. In Greece, the people riot in the streets—lethally, as I have noted before—for their "right" to continue to have their welfare benefits, even—especially—when these are paid for by others, including by the taxpayers of other nations.[30] In France, the people riot over the need for the government to raise the retirement age to 62 years old from 60 because the existing government-guaranteed pension programs are unsustainable as they are. In Great Britain, students riot over the new requirement that they should pay more for their education because the British government no longer can afford handouts for education costs,

---

30   Including as war reparations: then Greek Deputy Prime Minister Theodoros Pangalos, supported by then Prime Minister George Papandreou, insisted that Germany should continue to fund Greek welfare as part of claimed World War II reparations.

which costs are rising largely due to the existence of current government subsidies. These all are demonstrations of the moral collapse engendered in men by government welfare-pushing.

In the end, government intervention into free markets leads solely to a Ptolemaic construction of epicycles as the government needs to add new layers of bureaucracy, new layers of regulation, enact new laws to oversee and to try to redress the shortcomings of the prior round of "controls." We've encountered examples already: FDR's food stamps in response to the artificially inflated prices from his New Deal; the present administration's addition of agencies and "clarifications" to existing regulations and wholly new regulations in order to implement, and then to oversee, the PPACA; and PPACA itself, which is an attempt to redress shortfalls from those prior government interventions in the medical services industry.

Further, intervention is far worse than the creative destruction cycles of the free market. When the conflagration comes (as it must), it will be far worse for the government's interference, just as forest fires ultimately exploded out of control when firefighting was devoted to outright prevention of any forest fire whatsoever. The commerce of men, and the national economies that are the aggregate of this, are forces of nature, and they cannot be controlled any more effectively than nature's fires. Economies must be free to clear the detritus of normal business growth and failure. They must be free to go through their normal cycles of creative destruction and growth in order to facilitate—to foster—development of new businesses, new technologies, new ways of conducting commerce, and so to produce better products, better technologies, better quality of life. And this only redounds to the nation as a whole as these improvements aggregate to greater national wealth, greater national well-being, greater national power.

In sum, government's interventions don't work. "We have tried spending money. We are spending more than we have ever spent before and it does not work." Treasury Secretary Henry Morgenthau wrote these words in his diary in the depths of Franklin Roosevelt's New Deal-Great Depression debacle. He continued, "I want to see this country prosper. I want to see people get a job. I want to see people get enough to eat. We have never made good on our promises. I say after eight years of this administration, we have just as much unemployment as when we started. And enormous debt to boot."[31] Neither the current administration, nor its Treasury Secretary, have understood this lesson. Yet these are just the bookends—all the interventions in between, as we have seen, have been failures, as well.

If government intervention doesn't work, the alternative is for government not to intervene (which is not the same as "do nothing"), and so it's reasonable to ask what Americans might have done without these government interventions. The general question is one of potential outcomes had the controls and redistributions in their various guises not been imposed and had existing law been applied to actual misbehaviors. What were the costs of the opportunities lost from imposing the government's hand on our economy rather than leaving it free to operate under the invisible hand?

Had the Theodore Roosevelt administration chosen to apply existing law to the railroads' apparent price collusion, instead of taking advantage of the situation to impose controls over a sector of the transportation industry, the railroads would have been capable of competing on an equal (or at least more equal) footing with the trucking companies, and at least as importantly, both industries would have been equally bound by existing law. It's entirely likely that the railroads' securities would not have fallen so catastrophically, and so not have contributed to banking failures, and the Panic of 1907 would have been just another recession.

Absent Franklin Roosevelt's wage and price controls, absent his controls on the conditions under which (farm) products could be produced, the costs to consumers (who were laborers) would not have been artificially high. Labor costs, too, would not have been artificially high, with their cascade effects of fewer jobs (with businesses unable or unwilling to hire at those costs) and artificially elevated prices, generally (from the propped up labor costs). Absent his confiscation of the privately owned gold,[32] more wealth would have remained in private hands, allowing more goods to be bought. In a period of enormous unemployment, more goods and services would

---

31   Quoted in *The Journal of Economic History,* Vol. 43, No. 2 (Jun., 1983), pp. 487–493, esp. p 488

32   In 1933, as a result of FDR's Executive Order, 500 tons of gold were "voluntarily" surrendered to the Federal government. At $20.67/oz., this works out to roughly $330 million dollars (approximately $4.68 billion dollars in 2011) of private wealth seized outright.

have been more affordable to more people, more money would have been available for private spending—or saving—and the long period of national unemployment would have been far shorter: the increased (or, at worst, less depressed) private demand would have facilitated increased production, which would have facilitated increased employment (or at least reduced unemployment), which would have facilitated increased demand, which would have…. This positive feedback loop would have greatly shortened or eliminated the Depression; a recession, instead, would have been far less catastrophic for Americans. The recovery that tried to begin in the mid-30s would have succeeded.

It's true enough that without the farm controls imposed, more farms might have failed (though with increased demand—or less reduced demand—for farm produce, perhaps not so many). But without the government's interference, other businesses would not have failed. In the end, there was, and is, no reason to single out one small business, or one industry, for special treatment at the expense of other businesses or other industries.

What of all the money spent on the wealth redistribution of the retirement and health care market interventions? The Federal government spent the equivalent of 40%[33] of its $3.1 trillion 2009 budget on Social Security, Medicare, and Medicaid alone—over $1.25 trillion dollars. Much of this money was absorbed by the middleman layers described earlier and so never provided actual medical or support services. These one and a quarter trillion dollars, though, amount to roughly $4,000 for each man, woman, and child in the United States in 2009, or assuming a two-parent, two-child family, roughly $16,000 per family.

The Federally defined poverty level for 2009[34] was $22,050. If the money had simply been given directly to those American families below that line, far fewer families would have remained in poverty status. The median house price in the Northeast United States, the most expensive housing market in 2009, was $239,000. If the money had simply been given directly to American families, they would have been able to put down an additional 6% on that home; in the Midwest, the cheapest market then, those $16,000

---

33   That's not a typo. President Obama's 40% was not unique to him; it was simply a continuation of a long-standing allocation trend.

34   Officially, the Federal Poverty Income Guideline

would have represented an additional 11% for a down payment. Think about the affordability of mortgages with those larger down payments, think about the affordability of existing mortgages with that extra money available for the payments, think about the ability to meet rent payments with that extra money. At the rates of the Obama administration's "Cash for Clunkers" program ($3,500 or $4,500 per car, depending on some factors), if the money had simply been given directly to American families, Mom, Dad, Junior, and Baby Janet each could have bought a car with their trade-ins. It's easy to imagine the value of returning this money to individuals. Of course, these examples as offered greatly simplify the situations, but the point remains.

Suppose the money lost to these retirement and medical services interventions had been left in the individual citizen's hands, rather than confiscated by a government bent on redistributing the wealth. Presently, working individuals must pay a total of 7.65% of every one of their paychecks for Social Security and Medicare.[35] Their employers must pay the same amount for the same purposes; thus, every job contains a more than 15% tax payroll. Further, under current conditions, the individual will not ever see very much of this money.

The Social Security tax, far from being held in trust (and earning market rates while in that trust), goes right back out the Treasury's door to a currently retired person, or into the general treasury to be spent by the government on other matters. Legally, the Social Security Trust Fund is a separate budget and a separate account from the general treasury accounts, and any monies left over after the immediate retirement outlays are required to go into this Trust Fund. However, the Federal government routinely uses this Trust Fund as its private piggy bank, constantly raiding the Fund and spending the money for other purposes. Of course the money taken is "replaced," by debt instruments of the Federal government (the IOUs some have mentioned), but these IOUs are not marketable in any way. Further, given the currently exploding national debt and the magnitude of the current social security commitment (some 21 trillion dollars over the lifetimes of all those currently in the system—both payers and retirees), whether those IOUs will be paid at all is highly problematic.

---

35   This ignores the temporary reduction in Social Security taxes paid by the individual, as the reduction is valid only for the 2011 tax year. Also, Medicaid expenditures are from the general budget: California taxpayers subsidize Illinois' Medicaid program, among other states'—and vice versa.

In just two presidential election cycles as I write this, the Trust Fund will need to start calling in those IOUs, though, as the required outlays will exceed the redistribution tax revenues coming in (and continue to exceed them forever). The situation with Medicare is worse: this "benefit" will be bankrupt by 2017. It's worse yet for the States: although State participation in Medicaid is voluntary, all States have participated since 1982, and leaving the program is politically extremely difficult. This simply makes manifest the problem that, while Federal transfer payments currently cover 50% or more of each State's outlays, those transfer payments are at the same risk as Social Security and Medicare—the government is running out of money. (And this ignores the State programs that individual States might support with these funds, instead, if they could.)

The PPACA is represented as fixing this by, among other things, allowing the States to opt out of their part of the program. However, States can leave the program only if they provide their own, identical to the just departed-from Federal one. This is Hobson's choice, since a State that cannot afford the Federal program clearly cannot afford its own identical program.

Think, though, about alternative uses for the money, if these wealth redistributing payroll taxes did not exist. Think about the value to the individual of an immediate 7.65% raise in take-home pay. This money might be rent[36] or mortgage payments, food for the table, car maintenance and fuel (or saving for a new car)—or money for a retirement investment, and if desired, an insurance policy of his own choice. Think about the value to the employer of an immediate 7.65% reduction in his labor costs. This money might be more jobs (driven by increasing spending by consumers with their take-home pay raise); capital improvements and new capital investment (with associated increases in worker productivity and the cascade of lower costs of production, lower prices to consumers, increasing demand for those cheaper goods and services, etc.); increases in research and development for new products and improvements to existing products; increases in effectiveness, breadth, and quality of (health) insurance coverage (I'll have more to say on this when I talk about competition vs. wealth redistribution taxation below).

---

36   For our family of four at the 2009 poverty line, this 7.65% tax, over the course of a year, amounts to nearly two months' rent on a two-bedroom apartment in an upper middle class Dallas, TX suburb.

What of the money expected to be spent on PPACA, both in expanded government funding for associated government programs and the money demanded by government to be spent by American citizens, whether they wish to spend "their" money on that item or not? PPACA adds nearly a trillion dollars to Federal expenditures over the next ten years via dozens of new regulatory functionalities (each of which will siphon off its own "share" of the money for its own costs of operation), according to the Congressional Budget Office (CBO).

It's important to keep in mind that the actual costs are far worse, though. Not included in the figures provided to the CBO is the "Doctor Fix," one of those Ptolemaic epicycles. The doctor fix was another $240+ billion that was intended to essentially cancel the effect of a legislatively mandated reduction in Medicare reimbursements to doctors, and it was taken out of the PPACA explicitly to hold the cost of the remaining health care "reform" bill to less than the $1 trillion "required" by President Obama for health care reform generally. The Doctor Fix was passed as separate legislation, continuing the explosion in government-driven medical services costs, the deficit, and the debt.

It's also important to consider the nature of the figures given the CBO for their evaluation. The CBO is required to evaluate bills on the basis of the figures given them including, critically, the underlying assumptions to be applied—the CBO is not allowed to alter these underlying assumptions to better align them with reality. The Congressional staffers can do simple arithmetic as well as the CBO's accountants, and it's therefore easy to adjust assumptions about growth rates, inflation rates, participation rates, program savings,[37] and so on, so as to arrive at a set of assumptions that will yield the required answer when the CBO pulls their adding machine's crank on Congress' figures and assumptions.

We have, then, a minimum expenditure of an additional $1.25 trillion from

---

37   Congressional Progressives insisted, for instance, and required the CBO to evaluate on this basis, that PPACA would eliminate $500 billion in fraud, waste, and abuse in existing Medicare and Medicaid programs. However, when pressed, these Progressives were unable to identify a single instance of current fraud, or current waste, or current abuse. Of course, had they named examples, they would have had to explain why those had not already been corrected. This is not a matter of playing "gotcha" with Congressmen, though. The point is that were these "savings" concretely identifiable, they would already have been realized.

health care "reform" beyond the $1.25 trillion already described, and the costs of PPACA are proving empirically to be far worse, as the charges and waivers described earlier demonstrate. Think of the value of these additional $4,000+ for every man, woman, and child in America left in the hands of us Americans to be spent, or saved, according to our needs rather than the government's diktats.

Now it's appropriate to look at the strengths of a free market. What should direct a man's use of his property? There are only two things that can legitimately govern this: his own self-interest and the moral obligations inherent in him. I described the latter in Chapters 4 and 5, and I'll not pursue it here.

"Greed, for lack of a better word, is good," said Gordon Gekko.[38] Not entirely; however, never underestimate the power of greed to do good in the world. As Adam Smith saw, and generations of economists since have described, markets have a way of using individual self-interest to enhance the common welfare: individuals seeking only gain for themselves are led, "as by an invisible hand," to produce goods that other people need or want, and the transaction prices are determined by what those buyers are willing to pay and what the producers are willing to accept.

What is "our" property? This goes back to each of us, as an individual, as the primary means of production: our labor and what we produce, or gain from trading what we produce, whether money,[39] or other goods, or other services, is ours and ours alone. Locke understood this 320 years ago when he wrote in his **Second Treatise** that every man has a property in his own person, and whenever he manipulates a thing in the environment, whether through physical or intellectual labor, he gains ownership over that thing and the manipulation of it.

Without this natural right of private property, several things inevitably occur, none of them good. The output of one man's labor can be appropriated by another, either directly or through a government's redistribution tax. This can only harm the incentive to produce, since the productive man will

---

38   **Wall Street**, 1987, directed by Oliver Stone, written by Stanley Weiser, Oliver Stone
39   which, in the end, is nothing more than a means of storing and transporting the value of our labor.

THE ECONOMY

be deprived of some, or all, of the fruits of his own labor with neither cause nor compensation. This combination of the arbitrary removal of one's labor output and the loss of incentive to produce can only reduce the amount of production and the breadth of products created, at the direct expense of the quality of life for all of us.

To be sure, there are, in free market, capitalist economies, ups and downs, periods of prosperity and of loss, and some of these cycles are severe. But in the government's attempts to force smoothness onto this type of powerful, create-wealth-for-all free market economy, in its attempts to clamp such an economy into a steadfast vice, government destroys the power and the genius of that free market: the creative destruction of these cycles that always and invariably leads to significant increments, compared with conditions before the dislocation, in wealth, in standard of living, in breadth and freedom of choice for the individuals as the economy comes out of its period of dislocation and loss into a new period of growth.

Indeed, the inevitable outcome of these cycles, while destroying some jobs, certainly, is the creation of many more jobs and broad, new industries, each with its own vast array of new jobs. A graphic illustration of this is a situation that happened when word processors, as specialized computers, were first becoming commercially feasible. The United States Air Force squadron to which I was assigned at the time had the mission of final testing of various aircraft improvements before they went into production, and this work kept a pool of secretaries fully employed typing the test reports for dissemination. As we got the word processors and printers, the secretaries worried about their jobs; after all, these computers would make the work easier and faster. The work was easier, and it did go faster, but the secretaries needn't have worried: the squadron's ability to publish the results of its testing expanded by an order of magnitude and those secretaries gained even more work. Additionally, new tasks appeared in the Squadron: those computers and printers had to be maintained and their software packages had to be updated and bugs corrected.

If our Progressive Patricians have their way, though, today there would still be support subsidies for the buggy-whip manufacturers of a century ago—subsidies paid with our tax dollars—solely in order to protect the continued existence of these no longer useful jobs. Those tax collections also would have inhibited the ability to develop new and better transportation technologies. Look again at the protected monopoly (and so, subsidized) company that was Ma Bell. Recall how rapidly our telecommunications system began to improve and its costs to the individual began to fall when that subsidy was removed, when Ma Bell's monopoly status was terminated. Progressives focus on the ebb and flow of the differences in wealth between our richest and our poorest; they ignore the fact that all are better off within the growth of a free economy, with the poor richer in absolute terms; they seek, instead, to hold back those more successful. And these Progressives ignore the upward economic mobility available to individuals—and to families—that a free market economy facilitates for everyone, especially the poor. The children of today's poverty-level family are part of the next generation's middle class families. Today's poor young man is tomorrow's middle-aged middle class man. Indeed, as one Treasury Department report notes, "80 percent of taxpayers had incomes in quintiles as high or higher in 2005 than they did in 1996, and 45 percent of taxpayers not in the highest income quintile moved up at least one quintile."[40]

It is imperative that this welfare dependency creation in the United States be broken and the damage already done be corrected. One way to accomplish this (there are other ways that also must be pursued) is to address the dependency on government-provided health and retirement welfare programs rampant today. While our current elderly, who have been dragooned into this dependent state already, must be protected, we can stop this part of the damage and reverse it by privatizing the Social Security and Medicare programs, beginning with our currently younger citizens; by privatizing Medicaid; and by enabling competition in the health insurance and medical services industries (where, in fact, it does not exist today). It is a legitimate concern of society to ensure that our futures and our health are seen to so that we do not fall (again) into dependency on our neighbors or on government (which is our neighbors, ultimately, as has already been shown). But our future and our health can be our own only if we are responsible for these ourselves. Letting government seize this moral obligation will

---

40   "Income Mobility in the U.S. from 1996 to 2005," A Report of the Department of the Treasury, November 13, 2007. Further data that show with similar clarity this economic mobility can be found at "Getting Ahead or Losing Ground: Economic Mobility in America," EMP Reports, February 2008.

THE ECONOMY

surrender that future and that health to the control of that government, and it will reduce us from moral and responsible adult to government ward.

One way to achieve this privatization would be to repeal the payroll taxes altogether (with the immediate boost to business and personal wealth mentioned earlier), but to require us to commit our portion of these repealed taxes to retirement and health savings accounts under our direct management, using whatever savings and/or investment vehicles we see fit to use. We will do a far better job than the government has done over the last 80 years of Social Security and 40 years of Medicare/Medicaid failure. We can, and must, accumulate our own wealth, rather than continue the current system of the government, our employee, taking large portions of our wealth, leaving us to live off the labor of others. Aside from the immorality of this, with our current and projected demographics, there aren't enough "others;" the system is rapidly collapsing as it currently exists. The Progressives have two objections to such a plan, though: we Americans are too stupid to understand how to manage our own money; they, who know better, must do so for us. The second objection is even more appalling (and the Progressives won't admit this, even to themselves): it would allow all those dependent Americans to stop being field hands on the Progressive plantation, to escape, instead, and recover their freedom.

Health insurance premiums and medical costs (including those of the insurance companies) are too high, but these are inflated by government intervention and by the lack of market competition. Currently, fifty states each have their individual requirements for health insurance, the various coverages which must be provided, and the premiums that are permissible to be charged; additionally, one State's resident cannot buy a policy that is sold in another State. This interference must be stopped. Health insurance policies must be saleable nationwide. Here is a legitimate application of the Commerce clause. This restriction by one State on the sale of policies from other States is a restriction by the former of the latter's ability to engage in the interstate commerce of a product. Competition among insurance companies for the policies marketed will drive premiums down, and the individual can make his own choice for desired coverage—including none at all—rather than having that "choice" defined by government mandate.

Insurance companies, currently restrained from charging risk-based premiums, must be allowed to charge premiums consistent with the risk being assumed, and they must be allowed to devise policies that both are consistent with that risk and that match their customers' needs and desires, rather than that satisfy government diktat. With the actual customers—businesses and individuals—able to shop in a free market for the best policies, the policies that suit their individual needs will be developed, and premiums overall will decline. The new policies will have greater effectiveness and efficiency, and broader ranges of coverage and of options for coverage will become available. With insurance companies able to price their policies consistently with the risk being assumed, and not forced to subsidize one risk with premiums from another risk, some premiums necessarily will rise: coverage for pre-existing conditions, for instance. But coverage will appear for pre-existing conditions, there will be no need to drop coverages or customers. Further, policies with coverage caps, no-cap policies, and other options will become available. Premiums for other coverages will fall, and total costs will fall.

Now we can begin to develop an answer to a question concerning the purpose of taxation (this will be developed more fully in Chapter 8). I assert in the context of this chapter that the only appropriate purpose of taxation is to provide funds for matters serving the national good: for instance, the common defense of the United States, and the nation's infrastructure, as Article I, Section 8 of our Constitution says quite clearly.[41] Illegitimate purposes of taxation all are attempts at social engineering or wealth redistribution, for instance, attempts to "persuade" or openly to coerce, a man to do, or not to do, that which his subordinate government tries to dictate to him is right or wrong. Such "persuasions" include attempts to punish or to discourage this behavior (*e.g.*, a decision not to purchase health insurance or a business to accumulate earnings), or to encourage or to reward that behavior (*e.g.*, to purchase housing regardless of its affordability). Such "persuasions" include Congressman Weiner's excuse that the lack of a tax would add so greatly to the national debt[42]—which carefully elides the immorality of the argument that the government has a claim on the estate in the first place. (And, of

---

41   "The Congress shall have Power To lay and collect Taxes, Duties, Imposts and Excises, to pay the Debts and provide for the common Defence and general Welfare of the United States; but all Duties, Imposts and Excises shall be uniform throughout the United States."
42   In 2009, when estates were taxed at 45%, $25,000,000,000 were raised by this tax. This compares with the Federal deficit in 2009 of $1,400,000,000,000—or less than 2% of the deficit.

course, the lack of an estate tax cannot add anything to "our debt:" it is costless for the government not to receive that which does not belong to it in the first place. I'll have more to say on this in the Chapter 8.)

We do, indeed, pay for the gains of a free market with periods of bust, of creative destruction, and with periods of instability, but we gain hugely in advances: in wealth, in technologies, in quality of life and the protection of our morality. We pay for stability in our economy, a government-managed economy, with the sacrifice of those gains of the free market, together with the sacrifice of freedom—government determines what we will buy (and what is available to buy in a managed economy is itself severely circumscribed)— and with loss of morality, through loss of personal responsibility. And in the end, we still don't have a smooth, stable economy or life, as the collapse of the government-managed economies of the USSR and of the German Democratic Republic have shown, and as the riots in the welfare states of Europe currently demonstrate. There are always busts, but they are enormously worse when not allowed to clear themselves: no free-market nation has ceased to exist through its own economic dislocation.[43]

Free markets, unconstrained by arbitrary and erratic government intervention, allow societies to do what truly free societies always do better than any other: bungle hugely, fix it, and generate even more well-being. But in the fixing, and in the ordinary course of development (importantly, both paths are available to free societies and their free market economies, and only to them), lie the capabilities to make improvements, to develop new methods, to develop new products and technologies—and the realization of those capabilities. That's business in America. That's the commerce of free individuals in America. In free market systems, the self-correcting mechanisms are built in. Further, in the contest between free societies and those led by authoritarians or by Progressive elites, the claims of the former typically rest on this supreme moral foundation: free societies respect human decency and trust the wisdom of their members. Welfare states, "managed" economies of any sort, have no such respect or trust, and so they fail everywhere.

---

43   Some might suggest the disappearance of Weimar Germany is such a failure. However, leaving aside questions of how free that nation's economy truly was, its economic failure was guaranteed by the usurious reparations imposed on Germany by the European victors of World War I.

I'll close this chapter with a parable from our Revolutionary War. A Tory, standing at his door with his child at hand held forth on the state of things, and he finished with this statement, "Well! Give me peace in my day." Yet a proper parent, a generous father, would have said, "If there must be trouble, let it be in my day, that my child may have peace."[44] And so it is today. We cannot put off onto our children, or our children's children, or yet their children the crisis at hand today. We must resolve this crisis today, for the sake of our children and of their posterity and for the peace of our children and of their posterity.

---

44   The parable is provided by Thomas Paine in his *The American Crisis, No. I*, December 19, 1776

CHAPTER 8—THE GOVERNMENT

There are men in all ages who mean to govern well, but they mean to govern. They promise to be good masters, but they mean to be masters.
— Daniel Webster

A primary purpose of government is to protect and enforce the rights that men have and to create and protect an environment in which men, acting on their own imperatives, can satisfy their duties. I have written repeatedly, as have better men than me—Locke, Rousseau, Paine, *et al.*—that these are inherent in men; they exist in us because of our status as creations of our Creator.[1] As a result of this, neither these rights nor these duties can be taken away from us, or abridged in any way, by anything men might do.

Let us suppose, now, that this is not true, that contrary to the arguments of those men, contrary to the assertions in our Declaration of Independence, our rights are not inherent in us, these are not *natural* rights. Let us suppose, instead, that these rights originate from a government, while supposing, also, that this government is legitimate to the extent of our original acceptance of it; *i.e.*, this government's rule still gains its legitimacy from a foundation of an original consent of the first generation of the governed. Let us suppose, finally, that this government begins well-intentioned. What outcomes result from this? What rights originate from, and are preserved by, this condition?

We have, in the beginning, a set of rights from our condition as individuals in our original state of nature. This set comprises, again, our rights to do as we will and to own the results of our own labor—our own property—so long as these do not interfere with another's rights to the same ends. In this state

---

1   Another purpose of government is to create and protect an environment in which men, acting on their own imperatives, can satisfy their wishes. However, since their wishes cannot be satisfied effectively until their rights and duties are protected, I will focus on the latter in this chapter.

of nature, though, we are not constrained in any way—the strong can prey on the weak without fear of obstruction, except by the yet stronger.

From within this state of nature, then, we formed a government to act for us to protect these rights, and now the government, as part of our assent, has assumed these rights. The first, and most obvious, outcome is that our rights and duties, now under government control, are those defined and passed to us by that government. This seems innocuous, as these rights and duties, flowing from a government that had its creating generation's permission to exist and to govern, ultimately must flow from that first generation—from the men themselves. Included in that original endowment to government would be those things identified by Locke, Rousseau, and Paine (and others) such as the right, and the duty, to rid ourselves of a government that oversteps its bounds too far, too much, too abusively—that threatens, or actively interferes with, or eliminates, these rights. Yet if rights and duties now flow from the government, then it is but a moment's deliberation and the stroke of a pen to pass a law eliminating this right and duty, thereby guaranteeing a type government in perpetuity. Future generations no longer could give or withhold their consent, and the government will have become self-perpetuating, heritable.

Further, if this right and duty of throwing off a government that has produced a train of abuses is not inherent in our existence, then on what basis did these United States throw off our government of England, a government that already had asserted its right to rule without regard to the consent of its subjects, those two hundred years and more ago?

With our rights and duties being those assigned us by our government, there would seem little to legitimize this overthrow beyond—we won the fight. If the Rebellion is justified only by naked force and did not stem from our natural rights, then the government set up by the Rebellion's apparent success must, in fact, be illegitimate from its inception, and all the acts of this usurper government must be illegitimate. Among these illegitimate acts are the elimination of that most reprehensible of crimes, slavery. By what right were the slaves freed? Their freedom must have been an attribute of their natural rights as human beings, but if they have no such rights save those a government grants, then it would seem they cannot be free in and of themselves. Surely they could not have been freed—and no duty could have existed to free them—if the government that did so is illegitimate, or if these men had no inherent right to their own freedom.

This is an extreme outcome, but it flows inexorably from the logic of rights and duties flowing from government rather than being *of* man. And it's not an isolated result. Another outcome of our rights not being *natural*, not being *inherent in us*, but flowing from government is the premise that all men are created equal. If this, in fact, is not a (self-evident) truth, and what we are flows from government rather than from our being, then it is just another moment's deliberation and the stroke of a pen to pass a law creating classes of men, with these classes differentiated by the rights and duties assigned to each. The first two classes to be created will be the class of men suited to govern, and the (much larger) class of men suited to be governed, and we must ask the basis by which an individual is put into this class, or that one. I suggest that the second class named here is a slave class.

Another outcome of our rights and duties not being *natural*, but flowing from government, is the premise that we have a right to liberty. That which a government grants, it can withdraw with another moment's deliberation and pen stroke to create the effecting law. Our liberty then becomes what the government chooses for us, rather than what our Creator imbued in us. Now we must ask exactly what liberty is. A right flowing from government gains its definition solely from government. This government, which began with consent, arrogates to itself all of the rights of the consenting, and it creates whatever laws suit the purposes of the ruling class and defines these as preserving liberty either by asserting so, or by adjusting the meaning of "liberty" at need. Or the Rulers ignore the need of definition or of preservation altogether.

Another outcome of our rights and duties flowing from government is the premise that we have a right to the pursuit of happiness. Here, as with liberty, there inevitably will be abuse. My argument is the same, only substituting "happiness" for "liberty."

I'll not pursue the point concerning the right to life and what happens when that right flows from government; where this leads already is plain.

We see from this that we have arrived at a logical contradiction, in that the argument appears to legitimize some men holding dominion over other men—holding the very power of life or death—not because these other men have behaved so abjectly or so egregiously immorally, but only because some men are stronger than others: the very condition against which this government was formed by its founding generation. It's not necessary to repeat the argument for the inalienability of our rights; simply recall the discussion in earlier chapters. Our rights and duties are inherent in us from our status as our Creator's creations.

Then from where does any government get its perpetual legitimacy? To summarize, briefly, related earlier discussions (especially those of the other men I've named), there cannot be a government until there are, first, individuals. These individuals then must agree among themselves to be a body politic, and only then can they agree to have a government of some form. Note that men must first agree as individuals; they cannot first agree as a group because the group cannot exist until individuals exist. Thus, it is the individuals who are Sovereign in any body politic; not any group; not any government of theirs, each of whose very existence was created out of nothingness by those individuals severally consenting to creation of their government, via their social contract. And these Sovereigns cannot divorce themselves, or each other, by any mechanism, from their own endowment.

It's useful to explore, briefly, how this chain of sovereignty works in the American context. We have a republican form of government, rather than a popular (for instance) democracy. Individuals, in exercising our Sovereignty, act to support and to elect representatives to our government who then act in our name, while remaining subordinate to us, and to defeat the (re)election of those who have failed at this representation. This results from all of our individual choices: some of us may choose to exercise our Sovereignty by acting alone, and some may choose to exercise it by acting in concert with a collection of like-minded individuals. Finally, this steady, faithful sequence of elections, across generations of American citizens—the members of our social contract—together with the prescribed means of altering that contract (Article V of our Constitution) are the legitimacy of our government across those generations.

Note that, even though individuals may choose to abide by the decisions of their group, this transfers no Sovereignty to that group; especially, that group gains no Sovereignty over all the individuals of the nation: no group can gain Sovereignty, including the group selected to act as our representatives in the government.

Take careful notice of Webster's remark at the head of this chapter. The American social contract devised our government, with the structure described in other chapters, explicitly with that risk in mind. Following is a coarse summary of the various episodes of negotiation, renegotiation, and adjustments to our social contract.

Our contract has, in fact, gone through these processes several times in our history. The first period of negotiation began in earnest roughly in the 1770s, generally beginning with skirmishes between colonials and the British regular army. This period also included the development of our Declaration of Independence with its annunciation of our fundamental principles: the acknowledgment that all men have certain natural, inalienable rights and duties. This document also contains a list of the violations of those rights that justified our claiming our right to our independence as a nation. The men who drafted and signed it formed the core of an explicit pledging of men to this new, unique, and developing social contract. There followed a period of war, wherein the new nation successfully enforced its freedom, culminating in an essential end to the fighting in 1781 and a formal end to the war and Great Britain's acceptance of American independence in 1783.[2] The Articles of Confederation, which were part of an early draft of our social contract, had been drawn up and put into use during the Revolutionary War. The Constitution of the United States of America, whose drafting was driven in part to redress deficiencies in the Articles that had been exposed in the fighting and subsequent peace, was ratified in 1788, following an extended debate in the major newspapers of the time over its own deficiencies.[3]

---

2   Limited fighting continued after Cornwallis' surrender at Yorktown with skirmishes against Loyalist-led American Indians in the northwest and west. The Treaty of Paris, which constituted the British acceptance of the outcome, was signed 3 September. Related to this were the Treaties of Versailles, also signed 3 September 1783, formally ending hostilities between Great Britain, on the one hand, and France and Spain, on the other hand. The latter two had given critical support to the US as a means of attempting to take advantage, in the Caribbean and elsewhere in North America, of Great Britain's difficulties.

3   The printed articles and essays that constitute the core of the favorable side of the debate have been gathered into **The Federalist Papers**, one edition of which is edited by J. E. Cooke. The core of the counter-arguments can be found in **The Anti-Federalist Papers**, one edition of which can be

The ratification proceeded on the commitment that the major remaining deficiencies would be corrected by several amendments; these amendments were approved, as the Bill of Rights, in 1791.[4]

This series of negotiations resulted in a social contract that, for the first time, explicitly recognized all men as being equal and that these men, we Americans, were—and are—Sovereign in our nation, not any government: the government is subordinate to, and works for, the people of our nation. The ratification came at a price far worse than the war, however: the so-called slave states were to be allowed to keep their slaves. This was the shameful compromise that persuaded the southern states to ratify the Constitution, and thereby allow the birthing of the United States. It was viewed as a necessary bargain that was the least evil of the several options: permit slavery for a few years in order to get passage of the Constitution, with the expectation of an ultimate end of slavery. But note where the shame lies. It's not in the compromise itself, terrible though that was, but rather in those who demanded the "right" to hold others in bondage as the price of agreeing to a larger good, the birth of our nation—and with not the slightest sense of irony on the part of the slave owners who demanded this as the price of their agreeing to Life, of Liberty, of the pursuit of Happiness, as our nation's moral fundament.

The first renegotiation of our social contract was borne of that terrible compromise. Although slavery nominally was supposed to end in 1808,[5] it did not. There followed a period of political conflict, as the nation grew and added states, over whether each new accession would be a slave state or a free state. This renegotiation period occurred in earnest in the period 1857-1870. The nature of the need for renegotiation and correction of this

---

found in The Gutenberg Project.

4   In fact, 12 Amendments were proposed; only 10 were ratified in 1791. Amendments 1 - 9 were passed as the "Bill of Rights;" the 10th Amendment is included under the rubric, since it was passed at the same time; however it is not an enumeration of a specific right, but a general reservation of rights to the States and to the people. One Amendment was intended to govern apportionment of Representatives as the nation's population grew; this was never ratified. One Amendment required an election of Representatives before a change to Congressional compensation could take effect; this was passed, finally, in 1992 as the 27th Amendment.

5   Article I, Section 9: "The Migration or Importation of such Persons as any of the States now existing shall think proper to admit, shall not be prohibited by the Congress prior to the Year one thousand eight hundred and eight...." Slavery, thus, was to end with a cutoff of the importation of slaves and the eventual dying out of existing slaves.

cancer was laid bare with *Dred Scott*.[6] In this case, to vastly oversimplify, a slave was transported by his owner from a slave state to a free territory, and the slave, Scott, asserted his freedom as a result, suing, ultimately, in Federal court for enforcement. The case went to the Supreme Court under Chief Justice Roger B. Taney. The Taney Court ruled, correctly under the Constitution as it was then (mis)understood, that since Scott, as a man of African descent, could never be a United States citizen and could not be a citizen of any State, he had no standing to sue; thus lacking an interstate controversy, the Supreme Court had no jurisdiction. Despite claiming that lack of jurisdiction, though, the Court went on to rule that Scott could not be ruled a free man, as that would deprive his owner of the latter's 5th Amendment property rights.

With this abuse of men's inalienable rights so nakedly exposed, the renegotiation was joined in earnest. The Civil War was fought over the relationship between States' rights and those of the Federal government, with slavery as the proximate rights issue, and later as the primary object of the war. This period of renegotiation concluded with the Union victory in 1865 and the ratification of the 13th through the 15th Amendments in 1865, 1868, and 1870, respectively. These Amendments explicitly abolished slavery in the United States, since so many had not understood the matter from the beginning, either legally or morally; made all persons born in the United States to be citizens, to eliminate the premise that no person of African descent could be one; and eliminated race as a legal bar to the right to vote. This renegotiation period ended with our nation having been drawn into closer compliance with our social contract: all men truly are created equal and have equal rights under law.

The next episode was a period of adjustment of our American social contract, not a negotiation at all, but a blatant usurpation of power by the Federal government at the direct expense of our liberties and our rights. This adjustment was the Franklin Roosevelt New Deal and related legislation.[7] This assumption of power ran from the early 1930s through the early 1940s, and its effects ran, with continued expansion of Federal power (resulting in further abnegation of individual freedoms and rights and duties) for

---

6   *Dred Scott v. Sandford*, 60 U.S. 393 (1857).

7   Although other moves had been made by Theodore Roosevelt and Woodrow Wilson, the first concerted effort was Franklin Roosevelt's.

an additional 70 years, into the 21st century. I've written about the FDR legislation and arrogation of powers in earlier chapters; I'll only summarize here. With the New Deal legislation, the government asserted an authority to mandate the price men would be allowed to charge for their labor by placing a floor under their price. The government also asserted an authority to mandate the price men would be allowed to charge for the produce of their labor by placing a floor under the prices, for instance, at which various farm products could be sold. Thus, government asserted that men could control their own bodies and the produce of their own labor only to the extent government would allow.

Further, in response to the Supreme Court's interference with these efforts,[8] Roosevelt began his attack on the third branch of the Federal government. Although his court packing bill failed to pass the Senate, the Court was thoroughly cowed by the effort, as demonstrated by their ruling in favor of the government in *West Coast Hotel v. Parrish*,[9] which was a ruling with the effect of allowing the government to set wage floors. With the *West Coast Hotel* ruling, the Federal government was now free to set the price of labor, and to denigrate an individual's right to enter into his own agreements. The success of the intimidation also is demonstrated in a number of other Supreme Court cases. A pair of 1937 decisions (*Helvering v. Davis* and *NLRB v. Jones & Laughlin Steel Corp*)[10] essentially gave Congress the power to redistribute and regulate at will. A year later, in *United States v. Carolene Products*,[11] the court deprecated property rights. And *National Broadcasting Co. v. United States* (1943),[12] allowed Congress to delegate significant amounts of its vastly expanded legislative powers to administrative agencies

---

8   *Schechter Poultry Corp. v. United States,* 295 U.S. 495 (1935), for instance, held that Roosevelt's National Industrial Recovery Act was an unconstitutional distortion of the Commerce Clause of the United States Constitution.

9   The ruling overturned a 1923 precedent set in *Adkins v. Children's Hospital*, which had found setting wage floors a violation of a worker's freedom to enter into contracts, and so a violation of the worker's 5th Amendment rights.

10   Respectively, since welfare spending (specifically, Social Security) is not a local issue, the taxes on employees and employers for the purpose are constitutional, and local unions, despite being intrastate in character, are subject to interstate regulation.

11   This was another distortion of the Commerce Clause and of due process by holding constitutional a Federal ban of filled milk from interstate commerce.

12   This ruling held that the FCC could, without explicit legislative authority, regulate the relationship between national broadcasting networks and their local affiliates.

in a similarly expanding FDR Executive branch and away from the oversight of the Sovereign people.

Ultimately, Roosevelt succeeded in packing the court, anyway: by 1941, he had appointed eight of the nine Justices then sitting. With a now thoroughly compliant Supreme Court, Roosevelt was able to win *Wickard*, functionally reversing the salient portion of *Schechter*, and so was able to successfully distort further the Commerce Clause, allowing the Federal government now to determine what a man might do with the product of his own labor: the government now could claim that any product was interstate commerce, and so subject to Federal government control.

Beginning in 2008, the American social contract has entered into another period of unilateral adjustment. At the beginning of the Panic of 2008, the Federal government passed a $700 billion bailout bill over intense public opposition. Americans strongly urged that businesses be allowed to suffer the consequences of their poor performance—to fail. In ignoring the will of the public, the Bush Administration considered that they knew better than their employers and proceeded with the bailout bill and the expenditures.

With the passage of the Patient Protection and Affordable Care Act (PPACA), the Obama administration distorted the Commerce Clause even further to claim that, since a man exists, the government can control his behavior: every man must buy, for instance, a health insurance product for no better reason than the government has decided that he must. In addition to this naked power grab, the technique used to gain passage of the legislation is instructive. Key aspects of the Bill were negotiated in the back offices of the then Democratic Party Senate Majority Leader and the then Democratic Party Speaker of the House, with the Republican Party membership excluded. Key votes were openly purchased in the Congress' open auction market: Senator Mary Landrieu, (D) Louisiana, and Senator Ben Nelson, (D) Nebraska, in the Senate, and Representative Bart Stupak, (D) Michigan, and Representative Luis Gutierrez, (D) Illinois, in the House each sold their PPACA votes[13] to their Senate and House leaders, respectively. PPACA passed strictly along party lines in early 2010.

---

13   Respectively, the Louisiana Purchase, in which Sen. Landrieu sold her vote for PPACA for a one-time $300,000,000 Medicaid payment to Louisiana; the Cornhusker Kickback, in which Sen. Nelson agreed not to filibuster PPACA in return for 100% Federal funding of Nebraska's Medicaid

The conflict became increasingly vitriolic, as the Obama administration and its Congressional supporters, pushing PPACA, became increasingly frustrated with the failure of Americans—free individuals—to accept the government's superior understanding, and these government members attempted to suppress debate through *ad hominem* attacks on all who disagreed with them. We've seen the behavior in earlier chapters: the Senate Majority Leader likening the attempts by Republicans to block PPACA's intrusion into American freedoms with the delaying tactics of those who had attempted to block anti-slavery legislation 160 years prior; the then Speaker of the House and the then House Majority Leader calling those of us who opposed the then-proposed health reform bill (and cynically positing that PPACA was the only way to achieve health reform) Un-American; the President of the United States saying that Americans were simply too stupid to understand the Progressive message, and we weren't thinking clearly in our fear.

These two periods of adjustment represent moves by Liberals and then Progressives to alter our social contract drastically, with the effect of limiting individual rights and freedoms, and to do so without following the procedures for legitimate change prescribed by our Constitution. Indeed, these moves even deprecate we individual Americans in favor of big government; the latter should assume responsibility for these rights and duties because we are viewed as not competent for either. Worse, the moves were insidious, with limited public debate: they were only carried out by legislation which, in the 1930s, was facilitated by a compliant Supreme Court, and post-2008, was first worked out secretively, behind closed doors, with the results then passed unilaterally by a Democratic Party membership that could not be troubled to read the bill before voting.

The next phase of the sequence of negotiations and adjustments is the present renegotiation, which began during the run-up to the mid-term elections in 2010. At town hall meetings nationwide, Americans universally rejected

---

costs, in perpetuity; Rep. Stupak led a group of Representatives opposed to abortion who would vote against PPACA if Federal funds were used to pay for them, as he considered PPACA to do. In return for a personal meeting with President Obama, following which the President signed an Executive Order upholding the Hyde Amendment, Rep. Stupak brought his group over to favor PPACA. In the last case, Rep. Gutierrez threatened to hold PPACA hostage against getting immigration reform satisfactory to him passed. In return for President Obama's promise to discuss (this completely unrelated issue of) immigration reform, Rep. Gutierrez delivered his vote.

the Obama administration's and Democratic Party-led Congress' behavior and legislation. This was followed by even more Americans organizing themselves spontaneously into various Tea Party organizations which then elected a number of Tea Party members to Congress. These grass-roots Americans voted out of the House of Representatives a net 60 Democrats, and out of the Senate a net 5 Democrats. This stage remains in progress as I write, with the Obama Progressives continuing not to address the issues the American people have raised, instead continuing their *ad hominem* attacks: in response to the shootings in Tucson, AZ, in which a Representative was gravely wounded, a Federal judge murdered, and several other people also murdered or wounded, Arizona State Senator Linda Lopez (Dem) said "she heard" the shooter was an Afghanistan war veteran. On the floor of the House of Representatives, Rep Steve Cohen, (D) Tennessee, said the statements made by Republicans about PPACA were Goebbels-like lies reminiscent of the blood libel lies leading into the holocaust of NAZI Germany.

What, now, is the state of our present government and of its relationship to us, its Sovereign employer? Once again, the American social contract exists to guarantee an individual's freedom to do as he wishes and to be the master of his own property so long as these do not interfere with the ability of another to do the same. Our contract articulates a partial list of inalienable rights that give solidity to these underlying natural rights; this list contains the rights to Life, Liberty, and the pursuit of Happiness. In the milieu of a free country, free market economy, this means that each man has the right to buy, or not to buy, anything that is for sale; to produce, or not to produce, anything he might wish to sell—or to give away—and to develop new items not yet available. Our inalienable right to our private property supports this, also. Instead, though, we have a government dictating to us what industries are allowed to operate and whether those industries will be permitted to operate at all without direct government intervention or outright government ownership.

We have, presently, a government that asserts a right to decide for us what we as individuals might produce and how much, and the conditions (the prices) under which we will be allowed to sell our produce. This assertion is an outcome of the fiction that interstate commerce begins when a man produces a thing, rather than when he sends his produce to another state for sale there, and of the fiction that regulation of interstate commerce extends beyond the commerce among States as trading entities to the commerce of individuals who happen to reside in differing states.[14] We have a government that asserts a right to dictate what a man might do with his own property: he must exchange it, so asserts this government, for a product of the government's choice, when the government requires it, rather than retain it, or exchange a part (or all) of it for a product that suits his own needs or wants; indeed the government asserts that it can seize private property and, rather than use it for public good, simply transfer it to another private entity for that one's private use.[15] We have a government that actively seeks to suppress dissent, to keep opinions differing from its own from being spoken at all through its *ad hominem* attacks on those who disagree. We have a government that actively condones interference with voting.[16] We have a government that insists that, at the end of a lifetime of work creating value and accumulating wealth for family, that accumulated wealth must be turned over to the government, at least in significant part, for the government's purposes, claiming in Orwellian doublespeak, that it's moral to surrender a family's accumulation to the government.

Now let us explore the proper role of government. This exploration is well done in the context of some specific activities: taxation, spending, and the Federal government's relationship with the States of the United States. The Constitution (Article I, Section 8, first clause[17]) mandates the purpose of taxation by the Federal government, and the 16th Amendment

---

14   In Judge Roger Vinson's ruling striking down the Individual Mandate, and the PPACA as a whole, he provided a brief history of the Commerce Clause and of its intent. According to the Constitution's original intent, "commerce" was understood to encompass "...the activities of buying and selling that come after production and before the goods come to rest." Judge Vinson, citing Chief Justice John Marshall in *Gibbons v. Ogden*, further wrote that "Commerce, undoubtedly, is traffic, but it is something more: it is intercourse. It describes the commercial intercourse between nations, and parts of nations...." Judge Vinson concluded, "...the primary purpose behind the Commerce Clause was to give Congress power to regulate commerce so that it could eliminate the trade restrictions and barriers by and between the states that had existed under the Articles of Confederation." And finally, Judge Vinson cites Justice Joseph Rucker Lamar in *Kidd v. Pearson*, "...it is a matter of public history that the object of vesting in congress the power to regulate commerce...among the several states was to insure uniformity for regulation against conflicting and discriminatory state legislation."

15   *Midkiff* and *Kelo*, for instance, described in the Chapter 7.

16   The Justice Department's decision to dismiss cases against members of the New Black Panther Party after guilty pleas had been entered, and the Department's decision to enforce voting rights laws only when government-selected groups are violated.

17   "The Congress shall have Power To lay and collect Taxes, Duties, Imposts and Excises, to pay the Debts and provide for the common Defence and general Welfare of the United States; but all Duties, Imposts and Excises shall be uniform throughout the United States."

extends the ability to collect taxes for these purposes to an income tax. The Constitution is silent on the explicit matter of spending; however, it is clear in its implications of what constitutes proper spending. We can conclude that the government does not collect taxes in order to accumulate wealth; the taxes collected are properly spent on the tax purposes identified. Section 8 also identifies other areas on which funds might be expended: regulating interstate and international commerce, a court system, coinage, and the like. The Constitution also is quite clear on the areas in which Federal funds cannot be spent. These limits are in Article I, Section 9, and in the 10th Amendment. No funds can be spent on anything not explicitly authorized by an Appropriation made by Law, and under no circumstance can funds be expended to favor the commerce of one State over another. The Constitution's position on the relationship between the Federal government and the States is equally clear. States cannot conduct their own foreign policy or coin their own money, among a short list of prohibitions. Beyond these, as the 10th Amendment so famously and plainly says, if it's not an explicitly enumerated power of the Federal government or explicitly forbidden to the States, it's reserved to the States and to the people. Finally, the Supreme Court (on matters where it has not been intimidated by the Executive branch) has held, via the 14th Amendment, that the Bill of Rights is binding on, and within, the States as well as the nation as a whole.

The only appropriate purpose of taxation is to provide funds for matters of national welfare and for the common defense of the United States, and for very little else at all, as that first clause of Article I, Section 8 says quite clearly. There is nothing about taxing for farm supports, for instance, or tailoring the tax structure to favor government purposes such as a mortgage interest deduction, or taxing some explicitly to "redistribute" to others—these are not for the national welfare; rather, they are targeted for select groups. Nor can the market distortions resulting from such narrowly targeted tax policies be "for the general Welfare;" they actively harm it. We saw, in Chapter 7, the impact on our general welfare of farm subsidies' artificially elevated food prices, so that taxes had to be collected to pay for food stamps to assist those who could not (and still cannot) afford the (still) artificially high prices. We saw the impact on our general welfare of the mandated/ pressured easing of credit standards in the housing bubble and collapse and of the ensuing Panic of 2008.

When taxes are taken for a government's purpose in influencing the economy, or specific segments of it, this is simply wealth redistribution by another name. Taxing for the purpose of spending the money so collected to stimulate job creation, even assuming this failed Keynesian spending achieves some part of this goal, also is nothing but wealth redistribution, and the Keynesian notion is just another government claim that it knows better how a man's money should be spent than does that man.

On the other hand, a free market, unhindered by government tax (or any other) interference, encourages production, buying, and selling for purposes satisfactory to all participants and so does a far more efficient job of "redistributing" wealth. It achieves this by distributing that wealth according to each man's own purpose, thereby making all men wealthier and enabling all men to enrich their own lives and their own condition in ways determined by, and suited to, those men. Thus, commerce in a free market produces a redistribution of wealth through mutual consent. Through this mutually consented redistribution, a mechanism for enriching men's morality is facilitated, also. A man's morals cannot be satisfied by any other than himself, and so he must act first, and he must be free to act. This increased wealth enhances men's economic freedom to act to satisfy their moral obligation to help those less fortunate. We see, then, that citizen-driven commerce is a far more productive, efficient, moral means of wealth distribution, and one that increases total wealth, than is any redistribution by government taxation.

We return to the purpose of taxes. It's time to discard the tired, 100-year-old idea that the first purpose of a system of taxation is to satisfy an imperative to redistribute private wealth. To ensure American well-being, the pre-eminent purpose of a tax system must be to protect and to enforce our inalienable rights and to support satisfaction of our inalienable duties. It's instructive that our first tea party was about taxes, not about spending. The proper system of taxation is a system that leaves our money, first, in our hands, for our purposes, and secondarily, funds our government to satisfy its limited purpose: to protect and enforce our rights and to support our duties, rather than to feed an expanding government.

Some argue that not collecting taxes (generally; the death tax is only one example) is exceedingly costly, and the failure to collect adds enormously to the annual deficit and to the national debt. The argument is a threat to our freedoms and to our rights made manifest: it reverses the sovereignty laid out by our social contract. Since our money is our property, flowing from the outcome of our labor and those things we obtain by exchanging the produce of our labor, it cannot be the government's. Of course, it can cost the government nothing to not receive that which does not belong to it. It cannot add to any annual deficit, nor can it add to any national debt.

What does add to our deficit and to our debt is our government spending more than it receives in those tax funds we do authorize it to collect. The appropriate response, thus, is to reduce spending (including debt reduction spending after having reduced the present astronomical debt) to fit within available revenues, not increasing tax rates in a misguided, and ineffective, attempt to raise revenues to match (increasing) spending.

This brings me to the role of spending by our government.

The government spends huge amounts on the social engineering of wealth redistribution. We've already seen the vast amounts spent on wealth redistribution in the health services and retirement industries. We've also seen its fundamental counter-productiveness: the attempts, in the end, increase the price of the target product, and they damage the morality and the independence of the government-driven redistribution program "beneficiaries." So it is with wealth redistribution spending, generally.

James Madison had this to say on the matter of wealth redistribution by government fiat:[18]

> Mr. Madison wished to relieve the sufferers, but was afraid of establishing a dangerous precedent, which might hereafter be perverted to the countenance of purposes very different from those of charity. He acknowledged, for his own part, that he could not undertake to lay his finger on that article in the Federal Constitution which granted a right of Congress of expending, on objects of benevolence, the money of their constituents.

18   James Madison, in *Annals of Congress*, House of Representatives, 3rd Congress, 1st Session. At the time, the Annals summarized speeches in the third person.

Mr. Madison clearly recognized the dangers inherent in setting a precedent of government-driven welfare: the Constitution gave the Federal government authority to pursue certain limited ends only. These ends do not include authorization to provide the vast array of goods and services that today reduce so many of us to government dependency. The benefit objected to by Mr. Madison, in fact, was aid to refugees of a Haitian revolution. Instead, such assistance is properly first the obligation of private individuals and private organizations, as we saw in the Chapter 4.

Justice William Paterson wrote this in *Vanhorne's Lessee v. Dorrance*[19] as long ago as 1795 (it is clearly apparent, also, that Justice Paterson's words are relevant to the question of eminent domain) [italics in the original]:

> ...it is evident; that the right of acquiring and possessing property, and having it protected, is one of the natural, inherent, and unalienable rights of man. Men have a sense of property: Property is necessary to their subsistence, and correspondent to their natural wants and desires; its security was one of the objects, that induced them to unite in society. No man would become a member of a community, in which he could not enjoy the fruits of his honest labour and industry. The preservation of property then is a primary object of the social compact, and, by the late Constitution of *Pennsylvania,* was made a fundamental law. Every person ought to contribute his proportion for public purposes and public exigencies; but no one can be called upon to surrender or sacrifice his whole property, real and personal, for the good of the community, without receiving a recompence in value. This would be laying a burden upon an individual, which ought to be sustained by the society at large.

This includes, of course, a man's property in the form of money received,

---

19   *Vanhorne's Lessee v. Dorrance*, 2 U.S. 304 (1795). A Pennsylvania law sought to seize land from one private person and transfer it to another private person without compensation, not only in violation of the Constitution of the United States, but in violation of the Pennsylvania state constitution, as well. The U.S. Supreme Court found the Pennsylvania law unconstitutional on both the takings ground and as a violation of the sanctity of contracts guaranteed by the state's constitution.

perhaps in exchange for the produce of his labor, perhaps inherited from an antecedent who received the money property through a lifetime of labor and exchange.

Regarding the redistribution of wealth from the citizens of one State to another State (or the citizens resident there), it is a false premise that the citizens of New York are responsible for making whole a bankrupt California or that the citizens of Texas are responsible for making whole a bankrupt Illinois. President Gerald Ford was right when he refused to authorize federal funds to bail out a bankrupt New York City[20]. The principle concerning wealth redistribution applies to the States, as well. We remain a federation of States; the States are not a communal piggy bank to be tapped *ad libitum* by an overreaching Federal government.

The government also spends a tremendous amount of money in attempts to stimulate the economy—another form of wealth redistribution. The enormous sums spent by the Franklin Roosevelt administration accomplished two key things: they exploded the national debt by nearly 75% in the four years through 1936, and they prolonged the depression by crowding out and holding back the private economy. They did succeed, though, in creating no jobs, as unemployment remained above 15%, and generally above 19% until World War II. The enormous sums spent by the Bush and Obama administrations for the same purpose accomplished the same things: the national debt was exploded by roughly 55% in the four years since 2007, and they are prolonging the Panic of 2008 by holding back the private economy. And like Roosevelt's stimulus spending, the current stimulus spending is succeeding in creating no jobs.

Now we can develop an answer to the proper role of government spending, and it flows from the only proper role of government taxation. Our

---

20   In October 1975, President Ford said he would veto any bailout funds for New York City, which was approaching default on its debts and subsequent bankruptcy, a condition brought on by the city's profligate and uncontrolled spending. In the ensuing month, under the pressure of knowing the city would no longer be permitted its profligate ways, all interested parties came together: drastic reductions were made in the city's surplus work force, bankers restructured bond issues, the new Municipal Assistance Corporation was established to sell securities. In late November 1975, as a result of this restructuring, President Ford asked Congress to approve a series of seasonal loans over the next three years, at 1% over the nation's cost of money to facilitate the finalization of the city's budget and debt restructuring.

Constitution says quite clearly what our taxes are for: "...to pay the Debts and provide for the common Defence and general Welfare of the United States...." Article I, Section 8 lays out the remaining Congressional powers, and Articles II and III create the Executive and Judicial branches. Aside from the Taxing and Spending Clause's purposes, then, the only legitimate roles for taxing is to fund the structures of the three branches of government and to provide funds for the satisfaction of those remaining enumerated powers of Congress. There is no other purpose than these for Federal taxation.

Government spending must be for no other purposes than these, since these are the only legitimate purposes of our taxes. "Debts" and "the common Defence" are clear on their face. What is the "general Welfare," though? This is nothing more or less than leaving men free to see to their own ends, to make their own fortunes, which includes failing in the attempt, then recovering, and ultimately succeeding, or not. Providing for the "general Welfare" is best done through protecting men's wealth, rather than confiscating it through taxation, through facilitating men's ability to determine for themselves what is their welfare (which means sound education and vocational training,[21] and facilitating an ability to create new things through "Writings and Discoveries"), through development and protection of the national infrastructure (transportation, power generation and transmission, and communications—all underlain by the vocations and trades), and through an ability to enforce agreements they might make (which means contract law, transparency, and enforcement).

Currently, spending must be heavily committed to paying down our exploded national debt—not just making interest payments, but actually paying it down. Keeping our national debt low, as well as current, forms the basis of a sound economy and facilitates all other economic efforts that men might make. This represents an additional demand that spending be kept low, so as not to run up the national debt, again. Thomas Jefferson was right in his admonition, and he foretold today's condition [italics in the original]:[22]

---

21   College is not for everyone. Some men are better off—happier—working at what might be termed vocations, or trades. These should be the individual's choice, not an outcome of governmental (or societal) pressure. These men are the ones working at the very foundations of our nation, upon which all else must be built.

22   Letter to Samuel Kercheval, Monticello, July 12, 1816

We must not let our rulers load us with perpetual debt. We must make our election between *economy* and *liberty* or *profusion* and *servitude*. If we run into such debts, as that we must be taxed in our meat and in our drink, in our necessaries and our comforts, in our labors and our amusements, for our calling and our creeds...[we will] have no time to think, no means of calling our miss-managers to account but be glad to obtain subsistence by hiring ourselves to rivet their chains on the necks of our fellow-sufferers....

This example reads to us the salutary lesson, that private fortunes are destroyed by public as well as by private extravagance....A departure from principle in one instance becomes a precedent for a second; that second for a third; and so on, till the bulk of the society is reduced to be mere automatons of misery.... And the fore horse of this frightful team is public debt. Taxation follows that, and in its train wretchedness and oppression.

The "general Welfare" is facilitated by spending for education at all levels; however, this should be done via block grants flowing to the local communities. These local communities know best, even in this modern, interconnected national community, their own educational needs. No government should be in the business of controlling the local education precepts; outright grants through the State governments are most effective at stripping off the Federal government's strings and influences. And these grants need not be large: locally generated property taxes, the traditional, and tried and true, means of education fund raising still is very effective at providing the bulk of the funds—especially with the reduced taxation generally, and reduced government spending generally, which will leave more money in the hands of the (local) individuals who actually earned it.

Spending should be freely done for basic research and development (R&D), with the results turned over to private enterprise for further exploitation and development. Note that this is not a substitute for privately funded R&D. Tax-funded R&D, even though turned over to private enterprise, should remain in the public arena—its "exclusive Right" already expired—while only privately added developments, and privately funded R&D, should be available to patent and copyright. Some will argue that this is the social engineering just decried, but it is a function of government, as stated in our Constitution: Article I, Section 8 says, in part "To promote the Progress of Science and useful Arts...." This clause is in the context of protecting inventions and copyrights; however, government funding of basic research also contributes to Science and useful Arts that are worth protecting by helping to fund research difficult, or too expensive, for private enterprise to pursue alone.

The nation's physical infrastructure, and the computer systems that control it and its components, are legitimate subjects of government spending. However, as the utility company and communications company models have shown, spending here should be limited to helping private enterprise— through loans, not grants—overcome initial high costs of entry[23] into the industry, and go no further. Existing government intervention into the utility and communications industries should end. The United States used to have the best telephone system in the world, until the protected monopoly of Ma Bell was dismantled. The resulting competition made the system even better, cheaper, more flexible and reliable, and with vastly improved, and improving, capabilities and technologies. Reducing government intervention into the utilities and enabling competition there can only have the same result.

I do not have any room for wealth redistribution spending. We have seen, already, the failure of government-driven welfare, of government-driven social engineering, of government-driven wealth distribution, generally, with the damage to our individual freedoms, our duties, and our morality that a government-determined "proper" society engenders. An enormous reduction in government spending—and therefore reduction in economic distortion[24]—can be achieved by eliminating the vast bulk of wealth redistribution. As was shown in the Chapters 4 and 7, with citizen-driven welfare and retirement, government spending will be a shadow of the present levels. Some will argue that, at best, this is a naïve point of view. However, the only politicians making such arguments are, to paraphrase Friedman,[25]

---

23   Within this, the model of drug development and patenting by drug companies is instructive.
24   The 40%, for instance, of our annual budget currently spent on retirement and health redistribution.
25   **Tax Reform**, December 1999, in **Independent Review**. Friedman actually was talking about

those enabling legislators (and presidents) who seek to raise campaign funds by inserting or removing loopholes in our present obscenely complicated wealth redistribution programs.

Like Madison, I can find no part in the Constitution that authorizes a government to take property from one man and give it to another, no matter how lofty the motive. And this was no act of forgetfulness by our Founders. When men are free from arbitrary government restraint or pressure, the need for government-driven wealth redistribution is at its minimum: men do honor their obligations to each other when allowed to do so. They generally manage to achieve those ends more efficiently and effectively, as well.

The Federal government attempts to play too great a role concerning the States of the Union, also. There is afoot a presumption that States' rights are subject to Federal review and approval. This view first was expressed decades ago by a Republican, Arthur Larson, who claimed that the 10th Amendment to the Constitution only creates a "general presumption" toward States' rights.[26] However, if the States are not, in the Federal government's sole view, responding appropriately to the needs of the people, than the Federal government, Larson asserted, is obligated to intervene within the internal affairs of the individual States.[27] Larson justifies this amazing claim by stating that for every right there is a corresponding duty, which certainly is true, but he then claims that the Federal government is solely qualified to define that duty. This ignores the fact that the Constitution is not a primer on the theory of governance, nor is it, as has been (rightly) said, a suicide pact. It is, rather, binding law, the supreme law of the land, and it says in so many words that the Federal government's rights and powers are strictly limited to those explicitly enumerated in that same Constitution. All other powers and rights—let me repeat that, for emphasis—*all* other powers and rights are reserved to the States and to the people. Clearly, this includes the sole authority to define the nature of "duty" as the other side of the rights coin, and to determine how that duty should be satisfied, or when. Deviating from that is the suicide, not adherence to it.

---

our obscenely complicated tax system, but his point easily extends to Federal spending programs.
26   Larson, Arthur, **A Republican Looks at His Party**, 1956.
27   It is a curious thought, indeed, that State governments, being closer to the people than the Federal government, are less responsive to them than the Federal government has shown itself to be.

As Thomas Paine wrote in **Common Sense**, "Society is produced by our wants, and government by our wickedness; the former promotes POSITIVELY by uniting our affections, the latter NEGATIVELY by restraining our vices. The one encourages intercourse, the other creates distinctions. The first a patron, the last a punisher. Society in every state is a blessing, government even in the best of states is a necessary evil." And so our Constitution explicitly limits our government in all of its legal powers, but especially in the scope and breadth of its taxing and spending.

In the end, all governments originate either from the consent of the people or by the naked exercise of power of a few over the many: usurpation. The consent of the governed in a republic occurs through a process of delegation; no other means exists; any other means is that usurpation. The only reliable mechanism for delegation, the only thing to which one can point and say, "These are the authorities and permissions We the People delegate to our republican government which we consent to work for us" is a Constitution. Only through a Constitution can We the People delegate these authorities and permissions, and at the same time retain sovereignty. This demands an ever vigilant population. We the People must always be on guard against government, well-meaning or ill, overreaching its granted permissions and authorities. We the People must always be on guard against the individuals we've selected to man that government overreaching the permissions and authorities granted to the government within which they are acting.

We have seen that government interventions into the nation's economy are failures. There are two additional objections to government involvement beyond those abridgements of men's freedoms and morality. The first is that when an activity is better done by individuals, government has neither need to intervene, nor capability to do so effectively. The second is that such interventions inexorably add to governmental power. Our Constitution has given our government all the power and authority it needs; it must accrete no more than that. These objections are not new; Mill wrote of them 150 years ago.

And so we arrive, through the principles of proper government taxing and spending, at the proper role of a conservative government. Government must be minimalist: if we want an individual in control of his own life, the individual must be free to exercise that control without government interference. If the individual is free to act, he will exercise control over his actions and his life. If we leave government free to act, we should expect it to do as individuals do—take control of the actions of individuals: it is, after all, a collection of individuals. The people are Sovereign, not the government. We need to act like it. The elections of 2010 were a start on resuming our proper role, but only a start.

CHAPTER 9—MODERN LIBERALISM AND PROGRESSIVISM

Falsus in unum, falsus in omnibus.

— *Latin Saying*

def: *National Democracy*: a political philosophy that considers it necessary for central government to regulate (i) the powers of the key institutions and structures of the state, and (ii) the rights and duties of citizens.[1]

def: *welfare state*: a social system based on the assumption by a political state of primary responsibility for the individual and social welfare of its citizens.[2]

Let's listen, for a bit, to what the Progressives have to say about us, about their position, and about our social contract.

"If they bring a knife to the fight, we bring a gun."[3]

"I won."[4]

"We don't mind the Republicans joining us. They can come for the ride, but they gotta sit in back."[5]

---

1   From Saleam, Jim, **On National Democracy**. He continues with "National Democracy, by establishing new organs of political representation, would ensure the control of economics by politics."

2   Merriam-Webster Online.

3   Remark made by then-candidate Obama at a 2008 fundraiser in Pennsylvania.

4   Statement reported by participants as having been made by President Obama to terminate a discussion on tax policy during a private "bipartisan" meeting with Congressional leaders of both political parties in January 2009.

5   Statement by President Obama during an October 2010 mid-term Rhode Island campaign fundraising speech at a Woonsocket factory.

"We're going to punish our enemies and we're gonna reward our friends who stand with us on issues that are important to us."[6]

The foregoing illustrate the Progressive attitude toward bipartisanship.

Kathleen Sebelius, Director of Health and Human Services, threatened to lock insurance companies out of Patient Protection and Affordable Care Act (PPACA) health insurance markets if they persisted in criticizing PPACA and tried to raise their premiums more than the administration—she—deemed "reasonable" in response to the increased costs engendered by PPACA.[7]

"...have to pass the bill so that you can find out what is in it."[8]

When several large companies filed SEC documentation announcing extra charges against their revenues due to PPACA-caused increased costs, the then-Democratic Party Chairman of the House Energy and Commerce Committee threatened to summon them to hearings to explain their inappropriate actions.[9]

"Look, everybody has a role to play. And if people don't want to play that role, if they want to travel by some other means, of course that's their right. This is the United States...."[10]

These examples illustrate the degree of Progressive understanding of the consequences of the laws and regulations which they enact.

"It [the Constitution of the United States] has no binding power on anything.

---

6   Remark made by President Obama campaigning in October 2010 for his version of immigration reform. Although Mr. Obama (a week) later expressed reservations about the use of the word "enemies," ("I probably should have used the word 'opponents' instead of 'enemies.'"), he expressed no such reservations about the disdain in his statement for all who disagree with him.

7   Letter to America's Health Insurance Plans, September 2009.

8   "Pelosi Remarks at the 2010 Legislative Conference for National Association of Counties," Press Release, March 2010, available from the Speaker's Web site, http://www.speaker.gov/newsroom/pressreleases?id=1576, as I write this.

9   For instance, March 26, 2010 Rep. Henry Waxman (D), California, letter to Mr. Randall Stephenson, Chairman, President, CEO of AT&T.

10   Secretary of Homeland Security, Janet Napolitano's statement, 15 Nov 2010, in response to the hue and cry from a traveler advising a TSA agent (and filming a portion of the incident), "If you touch my junk, I'll have you arrested."

...the text is confusing because it was written more than a hundred years ago...."[11]

"It's an air kiss they're blowing to the Tea Party. ... Anything we're doing that's unconstitutional will be thrown out in court."[12]

"When I went to law school they said the law's what a judge says it is. Whether it is constitutional or not is going to be whether the Supreme Court says it is."[13]

Those three statements illustrate the Progressives' attitude toward the Constitution and their deprecation of it. Further, it seems that Congressman Waxman wasn't listening to his own oath of office when he took it.[14]

During these years of the Obama administration, there has been a steady drumbeat of blaming the prior administration, or of blaming President Bush's administration by name, for the nation's present ills. "It's all President Bush's fault." This is nothing more than a bad imitation of Flip Wilson's Geraldine routine.[15] And it exemplifies the Progressives' inability to accept responsibility for their actions.

Finally, I have described in earlier chapters Progressive attempts to suppress dissenting speech: the slurs against Tea Party members and affiliates by Representatives Pelosi and Hoyer; the slurs against Americans generally for our dissent; the slurs against the opposition party by Senator Reid and by Representative Cohen; President Obama's clear disdain for the intelligence of Americans who disagree with him, to recall a few.

---

11   Ezra Klein, Staff Writer with the Washington Post, in a December 2010 interview on MSNBC's "The Daily Rundown." The next day, Mr. Klein did clarify the "more than a hundred years" part.

12   Congressman Barney Frank on reading the Constitution to open the 112th Congress, quoted in The Daily Caller, 22 Dec 2010.

13   Congressman Henry Waxman, quoted in The Daily Caller, 22 Dec 2010.

14   "I do solemnly swear (or affirm) that I will support and defend the Constitution of the United States against all enemies, foreign and domestic; that I will bear true faith and allegiance to the same; that I take this obligation freely, without any mental reservation or purpose of evasion; and that I will well and faithfully discharge the duties of the office on which I am about to enter: So help me God."

15   Geraldine's routine excuse for avoiding responsibility was, "The Devil made me do it." For President Obama, it's "The Bush made me do it."

Progressives view the American social contract to be nothing more than a handbook, a guideline; they operate from a worldview that they can—and should—remake our nation according to their tenets, and the rest of us should quietly follow; and they disparage those of us who disagree with them without actually addressing the issues raised. Their own words cited above make this mindset clear. Following is a brief description of their view of the role of government in general, the relationship between government and individuals, and the relationship between Progressives and individuals—Progressive ideology and the outcomes of progressivism.

The Progressive sees government necessarily as large, growing, and of a Right intrusive because this growth in power is driven by the magnitude of "help" it must provide ordinary citizens and the amount of control it must exert over all of us in order to provide this aid. Government not only is to be the first resort for assistance; it must intervene preemptively. The aid of private citizens, which it is our duty to provide, as we have seen, is not to be relied upon. The aid of private charity organizations, which are manned and funded by private citizens, is not to be relied upon. This drives the Progressive assertion, for instance, of the primacy of the Federal government's claim on the property of Americans: it's driven by their view of the role of government in Americans' lives.

The Progressive movement, in our government and our discourse, also has indicated its disdain for a fundamental principle of American jurisprudence—innocent until proven guilty. David Axelrod (then Senior Advisor to President Obama), for instance, accused The U. S. Chamber of Commerce, during the 2010 election campaign, of using foreign money to pay for political advertising in the 2010 national elections (not just an unethical act: if true, this would be an illegal act), and then refused to provide any evidence to support the administration's accusation, asserting that it's the responsibility of The Chamber to prove its innocence in the matter.[16] President Obama made substantially the same claim during the same campaign season.[17]

We can also see that Progressives consider individuals to be subservient

16   CBS News "Face the Nation" Interview, Oct 2010
17   Eric Lichtblau, "Topic of Foreign Money in U.S. Races Hits Hustings," New **York Times**, October 8, 2010

to their Progressive government; no more should government work for us. President Obama asserted in an April 2010 speech in Quincy, Illinois that "at a certain point you've made enough money," although he continued that he doesn't "begrudge success that's fairly earned." It's clear that he intends his Progressive movement to be the definers of "enough" and of "fairly earned," and not the individuals doing the work. As he insisted in his 2008 campaign, it's necessary to "spread the wealth around." The individual who earned the wealth shouldn't be allowed to keep it.

Your family, say the Progressives, shouldn't be allowed to keep what you've earned after you've died; nor should you care: in the words of Representative Weiner, "You'll be dead."[18] This goes along with President Obama's just recalled "spread the wealth around" remark. Vice President Biden insists that it's "the patriotic thing to do"[19] for some groups to pay even more taxes than they do now, even though other groups are not paying more, and yet other groups are paying no taxes at all. This, though, ignores the taxation resolution of the 1765 Colonial Stamp Act Congress, which held that taxes, as "free gifts of the people," can be set only by the people.

We have, finally, a Progressive President who granted input to and influence over domestic law—American civil rights and duties—to foreign nations and foreign religious influences. President Obama explicitly allowed Mexico and 10 other foreign nations[20] to intervene in a domestic legal dispute between the State of Arizona and the Federal government over immigration law. A New Jersey state court granted a husband his right to rape his wife because an interpretation of Sharia law condones this;[21] President Obama was shockingly silent on this, though he was more than willing to intrude on other local matters (*vis.*, the "beer summit" affair).

In addition to insisting on the primacy of Government over individuals, Progressives view themselves a cut above the rest of us. The Progressive does not recognize his fellow citizens as capable of or interested in seeing to our

---

18   Interview with Megyn Kelly, "America Live," Fox News Channel, 8 December 2010.

19   In a September 2010 interview on ABC's "Good Morning America," vice President Biden said, "We want to take money and put it back in the pocket of middle-class people...It's time to be patriotic...."

20   Mexico, Argentina, Bolivia, Brazil, Chile, Costa Rica, El Salvador, Ecuador, Nicaragua, Paraguay, and Peru.

21   S.D. v. M.J.R., which overturned by the New Jersey trial court's ruling allowing the rape.

own needs and wants, or of seeing to our duties. Only the Progressive has the wisdom and the level of concern required, and so only the Progressive should have access to the controls and the money necessary to satisfy his moral duty (which duty he sees as including imposition of his moral precepts on the rest of us). Ordinary citizens and private charities need to be controlled by the Progressive government, to make sure they function correctly. This, of course, is nothing more than a recreation of the Patrician class of an earlier time and the separation of this class from the common man that was extant in our colonial, pre-Revolution period: some men are more polished, better educated, better suited to governance than are the rest of us. Some Americans are more equal than others.[22]

The development of the modern Progressive ideology really isn't development at all; it's simply 18th Century Conservatism brought forward to today and adopted by our modern Patricians. Some of the history has been described in earlier chapters; their central precepts are described here. The landed gentry in colonial America and the nascent United States did not trust the wisdom of the individual in the economy. Today's Progressives, like that early American aristocracy, consider ordinary citizens too venal, and too uneducated, even too stupid, to be entrusted with voluntary, unfettered participation in a free market. Rather, only the properly educated Progressives are fit to manage "commerce," and so we have diktats from government about what an ordinary citizen must buy, how much of it that citizen must buy, when it must be bought, and the price to be paid for the item. We have diktats mandating the products that may be produced, their quantity, the prices that must be charged for them, and the amount that must be paid for the labor used.

Herb Croly, a founder of the explicitly named Progressive Movement of the early 20th century wrote in his **The Promise of American Life**, "To be sure, any increase in centralized power and responsibility, expedient or inexpedient, is injurious to certain aspects of traditional American democracy. But the fault in that case lies with the democratic tradition; and the erroneous and misleading tradition must yield before the march of constructive national democracy." He wrote further that a large part of the fault lies in the fact that "the average American individual is morally

---

22   "All animals are equal, but some animals are more equal than others." This was the final version of what began as the Seven Commandments in George Orwell's **Animal Farm**.

and intellectually inadequate to serious and consistent conception of his responsibilities as a democrat." Here is the genesis of, and guide for, the modern Progressive imperative.

The Progressives' belief in National Democracy leads them to hold that individuals can expect—have a right—to be provided by government with their benefits and services. This is the modern Progressive creed which Abraham Lincoln scorned in his critique of Stephen A. Douglas: "...the same old serpent that says you work and I eat, you toil and I will enjoy the fruits of it."[23] Our Progressives, however, couch the matter in somewhat modified terms: government should form a welfare state to take care of you, for you are incapable of taking care of yourself (as President Obama emphasized in his campaigning for PPACA, we Americans just don't think clearly enough). Notice that this is another aspect of the soft bigotry of low expectations.[24] Government will achieve this by taxing those rich people who make, or whose businesses make, more than $250,000 per year. You won't have to pay for a thing. Progressives support this proposition through their contempt for the successful:

- You're rich. You must have done something immoral or illegal to gain such riches. Therefore you don't deserve to keep it.
- You're rich. Government wants. Therefore you must to yield it up.

We have seen, empirically, the effect of the Progressive's welfare state on morals in an earlier chapter.[25] As Mill feared, though (I'm paraphrasing

---

23   Lincoln's speech, a critique of Senator Stephen A. Douglas, delivered July 10, 1858, at Chicago, IL.

24   The original reference was by President Bush in his 2004 Republican nomination acceptance speech: "The principal [of Gainesville Elementary School, Georgia] expresses the philosophy of his school this way: 'We don't focus on what we can't do at this school; we focus on what we can do.' See, this principal is challenging the soft bigotry of low expectations."

25   To repeat: A man was cited in a December 29, 2010 **Wall Street Journal** article on home foreclosures: For two years, [a man] and his wife received $1,200 a month in unemployment payments, in addition to their $3,200 social-security checks. The unemployment payments have now run out, so [the man] said he was going back to work—not that he now had to, but that he now was willing to. Another man was quoted in a January 8, 2010 **Wall Street Journal** article on weak hiring as saying, "There are jobs around if I want to make less than what I'm making on unemployment, but that would put me in a worse spot." Social liberalism saps the morality of men who are not in dire straits, when they see the lack of morality around them. A 27-year-old real-estate investor was cited in the same December article: "He said he had no difficulty paying [his] monthly mortgage.... Concluding that the home, now worth about half of what he paid, won't recover..., [the owner] decided to walk away

his **On Liberty** Introductory remarks), "The [Progressives] have…learned to feel the power of government their power…."

When the Federal government mandates welfare, as we have seen in an earlier chapter, three essential things result. The recipient, however great or small his need, is reduced to dependency on that government, and on that politician who presses for the welfare payments. Further, the recipient, having been so reduced, is denied any ability to correct his condition, and so is denied any opportunity to satisfy his own moral obligation to achieve his own self-sufficiency, to see to his own imperatives: he cannot even try from within his state of dependency. The second result is that the person taxed to provide this welfare is denied his right to use his property for his own ends. Further, this person is denied the right to completely satisfy his moral duty, or to satisfy it in the manner he deems appropriate. On the other hand, the man who votes for this welfare program, no matter the loftiness of his purpose, not only is seeing to his own moral end (as is entirely appropriate), but is seeking to impose his terms of morality on everyone else (which is simply arrogance). The third result is the dependency of the Progressive on his own program. He comes to need the dependency of his "beneficiaries" as much as those persons trapped in their dependency need him. The Progressiveiscompletely addicted to this dependency of others on him.

Further, the Progressives' behavior is tinged with hypocrisy. All we have to do to see this is to ask our Progressive elected official (actually, each of our elected officials), the next time that person presses for increased taxes and spending (because we must help those less fortunate), these two simple questions:

- What was your total income last year from all sources?
- How much money did you give to charity last year?

The answers will be illuminating. Individual Americans, as a whole, donated over $300 billion to charity in 2008; the second year in a row we have donated to charity more than $300 billion in a single year.[26] Within this, according to a Gallup poll for that same year, Conservatives donated 3.5% to 4.5% of

---

[and default on his mortgage]." "It's a no-brainer once you do the math," the owner said.
26   "Giving USA 2009," GivingUSA Foundation.

their incomes; Liberals donated 1.25% to 1.5%.[27] Vice President Biden, who considers it the patriotic thing to do to pay lots of taxes, donated 0.1% of his income in each of the years 2001-2004 when he was in the United States Senate.[28] Americans—conservative Americans, at any rate—are going to do their duty, they're going to help their fellows. Recall from an earlier chapter the amount of Federal government spending on the various wealth redistribution programs, and think about how much more we could help our fellows if we were allowed to keep these taxes that are spent on government-driven welfare. Think also about how much more we, as a nation, could help our fellows if Progressives caught up with their conservative brothers in doing their moral duty through their donation rates.

And so we have this contrast. 18th Century Liberalism—classical liberalism, modern conservatism—is committed to limited government, and it is grounded on the economics of free markets, an understanding of individual liberty and of natural law, a belief in progress and in the ability of men, acting without government intervention, to improve their own lives and to satisfy their own moral imperatives. And they actively seek to help their fellow men in need.

18th Century Conservatism—Modern American liberalism, progressivism—on the contrary, claims the primary role for government, and it openly supports a welfare state, without regard for cost or for whose money is being spent. And they are not at all active in seeking, personally, their fellow men in need: Progressives will only help the unfortunates with other people's money.

Here's one more spending example, from the Federal Transit Administration's (FTA) 2009 survey of public transit authorities, reported by Coyote Blog.[29] Looking at light rail transportation systems, the FTA reports that, for all US light rail systems, we have the following costs:

---

27   Reported by Arthur C. Brooks in his column, "Conservatives Have Answered Obama's Call," **Wall Street Journal,** January 22, 2009.

28   Reported by The Conservative Thinker, April 21, 2009, in "Conservatives are More Charitable," http://conservative-thinker.com/blog/2009/04/21/conservatives-are-more-charitable/, as I write this in Fall 2011.

29   http://www.coyoteblog.com/coyote_blog/2011/02/light-rail-and-sustainability.html as I write this.

- User fares paid per passenger-mile: $0.18
- Total cost per passenger-mile: $2.22
- Taxpayer subsidy per passenger-mile: $2.04

For Phoenix, Arizona, in particular, we have the following costs:

- User fares paid per passenger-mile: $0.07
- Total cost per passenger-mile: $3.89
- Taxpayer subsidy per passenger-mile: $3.82

We see that non-users, nationwide, pay 92% of light rail's costs. In Phoenix, non-users pay 98% of the costs. In Phoenix alone, money is taken from millions of people[30] in the form of wealth redistribution taxes so that roughly 17,000 can ride the light rail each day. Progressives simply have no concern for other people's money. Once again, I suggest you think about what Americans could do with that money left in their pockets.

Progressive causes include government-created and -mandated entitlements, and Progressives insist on funding these through wealth redistribution programs. Indeed, the recipients of these programs' payments already have been swelled, by Progressive policies, to nearly half the families of the United States. Forty-seven percent of our households paid no Federal income tax for 2009, either due to low income, or because there were enough tax credits, deductions, and exemptions (our Byzantine tax system) to eliminate their tax liability. Half of us are working to support the other half (Stephen Douglas' goal), and this is just in those areas supported by income taxes;[31] it does not include those whose retirements are being supported by the rest of us.

The inexorable outcome of the Progressives' attempts to change the structure of our economy and of our government will be a condition where state regulation will have eliminated the freedom and wealth-for-everyone power of capitalism and replaced it with a system of positive law that defines what rights we are allowed to have and that demands that some of us will work for the benefit of others of us who do not work. And they seek to force these

---

30   Phoenix proper had a 2010 population of 1.4 million; the Phoenix Metropolitan Statistical Area had a 2009 population of 4.4 million.

31   "47% of Americans Pay No Federal Income Tax," Associated Press, April 8, 2010.

reforms through regardless of the views of Americans or the limits applied by our Constitution, all while claiming a desire for bipartisanship, decrying its absence, and disdaining actually to have any.

Chapter 10—Conclusions

Freedom is never more than one generation away from extinction. We didn't pass it to our children in the bloodstream. It must be fought for, protected, and handed on for them to do the same, or one day we will spend our sunset years telling our children and our children's children what it was once like in the United States where men were free.

— **Ronald Wilson Reagan**

As we have just seen, we have a Progressive government that is the result of a long period of deviation, indeed of separation, from our 18th Century Liberal founding principles. This Progressive government actually is accelerating that separation, returning us to that 18th Century Conservative aristocratic principle of government knows best, and it is doing so without the consent of Americans—in defiance of us, in fact. And the present government's incumbents seem incompetently amateurish in the process. Paraphrasing Shelby Steele, writing for the **Wall Street Journal**,[1] this government's policymaking has been grandiose, thoughtless, and bullying; its health-care bill was…finally, so chaotic that today no citizen knows where they stand in relation to it; its financial-reform bill seems little more than a short-sighted scapegoating of Wall Street. In foreign policy…we don't know why we do what we do.…

One response to this has been the multitude of self-organizing tea parties everywhere in our country, and the demand of these mainstream Americans for a return to our foundational principles—the very precepts that made the United States great, and exceptional. Today, for all the damage done, we still are the only nation on Earth founded on the First Principles of the inherent equality of man before our Creator and before law, and on the indivisibility and inalienableness of our natural rights. These tea partiers, these Americans, so routinely denigrated by Progressives as, variously, racist; un-American;

---

1   Steele, Shelby, A., "Referendum on the Redeemer," **Wall Street Journal**, 28 Oct 2010

not even the people, *per se*; have stood up and objected to the Progressive's inherent distrust of ordinary Americans; of our fundamental decency; of our capability for seeing to our own needs and wants; of our willingness and capacity for satisfying our own moral imperatives. And we have seen these same disparaged tea partiers, and other Conservatives everywhere, affiliated with the tea partiers only through a commonality of purpose and fundamental respect for our social contract (with its respect for Americans), utterly reject the Progressives, their policies, and their denigration of us and our principles in the 2010 mid-term national elections.

What may we conclude from this, and what must be our next (and continuing) steps? We have seen in the examples of earlier chapters that if there are no Creator-given rights, then there cannot be inalienable rights, natural rights. The entire matter becomes irrelevant, for if there is no higher level of authority, then all rights must originate either from us acting on our own or from the government which we create. And so there are no rights which cannot be severed from us; all rights awarded by men or by a government of men can be modified or taken away altogether by those men or that government. Our rights, should they flow from governments, or ourselves, and not from our Creator, can only lead directly and speedily to the slavery of most of us to the few. We have seen how the 21st century Progressive, building on the 20th century Liberal's output, is seeking to entrench government authority in place of individual, personal responsibility.

It's important to keep firmly in mind, though, that as we speak of the Democratic Party-controlled Senate, or the Republican Party-controlled House of Representatives, or the Democratic Party Presidency, these two Legislative branch houses and the Executive branch of our government are not the possessions of these parties or of their underlying ideologies (I hesitate to call them philosophies). These sections of our government are the people's branches; they belong to us, they work for us, they are ours to command: We the People. (So, also, is the Judicial branch our branch, but we inure this one from day to day—or election cycle to election cycle—variations in political demands by putting these selectees through an arduous vetting and acceptance process and then granting them a lifetime tenure.)

We see, also, that Progressives engage in the politics of despair: man is fallen and cannot improve himself, and so we must constantly be redeemed by our betters; we have no hope, save through their leadership. Yet this leads directly to a logical conundrum. On the one hand, if man is irredeemably fallen, the Progressives who would lead us must not be men, but rather some set of superior beings. On the other hand, if the Progressives who would lead us acknowledge their own humanity, then they, too, are irredeemably fallen, and so they cannot be any more fit to lead us than the rest of us.

Conservatives, however, practice the politics of hope and optimism—man is fallen, but through our own strength and wisdom, and with the aid of our Creator, we can improve ourselves; we need none of the opium of the welfare of our "Betters." Today's Conservatives respect the wisdom of us all and hold no pretense that some men are better than others. Each man is as fit to lead—or to follow—as any other; he has only to convince his fellows in the next election.

I offer, in summary, these fundamental principles as the foundation for one man's conservative manifesto.

1. All men are created equal.
    a. Corollary 1: No man has a claim on any other. Thus, for instance (but not exclusively), charity both is voluntary (albeit a donor's moral imperative) from the donor and can have no result of claimant on the part of the recipient.
    b. Corollary 2: Each man is sovereign over his own person and his own mind and conscience. A man's belief is between himself and his Creator, and no government can interfere, except in narrowly defined aspects related to that man's repeated infringements on another man's rights and duties—never at all with his mind and beliefs.
    c. Corollary 3: Every man is responsible for the outcomes of his own behavior and of his own choices. No other man can be held responsible for the first man's outcomes or for his duties. To do so would infringe the rights and duties, and so the morality, of the first man as well as of the second man.
    d. Corollary 4: Every man has both the capacity and the obligation to improve himself in both his material and his moral condition, and to work to help those he has accepted into his care—his family and those with whom he voluntarily

associates—to improve theirs. A government which men voluntarily form for themselves can assist in these efforts, but it can never mandate, nor can it ever act before men have acted except in accordance with Corollary 2 above.

e. Corollary 5: Government is subordinate to men; it can never legitimately claim sovereignty over men.

1. Government can have only those narrowly prescribed authorities and powers assigned it in our American social contract, and it must be kept small in size, scope, and capacity.

2. Government has the sole purpose of protecting men's rights and creating an environment within which men can satisfy their own duties. As with Corollary 4, government can assist, but it can never mandate.

3. If we yield on either of these to government, our fall will be both long and steep.

2. A man is the primary means of production—it is the man's body and his mind that are the source of his labor and so of all product of that labor. From this, each man has a property—an ownership—in all that he produces.

a. Corollary 1: No man or man-made agency can have dominion over what another man produces. This is strictly his own to trade according to terms with which he and his trading partner voluntarily agree.

b. Corollary 2: The right to private property, and to control the disposition of that private property, is as inalienable in men as is our equality. This right also forms the practical foundation of our freedom: our ability to create wealth for ourselves and for our nation as a whole and our capacity for continued improvements in the quality of our lives both material and moral.

c. Corollary 3: A man's money, as a product of his labor, is never the government's; it is his own. We give some of our money to our government, in the form of taxes, for our own future well-being and for the common welfare of our fellows and the nation as a whole. The government cannot take as much as it wishes, leaving us an amount it determines to be appropriate.

     d. Corollary 4: There can be no government-mandated redistribution of wealth, save the extremely limited form described in Chapter 4. The irreducible minimum of redistribution must include a redistribution of rights and of morality because these are inherent in the property being redistributed. Redistribution of rights flows by giving the recipient a claim on the original owner's property at the direct expense of that owner's rights in his own property. Redistribution of morality flows by reducing the recipient's moral obligation in his own welfare and placing that decrement directly into the obligations of the original owner of the property being redistributed.

3. *Eternal vigilance is the price of liberty.* But, *The tree of liberty must be refreshed from time to time with the blood of patriots and tyrants.* -- Thomas Jefferson

The steps we take on the long road to our nation's recovery must include the following:

1. We must repair our government's borrowing schemes and reduce the national debt, which today stands at an enormous and expanding level and represents a threat to our freedom of action on the global— and domestic—stage, and so threatens our security.

2. We must repair our government's spending schemes and reduce the nation's annual budget deficit. The repair must include our entitlements and the nation's defense, for in the end, *all* government spending is discretionary, not just those portions useful to a politician for buying votes. The deficits underlie and expand the national debt.

3. We must repair our government's taxing schemes, simplify our tax code, and reduce our overall tax rates. Taxes do not exist to support government spending; spending must be fit into the available tax revenue, and those tax revenues must be what We the People determine is appropriate, not what an unresponsive government imposes on us.

These three must come first; there can be no economic recovery, no improvement in private employment rates, no restoration of freedom or of morality, until the government's profligate borrowing and spending are brought under our control, and the government brought to a recognition that the monies being taxed are ours, not the government's.

4. Our laws and regulations must be aimed at transparency, not at controlling what we may produce or sell or buy, or the prices at which these must be done. When men can know the terms of an investment, when men can know the factors surrounding and underlying a transaction, we can, and do, make the best choices, for these are informed choices that satisfy our needs and wants. This also maximizes our ability to satisfy our moral imperative to see to our own ends first, and to assist our fellows, rather than looking to government to do that for us. Mandating behavior, rather than mandating visibility, is an abridgement of our freedoms and of our duties that are associated with those freedoms.

5. We must greatly reduce the physical size of our Federal government. We have, currently, in the Executive branch alone 15 Cabinet-level Executive Departments, with bloated staffs, and 37 unaccountable, independent Czars ("Special Advisors to the President"). Many of these Departments should be eliminated (not by folding them into remaining Departments; rather eliminating the Departments, their functions, and their payrolls, altogether). Candidate Departments include the Departments of Agriculture, Commerce, Education, Energy, Health and Human Services, Labor, and Veterans Affairs. The functions of the first six of these Departments are much better done at the State level, where their output can more easily, and properly, be tailored to the individual States' needs. Veterans Affairs is better handled in a Department of Defense that is better focused on seeing to the nation's security (which includes seeing to the needs of those who have sacrificed for our security) and less focused on jobs protection for defense contractors as high-donation constituents of our representatives. The Czars and their staffs must be eliminated altogether. Our government has a Cabinet of Executive Departments which are led by people who must be openly nominated by the President and actively and openly approved by the Senate. The government has no functions, and so needs no staff, that benefit the nation through operations outside the oversight of the Congress, and so of we Americans.

6. We must legislatively reverse *Wickard*, the distortion of the use and meaning of the general welfare clause in *Nebbia*, and *Wickard*"'s precursor, *West Coast Hotel*. The court-sanctioned over-expansion of the Commerce and related clauses, the distortion of interstate commerce regulation away from its original purpose, and the misuse of the general welfare clause must be reversed.

7. We must legislatively reverse *Midkiff* and *Kelo*, and restore our property rights to their correct status. Our Constitution allows eminent domain appropriations for the public good, not for transfer to another private entity, and not as an excuse to increase a government's tax revenues.

8. The courts generally, and the Supreme Court specifically, must be instructed on the true meaning of the 10th Amendment; their ignorance of this Amendment remaining manifest from *Darby Lumber Co.*

9. There must be a single litmus test for those considered for appointment to a Federal judgeship, including the Supreme Court. This test must be for the candidate to attest that he or she adheres to strict constructionism or to originalism.[2] A judge cannot be expected to satisfy his/her oath to "support and defend the Constitution of the United States" if that judge considers him/herself free to adjust the meaning of the Constitution at will, according to personal beliefs or a newer, *au courant* interpretation. If the Constitution needs change, than it must be changed in accordance with the Article V prescribed methods, and not from the Judicial or Legislative benches.

If we can accomplish these, we will have made important progress in satisfying the list of goals provided at the end of Chapter 2. We took an important first step with the 2010 mid-term national elections, but we cannot stop there. The people we elected to represent us in the Legislative branch must know that they are on probation against their actual performance in restoring our

---

2   *Strict Constructionism*: The application of the text of the Constitution as it is written. There is only one clear meaning of the text, and once that text is understood, no further investigation into its meaning is required. *Originalism*: Find and understand the original meaning or intent of the text, and do not seek to impose any newer interpretations foreign to the author(s)' intentions. This contrasts with *textualism*, which holds that a statute's "ordinary meaning" governs interpretation of that statute; neither the intention of the legislature nor the problem intended to be remedied by the statute are relevant. The "ordinary meaning" escape simply gives activist judges license to interpret the statute, and the Constitution, in any manner convenient to them.

nation to its foundational principles, to our social contract. The Executive branch must face its own accounting in the 2012 national elections. The Legislative branch members and the President we elect in 2012, too, must know that they are on probation against their actual performance of our will. This will be a multi-election cycle struggle—indeed, a generational struggle—and at each election, those elected must be given to know that they are on probation against their actual performance. Election cannot be synonymous with life tenure.

We have our Pledge of Allegiance:

> I pledge allegiance to the flag of the United States of America, and to the republic for which it stands, one nation under God, indivisible, with liberty and justice for all.

And we have the oaths of office for our elected officials and our soldiers:

- I do solemnly swear (or affirm) that I will support and defend the Constitution of the United States against all enemies, foreign and domestic; that I will bear true faith and allegiance to the same; that I take this obligation freely, without any mental reservation or purpose of evasion; and that I will well and faithfully discharge the duties of the office on which I am about to enter: So help me God.[3]
- I, _____, do solemnly swear (or affirm) that I will support and defend the Constitution of the United States against all enemies, foreign and domestic; that I will bear true faith and allegiance to the same; and that I will obey the orders of the President of the United States and the orders of the officers appointed over me, according to regulations and the Uniform Code of Military Justice. So help me God.[4]
- I, _____ (SSAN), having been appointed an officer in the Army of the United States, as indicated above in the grade of _____ do solemnly swear (or affirm) that I will support and defend the Constitution of the United States against all enemies, foreign or domestic, that I will bear true faith and allegiance to the same; that I take this obligation

---

3   The oath of office for the House of Representatives and the Senate, enacted in 1884.

4   The enlisted man's enlistment oath.

freely, without any mental reservations or purpose of evasion; and that I will well and faithfully discharge the duties of the office upon which I am about to enter; So help me God.[5]

As Lt. Col. Allen West (USA, Ret.), now Representative Allen West (R, 22nd District, FL), has emphasized, there is no statute of limitations on the oath for those who are military veterans, and for those who are not, now is their chance to serve—to take this oath and join the fight to retrieve our country.[6] It would behoove all of us to repeat to ourselves the Pledge and one of the above oaths of office, to remind ourselves of the bond and duty we have to our nation.

I close with this thought from Thomas Paine:

> The summer soldier and the sunshine patriot will, in this crisis, shrink from the service of his country; but he that stands it NOW deserves the love and thanks of man and woman.[7]

---

5   The officer commissioning oath for the other services is substantially the same.

6   Statement made in his October 2009 speech at the American Freedom Tour in Fort Lauderdale, Florida.

7   Thomas Paine, "The American Crisis, Number 1"

BIBLIOGRAPHY

The following references have informed my thinking and the writing of this book. However, there are no particular citations from these, except where explicitly identified in the footnote(s) of a given page. In the end, my ideas should stand on their merits, not because some old, dead guys, or some live guys, agree with them; albeit these are some very important old, dead guys and very important live guys, and they are worth listening to.

Alinsky, Saul D., **Rules for Radicals**, Vintage, 1989

Amar, Akhil Reed, **America's Constitution**, A Biography, 2005

Amar, Akhil Reed, **The Bill of Rights**, 1998

Baumer, Franklin L., **Modern European Thought: Continuity and Change in Ideas, 1600-1950**, 1977

Carey, George W. editor, **The Political Writings of John Adams**, 2001

Cooke, J. E., ed., **The Federalist Papers**, 1961

Croly, Herb, **The Promise of American Life**, 1909

Friedman, Lawrence M., **American Law**, 1984

Goldwater, Barry, **The Conscience of a Conservative**, 2010

Hanson, Victor Davis, **Carnage and Culture, Landmark Battles in the Rise of Western Power**, 2001

Hayek, F. A., **The Road to Serfdom**, 1944

Kaplan, Abraham, **The Conduct of Inquiry**, 1964

Larson, Arthur, **A Republican Looks at His Party**, 1956

Levy, Leonard W., **Origins of the Bill of Rights**, 1999

Locke, John, **Second Treatise of Government, in Political Essays, Cambridge Texts in the History of Political Thought**, Mark Goldie, editor, 1997

Meese, Edwin III, **The Heritage Guide to the Constitution**, Matthew Spalding and David Forte, editors, 2005

Mill, John Stuart, **On Liberty**, Michael B. Mathias, editor, 2007

Morison, Samuel Eliot, **The Oxford History of the American People**, 1965

Morris, Charles R., **Money, Greed, and Risk**, 1999

Paine, Thomas, **Collected Writings**, Eric Foner, editor, 1995

Painter, Sidney, **Feudalism and Liberty**, Fred A. Cazel, Jr, editor, 1961

Rappleye, Charles, **Robert Morris: Financier of the American Revolution**, 2010

Rousseau, Jean-Jacques, **The Social Contract, in The Social Contract and other later political writings**, Cambridge Texts in the History of Political Thought, Victor Gourevitch, editor 2009

Skousen, W. Cleon, **The Five Thousand Year Leap**, 2009

Smith, Adam, **An Inquiry into the Nature and Causes of the Wealth of Nations**, R. H. Campbell and A. S. Skinner, editors, 1976

de Soto, Hernando, **The Mystery of Capital: Why Capitalism Triumphs in the West and Fails Everywhere Else**, 2000

Various, "Constitution of the United States of America"

Various, "The unanimous Declaration of the thirteen united States of America"

Walzer, Michael, **Just and Unjust Wars: A Moral Argument with Historical Illustrations**, 2d ed.

Wood, Gordon S., **The Radicalism of the American Revolution**, 1991

POSTSCRIPT

There are a few items, not central to the theme of this book, that may want expansion in a place of their own. While these each would warrant books of their own from someone more capable than I, I offer the following, to be understood within the context of their usage in the present book.

1. An astute reader will have noticed that I use "natural rights" and "inalienable rights" interchangeably and that I use "natural law", "rights," and "freedom" interchangeably, as well. In both cases, this is deliberate. As our Founders so clearly understood, our natural rights are endowments of our Creator, and so they are inalienable: they are indivisible from each of us. Thus, in the context of this book, the two terms refer to the same thing: the suite of rights imbued in each of us solely as a result of our existence as the product of our Creator. In the second case, the usage is less precise, as there are distinctions among the three. However, I do not consider those distinctions to be major in the context of this subject matter; although, they would be important in a treatment of law generally, or of American law specifically.

2. On the matter of freedom and rights, generally, there are two dimensions of duality that inhere in them. One duality is that of the obligations that are the other side of the rights (freedoms) coin. Every right carries with it a duty to protect and enforce it, not only for ourselves, but for our neighbors, also. This set of duties also includes an obligation to be active in our civic responsibilities, most especially in the oversight and control we must exercise over the governments we hire, from the local jurisdiction of our towns to the national jurisdiction of our Federal government. This set of duties also includes an obligation to use our rights and freedoms, in some sense, responsibly (where responsibility, in a free nation, is defined by the individual, rather than any government). We occasionally pass a set of laws (ideally, an abbreviated set), or receive a court opinion, to help us to satisfy these obligations. One such, in the context of responsible behavior, is the injunction against shouting fire in a crowded theater, even though a blanket

exercise of our 1ˢᵗ Amendment right would seem to include the freedom to do exactly that (here is an example of the clash between our right to do a thing ending at the right of another to do a thing: our "freedom" to shout fire in that crowd conflicts with the rights of others in that crowd to their safety, which would be threatened by a potential panic ensuing).

The other duality is the two-sided nature of any freedom or right: the concept of freedom to do or not to do. As the Reverend Dr. Martin Luther King, Jr., recognized in an earlier era of political (and economic) crisis, "none of us are free unless all of us are free." In this simple statement lies the dualism of our freedoms. We cannot be free to do a thing unless we also are free not to do that thing, for if we can only do, then we must do, and we are not free. Similarly, we cannot be free not to do a thing, unless we also are free to do it. For if we only cannot, then we must not, and again we are not free. It doesn't matter what it is that is being done or not done: if we must buy an item, then we are not free to not buy it, and so we are not free. If we are enjoined from selling our labor at a price of our own choosing, then we do not have control over our own labor, over our own bodies, and so we are not free.

3. The phrase "pursuit of Happiness" gets bandied about frequently, and it's used often in this book. What did our Founding Fathers mean with this phrase? John Adams was clear: "All men are born free and independent, and have certain natural, essential, and unalienable rights, among which may be reckoned the right of enjoying and defending their lives and liberties; that of acquiring, possessing, and protecting property; in fine, that of seeking and obtaining their safety and happiness."[1]

---

1   Carey, George W. editor, **The Political Writings of John Adams**. This particular quote is from Adams' offering for "A Declaration of the Rights of the Inhabitants of the Commonwealth of Massachusetts" and which was included in the 1780 Constitution of Massachusetts as Article I of the First Part, which had that title.

Appendix I: The unanimous Declaration of the thirteen United States of America

IN CONGRESS, JULY 4, 1776[1]

The unanimous Declaration of the thirteen united States of America

When in the Course of human events it becomes necessary for one people to dissolve the political bands which have connected them with another and to assume among the powers of the earth, the separate and equal station to which the Laws of Nature and of Nature's God entitle them, a decent respect to the opinions of mankind requires that they should declare the causes which impel them to the separation.

We hold these truths to be self-evident, that all men are created equal, that they are endowed by their Creator with certain unalienable Rights, that among these are Life, Liberty and the pursuit of Happiness. — That to secure these rights, Governments are instituted among Men, deriving their just powers from the consent of the governed, — That whenever any Form of Government becomes destructive of these ends, it is the Right of the People to alter or to abolish it, and to institute new Government, laying its foundation on such principles and organizing its powers in such form, as to them shall seem most likely to effect their Safety and Happiness. Prudence, indeed, will dictate that Governments long established should not be changed for light and transient causes; and accordingly all experience hath shewn that mankind are more disposed to suffer, while evils are sufferable than to right themselves by abolishing the forms to which they are accustomed. But when a long train of abuses and usurpations, pursuing invariably the same Object evinces a design to reduce them under absolute Despotism, it is their right, it is their duty, to throw off such Government, and to provide new Guards for their future security. — Such has been the patient sufferance of these

---

1   This particular version is Copyright ©2011 ushistory.org, http://www.ushistory.org/declaration/document/index.htm as I write this in Fall 2011).

Colonies; and such is now the necessity which constrains them to alter their former Systems of Government. The history of the present King of Great Britain is a history of repeated injuries and usurpations, all having in direct object the establishment of an absolute Tyranny over these States. To prove this, let Facts be submitted to a candid world.

He has refused his Assent to Laws, the most wholesome and necessary for the public good.

He has forbidden his Governors to pass Laws of immediate and pressing importance, unless suspended in their operation till his Assent should be obtained; and when so suspended, he has utterly neglected to attend to them.

He has refused to pass other Laws for the accommodation of large districts of people, unless those people would relinquish the right of Representation in the Legislature, a right inestimable to them and formidable to tyrants only.

He has called together legislative bodies at places unusual, uncomfortable, and distant from the depository of their Public Records, for the sole purpose of fatiguing them into compliance with his measures.

He has dissolved Representative Houses repeatedly, for opposing with manly firmness his invasions on the rights of the people.

He has refused for a long time, after such dissolutions, to cause others to be elected, whereby the Legislative Powers, incapable of Annihilation, have returned to the People at large for their exercise; the State remaining in the mean time exposed to all the dangers of invasion from without, and convulsions within.

He has endeavoured to prevent the population of these States; for that purpose obstructing the Laws for Naturalization of Foreigners; refusing to pass others to encourage their migrations hither, and raising the conditions of new Appropriations of Lands.

He has obstructed the Administration of Justice by refusing his Assent to Laws for establishing Judiciary Powers.

He has made Judges dependent on his Will alone for the tenure of their offices, and the amount and payment of their salaries.

He has erected a multitude of New Offices, and sent hither swarms of Officers to harass our people and eat out their substance.

He has kept among us, in times of peace, Standing Armies without the Consent of our legislatures.

He has affected to render the Military independent of and superior to the Civil Power.

He has combined with others to subject us to a jurisdiction foreign to our constitution, and unacknowledged by our laws; giving his Assent to their Acts of pretended Legislation:

For quartering large bodies of armed troops among us:

For protecting them, by a mock Trial from punishment for any Murders which they should commit on the Inhabitants of these States:

For cutting off our Trade with all parts of the world:

For imposing Taxes on us without our Consent:

For depriving us in many cases, of the benefit of Trial by Jury:

For transporting us beyond Seas to be tried for pretended offences:

For abolishing the free System of English Laws in a neighbouring Province, establishing therein an Arbitrary government, and enlarging its Boundaries so as to render it at once an example and fit instrument for introducing the same absolute rule into these Colonies

For taking away our Charters, abolishing our most valuable Laws and altering fundamentally the Forms of our Governments:

For suspending our own Legislatures, and declaring themselves invested with power to legislate for us in all cases whatsoever.

He has abdicated Government here, by declaring us out of his Protection and waging War against us.

He has plundered our seas, ravaged our coasts, burnt our towns, and destroyed the lives of our people.

He is at this time transporting large Armies of foreign Mercenaries to compleat the works of death, desolation, and tyranny, already begun with circumstances of Cruelty & Perfidy scarcely paralleled in the most barbarous ages, and totally unworthy the Head of a civilized nation.

He has constrained our fellow Citizens taken Captive on the high Seas to bear Arms against their Country, to become the executioners of their friends and Brethren, or to fall themselves by their Hands.

He has excited domestic insurrections amongst us, and has endeavoured to bring on the inhabitants of our frontiers, the merciless Indian Savages whose known rule of warfare, is an undistinguished destruction of all ages, sexes and conditions.

In every stage of these Oppressions We have Petitioned for Redress in the most humble terms: Our repeated Petitions have been answered only by repeated injury. A Prince, whose character is thus marked by every act which may define a Tyrant, is unfit to be the ruler of a free people.

Nor have We been wanting in attentions to our British brethren. We have warned them from time to time of attempts by their legislature to extend an unwarrantable jurisdiction over us. We have reminded them of the circumstances of our emigration and settlement here. We have appealed to their native justice and magnanimity, and we have conjured them by the ties of our common kindred to disavow these usurpations, which would inevitably interrupt our connections and correspondence. They too have been deaf to the voice of justice and of consanguinity. We must, therefore, acquiesce in the necessity, which denounces our Separation, and hold them, as we hold the rest of mankind, Enemies in War, in Peace Friends.

We, therefore, the Representatives of the united States of America, in General Congress, Assembled, appealing to the Supreme Judge of the world for the rectitude of our intentions, do, in the Name, and by Authority of the good People of these Colonies, solemnly publish and declare, That these united Colonies are, and of Right ought to be Free and Independent States, that they are Absolved from all Allegiance to the British Crown, and that all political connection between them and the State of Great Britain, is and ought to be totally dissolved; and that as Free and Independent States, they have full Power to levy War, conclude Peace, contract Alliances, establish Commerce, and to do all other Acts and Things which Independent States may of right do. — And for the support of this Declaration, with a firm reliance on the protection of Divine Providence, we mutually pledge to each other our Lives, our Fortunes, and our sacred Honor.

— John Hancock

New Hampshire:
Josiah Bartlett, William Whipple, Matthew Thornton

Massachusetts:
John Hancock, Samuel Adams, John Adams, Robert Treat Paine, Elbridge Gerry

Rhode Island:
Stephen Hopkins, William Ellery

Connecticut:
Roger Sherman, Samuel Huntington, William Williams, Oliver Wolcott

New York:
William Floyd, Philip Livingston, Francis Lewis, Lewis Morris

New Jersey:
Richard Stockton, John Witherspoon, Francis Hopkinson, John Hart, Abraham Clark

Pennsylvania:
Robert Morris, Benjamin Rush, Benjamin Franklin, John Morton, George Clymer, James Smith, George Taylor, James Wilson, George Ross

Delaware:
Caesar Rodney, George Read, Thomas McKean

Maryland:
Samuel Chase, William Paca, Thomas Stone, Charles Carroll of Carrollton

Virginia:
George Wythe, Richard Henry Lee, Thomas Jefferson, Benjamin Harrison, Thomas Nelson, Jr., Francis Lightfoot Lee, Carter Braxton

North Carolina:
William Hooper, Joseph Hewes, John Penn

South Carolina:
Edward Rutledge, Thomas Heyward, Jr., Thomas Lynch, Jr., Arthur Middleton

Georgia:
Button Gwinnett, Lyman Hall, George Walton

Appendix II: The Constitution of the United States of America

The Constitution of the United States of America[1]

Preamble

We the People of the United States, in Order to form a more perfect Union, establish Justice, insure domestic Tranquility, provide for the common defence, promote the general Welfare, and secure the Blessings of Liberty to ourselves and our Posterity, do ordain and establish this Constitution for the United States of America.

Article I - The Legislative Branch

Section 1 - The Legislature

All legislative Powers herein granted shall be vested in a Congress of the United States, which shall consist of a Senate and House of Representatives.

Section 2 - The House

The House of Representatives shall be composed of Members chosen every second Year by the People of the several States, and the Electors in each State shall have the Qualifications requisite for Electors of the most numerous Branch of the State Legislature.

No Person shall be a Representative who shall not have attained to the Age of twenty five Years, and been seven Years a Citizen of the United States, and who shall not, when elected, be an Inhabitant of that State in which he shall be chosen.

---

1   This particular version is used with the kind permission of USConstitution.net at "U.S. Constitution Online," http://www.usconstitution.net/const.html, as I write this in Fall 2011).

(Representatives and direct Taxes shall be apportioned among the several States which may be included within this Union, according to their respective Numbers, which shall be determined by adding to the whole Number of free Persons, including those bound to Service for a Term of Years, and excluding Indians not taxed, three fifths of all other Persons.) **(The previous sentence in parentheses was modified by the 14th Amendment, section 2.)** The actual Enumeration shall be made within three Years after the first Meeting of the Congress of the United States, and within every subsequent Term of ten Years, in such Manner as they shall by Law direct. The Number of Representatives shall not exceed one for every thirty Thousand, but each State shall have at Least one Representative; and until such enumeration shall be made, the State of New Hampshire shall be entitled to chuse three, Massachusetts eight, Rhode Island and Providence Plantations one, Connecticut five, New York six, New Jersey four, Pennsylvania eight, Delaware one, Maryland six, Virginia ten, North Carolina five, South Carolina five and Georgia three.

When vacancies happen in the Representation from any State, the Executive Authority thereof shall issue Writs of Election to fill such Vacancies.

The House of Representatives shall chuse their Speaker and other Officers; and shall have the sole Power of Impeachment.

Section 3 - The Senate

The Senate of the United States shall be composed of two Senators from each State, *(chosen by the Legislature thereof,)* **(The preceding words in parentheses superseded by 17th Amendment, section 1.)** for six Years; and each Senator shall have one Vote.

Immediately after they shall be assembled in Consequence of the first Election, they shall be divided as equally as may be into three Classes. The Seats of the Senators of the first Class shall be vacated at the Expiration of the second Year, of the second Class at the Expiration of the fourth Year, and of the third Class at the Expiration of the sixth Year, so that one third may be chosen every second Year; *(and if Vacancies happen by Resignation, or otherwise, during the Recess of the Legislature of any State, the Executive thereof may make temporary Appointments until the next Meeting of the*

Legislature, which shall then fill such Vacancies.) **(The preceding words in parentheses were superseded by the 17th Amendment, section 2.)**

No person shall be a Senator who shall not have attained to the Age of thirty Years, and been nine Years a Citizen of the United States, and who shall not, when elected, be an Inhabitant of that State for which he shall be chosen.

The Vice President of the United States shall be President of the Senate, but shall have no Vote, unless they be equally divided.

The Senate shall chuse their other Officers, and also a President pro tempore, in the absence of the Vice President, or when he shall exercise the Office of President of the United States.

The Senate shall have the sole Power to try all Impeachments. When sitting for that Purpose, they shall be on Oath or Affirmation. When the President of the United States is tried, the Chief Justice shall preside: And no Person shall be convicted without the Concurrence of two thirds of the Members present.

Judgment in Cases of Impeachment shall not extend further than to removal from Office, and disqualification to hold and enjoy any Office of honor, Trust or Profit under the United States: but the Party convicted shall nevertheless be liable and subject to Indictment, Trial, Judgment and Punishment, according to Law.

Section 4 - Elections, Meetings

The Times, Places and Manner of holding Elections for Senators and Representatives, shall be prescribed in each State by the Legislature thereof; but the Congress may at any time by Law make or alter such Regulations, except as to the Place of Chusing Senators.

The Congress shall assemble at least once in every Year, and such Meeting shall *(be on the first Monday in December,)* **(The preceding words in parentheses were superseded by the 20th Amendment, section 2.)** unless they shall by Law appoint a different Day.

Section 5 - Membership, Rules, Journals, Adjournment

Each House shall be the Judge of the Elections, Returns and Qualifications of its own Members, and a Majority of each shall constitute a Quorum to do Business; but a smaller number may adjourn from day to day, and may be authorized to compel the Attendance of absent Members, in such Manner, and under such Penalties as each House may provide.

Each House may determine the Rules of its Proceedings, punish its Members for disorderly Behavior, and, with the Concurrence of two-thirds, expel a Member.

Each House shall keep a Journal of its Proceedings, and from time to time publish the same, excepting such Parts as may in their Judgment require Secrecy; and the Yeas and Nays of the Members of either House on any question shall, at the Desire of one fifth of those Present, be entered on the Journal.

Neither House, during the Session of Congress, shall, without the Consent of the other, adjourn for more than three days, nor to any other Place than that in which the two Houses shall be sitting.

Section 6 - Compensation

(The Senators and Representatives shall receive a Compensation for their Services, to be ascertained by Law, and paid out of the Treasury of the United States.) **(The preceding words in parentheses were modified by the 27th Amendment.)** They shall in all Cases, except Treason, Felony and Breach of the Peace, be privileged from Arrest during their Attendance at the Session of their respective Houses, and in going to and returning from the same; and for any Speech or Debate in either House, they shall not be questioned in any other Place.

No Senator or Representative shall, during the Time for which he was elected, be appointed to any civil Office under the Authority of the United States which shall have been created, or the Emoluments whereof shall have been increased during such time; and no Person holding any Office under the United States, shall be a Member of either House during his Continuance in Office.

Section 7 - Revenue Bills, Legislative Process, Presidential Veto

All bills for raising Revenue shall originate in the House of Representatives; but the Senate may propose or concur with Amendments as on other Bills.

Every Bill which shall have passed the House of Representatives and the Senate, shall, before it become a Law, be presented to the President of the United States; If he approve he shall sign it, but if not he shall return it, with his Objections to that House in which it shall have originated, who shall enter the Objections at large on their Journal, and proceed to reconsider it. If after such Reconsideration two thirds of that House shall agree to pass the Bill, it shall be sent, together with the Objections, to the other House, by which it shall likewise be reconsidered, and if approved by two thirds of that House, it shall become a Law. But in all such Cases the Votes of both Houses shall be determined by Yeas and Nays, and the Names of the Persons voting for and against the Bill shall be entered on the Journal of each House respectively. If any Bill shall not be returned by the President within ten Days (Sundays excepted) after it shall have been presented to him, the Same shall be a Law, in like Manner as if he had signed it, unless the Congress by their Adjournment prevent its Return, in which Case it shall not be a Law.

Every Order, Resolution, or Vote to which the Concurrence of the Senate and House of Representatives may be necessary (except on a question of Adjournment) shall be presented to the President of the United States; and before the Same shall take Effect, shall be approved by him, or being disapproved by him, shall be repassed by two thirds of the Senate and House of Representatives, according to the Rules and Limitations prescribed in the Case of a Bill.

Section 8 - Powers of Congress

The Congress shall have Power To lay and collect Taxes, Duties, Imposts and Excises, to pay the Debts and provide for the common Defence and general Welfare of the United States; but all Duties, Imposts and Excises shall be uniform throughout the United States;

To borrow money on the credit of the United States;

To regulate Commerce with foreign Nations, and among the several States, and with the Indian Tribes;

To establish an uniform Rule of Naturalization, and uniform Laws on the subject of Bankruptcies throughout the United States;

To coin Money, regulate the Value thereof, and of foreign Coin, and fix the Standard of Weights and Measures;

To provide for the Punishment of counterfeiting the Securities and current Coin of the United States;

To establish Post Offices and Post Roads;

To promote the Progress of Science and useful Arts, by securing for limited Times to Authors and Inventors the exclusive Right to their respective Writings and Discoveries;

To constitute Tribunals inferior to the supreme Court;

To define and punish Piracies and Felonies committed on the high Seas, and Offenses against the Law of Nations;

To declare War, grant Letters of Marque and Reprisal, and make Rules concerning Captures on Land and Water;

To raise and support Armies, but no Appropriation of Money to that Use shall be for a longer Term than two Years;

To provide and maintain a Navy;

To make Rules for the Government and Regulation of the land and naval Forces;

To provide for calling forth the Militia to execute the Laws of the Union, suppress Insurrections and repel Invasions;

To provide for organizing, arming, and disciplining, the Militia, and for governing such Part of them as may be employed in the Service of the United States, reserving to the States respectively, the Appointment of the Officers, and the Authority of training the Militia according to the discipline prescribed by Congress;

To exercise exclusive Legislation in all Cases whatsoever, over such District (not exceeding ten Miles square) as may, by Cession of particular States, and the acceptance of Congress, become the Seat of the Government of the United States, and to exercise like Authority over all Places purchased by the Consent of the Legislature of the State in which the Same shall be, for the Erection of Forts, Magazines, Arsenals, dock-Yards, and other needful Buildings; And

To make all Laws which shall be necessary and proper for carrying into Execution the foregoing Powers, and all other Powers vested by this Constitution in the Government of the United States, or in any Department or Officer thereof.

Section 9 - Limits on Congress

The Migration or Importation of such Persons as any of the States now existing shall think proper to admit, shall not be prohibited by the Congress prior to the Year one thousand eight hundred and eight, but a tax or duty may be imposed on such Importation, not exceeding ten dollars for each Person.

The privilege of the Writ of Habeas Corpus shall not be suspended, unless when in Cases of Rebellion or Invasion the public Safety may require it.

No Bill of Attainder or ex post facto Law shall be passed.

(No capitation, or other direct, Tax shall be laid, unless in Proportion to the Census or Enumeration herein before directed to be taken.) **(Section in parentheses clarified by the 16th Amendment.)**

No Tax or Duty shall be laid on Articles exported from any State.

No Preference shall be given by any Regulation of Commerce or Revenue to the Ports of one State over those of another: nor shall Vessels bound to, or from, one State, be obliged to enter, clear, or pay Duties in another.

No Money shall be drawn from the Treasury, but in Consequence of Appropriations made by Law; and a regular Statement and Account of the Receipts and Expenditures of all public Money shall be published from time to time.

No Title of Nobility shall be granted by the United States: And no Person holding any Office of Profit or Trust under them, shall, without the Consent of the Congress, accept of any present, Emolument, Office, or Title, of any kind whatever, from any King, Prince or foreign State.

Section 10 - Powers prohibited of States

No State shall enter into any Treaty, Alliance, or Confederation; grant Letters of Marque and Reprisal; coin Money; emit Bills of Credit; make any Thing but gold and silver Coin a Tender in Payment of Debts; pass any Bill of Attainder, ex post facto Law, or Law impairing the Obligation of Contracts, or grant any Title of Nobility.

No State shall, without the Consent of the Congress, lay any Imposts or Duties on Imports or Exports, except what may be absolutely necessary for executing it's inspection Laws: and the net Produce of all Duties and Imposts, laid by any State on Imports or Exports, shall be for the Use of the Treasury of the United States; and all such Laws shall be subject to the Revision and Controul of the Congress.

No State shall, without the Consent of Congress, lay any duty of Tonnage, keep Troops, or Ships of War in time of Peace, enter into any Agreement or Compact with another State, or with a foreign Power, or engage in War, unless actually invaded, or in such imminent Danger as will not admit of delay.

Article II - The Executive Branch

Section 1 - The President

The executive Power shall be vested in a President of the United States of America. He shall hold his Office during the Term of four Years, and, together with the Vice-President chosen for the same Term, be elected, as follows:

Each State shall appoint, in such Manner as the Legislature thereof may direct, a Number of Electors, equal to the whole Number of Senators and Representatives to which the State may be entitled in the Congress: but no Senator or Representative, or Person holding an Office of Trust or Profit under the United States, shall be appointed an Elector.

(The Electors shall meet in their respective States, and vote by Ballot for two persons, of whom one at least shall not lie an Inhabitant of the same State with themselves. And they shall make a List of all the Persons voted for, and of the Number of Votes for each; which List they shall sign and certify, and transmit sealed to the Seat of the Government of the United States, directed to the President of the Senate. The President of the Senate shall, in the Presence of the Senate and House of Representatives, open all the Certificates, and the Votes shall then be counted. The Person having the greatest Number of Votes shall be the President, if such Number be a Majority of the whole Number of Electors appointed; and if there be more than one who have such Majority, and have an equal Number of Votes, then the House of Representatives shall immediately chuse by Ballot one of them for President; and if no Person have a Majority, then from the five highest on the List the said House shall in like Manner chuse the President. But in chusing the President, the Votes shall be taken by States, the Representation from each State having one Vote; a quorum for this Purpose shall consist of a Member or Members from two-thirds of the States, and a Majority of all the States shall be necessary to a Choice. In every Case, after the Choice of the President, the Person having the greatest Number of Votes of the Electors shall be the Vice President. But if there should remain two or more who have equal Votes, the Senate shall chuse from them by Ballot the Vice-President.) **(This clause in parentheses was superseded by the 12th Amendment.)**

The Congress may determine the Time of chusing the Electors, and the Day on which they shall give their Votes; which Day shall be the same throughout the United States.

No person except a natural born Citizen, or a Citizen of the United States, at the time of the Adoption of this Constitution, shall be eligible to the Office of President; neither shall any Person be eligible to that Office who shall not have attained to the Age of thirty-five Years, and been fourteen Years a Resident within the United States.

(In Case of the Removal of the President from Office, or of his Death, Resignation, or Inability to discharge the Powers and Duties of the said Office, the same shall devolve on the Vice President, and the Congress may by Law provide for the Case of Removal, Death, Resignation or Inability, both of the President and Vice President, declaring what Officer shall then act as President, and such Officer shall act accordingly, until the Disability be removed, or a President shall be elected.) **(This clause in parentheses has been modified by the 20th and 25th Amendments.)**

The President shall, at stated Times, receive for his Services, a Compensation, which shall neither be increased nor diminished during the Period for which he shall have been elected, and he shall not receive within that Period any other Emolument from the United States, or any of them.

Before he enter on the Execution of his Office, he shall take the following Oath or Affirmation:

"I do solemnly swear (or affirm) that I will faithfully execute the Office of President of the United States, and will to the best of my Ability, preserve, protect and defend the Constitution of the United States."

Section 2 - Civilian Power over Military, Cabinet, Pardon Power, Appointments

The President shall be Commander in Chief of the Army and Navy of the United States, and of the Militia of the several States, when called into the actual Service of the United States; he may require the Opinion, in writing, of the principal Officer in each of the executive Departments, upon any subject relating to the Duties of their respective Offices, and he shall have Power to Grant Reprieves and Pardons for Offenses against the United States, except in Cases of Impeachment.

He shall have Power, by and with the Advice and Consent of the Senate, to make Treaties, provided two thirds of the Senators present concur; and he shall nominate, and by and with the Advice and Consent of the Senate, shall appoint Ambassadors, other public Ministers and Consuls, Judges of the supreme Court, and all other Officers of the United States, whose Appointments are not herein otherwise provided for, and which shall be established by Law: but the Congress may by Law vest the Appointment of such inferior Officers, as they think proper, in the President alone, in the Courts of Law, or in the Heads of Departments.

The President shall have Power to fill up all Vacancies that may happen during the Recess of the Senate, by granting Commissions which shall expire at the End of their next Session.

Section 3 - State of the Union, Convening Congress

He shall from time to time give to the Congress Information of the State of the Union, and recommend to their Consideration such Measures as he shall judge necessary and expedient; he may, on extraordinary Occasions, convene both Houses, or either of them, and in Case of Disagreement between them, with Respect to the Time of Adjournment, he may adjourn them to such Time as he shall think proper; he shall receive Ambassadors and other public Ministers; he shall take Care that the Laws be faithfully executed, and shall Commission all the Officers of the United States.

Section 4 - Disqualification

The President, Vice President and all civil Officers of the United States, shall be removed from Office on Impeachment for, and Conviction of, Treason, Bribery, or other high Crimes and Misdemeanors.

Article III - The Judicial Branch

Section 1 - Judicial powers

The judicial Power of the United States, shall be vested in one supreme Court, and in such inferior Courts as the Congress may from time to time ordain and establish. The Judges, both of the supreme and inferior Courts, shall hold their Offices during good Behavior, and shall, at stated Times, receive for their Services a Compensation which shall not be diminished during their Continuance in Office.

Section 2 - Trial by Jury, Original Jurisdiction, Jury Trials

(The judicial Power shall extend to all Cases, in Law and Equity, arising under this Constitution, the Laws of the United States, and Treaties made, or which shall be made, under their Authority; to all Cases affecting Ambassadors, other public Ministers and Consuls; to all Cases of admiralty and maritime Jurisdiction; to Controversies to which the United States shall be a Party; to Controversies between two or more States; between a State and Citizens of another State; between Citizens of different States; between Citizens of the same State claiming Lands under Grants of different States, and between a State, or the Citizens thereof, and foreign States, Citizens or Subjects.) **(This section in parentheses is modified by the 11th Amendment.)**

In all Cases affecting Ambassadors, other public Ministers and Consuls, and those in which a State shall be Party, the supreme Court shall have original Jurisdiction. In all the other Cases before mentioned, the supreme Court shall have appellate Jurisdiction, both as to Law and Fact, with such Exceptions, and under such Regulations as the Congress shall make.

The Trial of all Crimes, except in Cases of Impeachment, shall be by Jury; and such Trial shall be held in the State where the said Crimes shall have been committed; but when not committed within any State, the Trial shall be at such Place or Places as the Congress may by Law have directed.

Section 3 - Treason

Treason against the United States, shall consist only in levying War against them, or in adhering to their Enemies, giving them Aid and Comfort. No Person shall be convicted of Treason unless on the Testimony of two Witnesses to the same overt Act, or on Confession in open Court.

The Congress shall have power to declare the Punishment of Treason, but no Attainder of Treason shall work Corruption of Blood, or Forfeiture except during the Life of the Person attainted.

Article IV - The States

Section 1 - Each State to Honor all others

Full Faith and Credit shall be given in each State to the public Acts, Records, and judicial Proceedings of every other State. And the Congress may by general Laws prescribe the Manner in which such Acts, Records and Proceedings shall be proved, and the Effect thereof.

Section 2 - State citizens, Extradition

The Citizens of each State shall be entitled to all Privileges and Immunities of Citizens in the several States.

A Person charged in any State with Treason, Felony, or other Crime, who shall flee from Justice, and be found in another State, shall on demand of the executive Authority of the State from which he fled, be delivered up, to be removed to the State having Jurisdiction of the Crime.

(No Person held to Service or Labour in one State, under the Laws thereof, escaping into another, shall, in Consequence of any Law or Regulation therein, be discharged from such Service or Labour, But shall be delivered up on Claim of the Party to whom such Service or Labour *may be due.)* **(This clause in parentheses is superseded by the 13th Amendment.)**

Section 3 - New States

New States may be admitted by the Congress into this Union; but no new States shall be formed or erected within the Jurisdiction of any other State; nor any State be formed by the Junction of two or more States, or parts of States, without the Consent of the Legislatures of the States concerned as well as of the Congress.

The Congress shall have Power to dispose of and make all needful Rules and Regulations respecting the Territory or other Property belonging to the United States; and nothing in this Constitution shall be so construed as to Prejudice any Claims of the United States, or of any particular State.

Section 4 - Republican government

The United States shall guarantee to every State in this Union a Republican Form of Government, and shall protect each of them against Invasion; and on Application of the Legislature, or of the Executive (when the Legislature cannot be convened) against domestic Violence.

Article V - Amendment

The Congress, whenever two thirds of both Houses shall deem it necessary, shall propose Amendments to this Constitution, or, on the Application of the Legislatures of two thirds of the several States, shall call a Convention for proposing Amendments, which, in either Case, shall be valid to all Intents and Purposes, as part of this Constitution, when ratified by the Legislatures of three fourths of the several States, or by Conventions in three fourths thereof, as the one or the other Mode of Ratification may be proposed by the Congress; Provided that no Amendment which may be made prior to the Year One thousand eight hundred and eight shall in any Manner affect the first and fourth Clauses in the Ninth Section of the first Article; and that no State, without its Consent, shall be deprived of its equal Suffrage in the Senate.

Article VI - Debts, Supremacy, Oaths

All Debts contracted and Engagements entered into, before the Adoption of this Constitution, shall be as valid against the United States under this Constitution, as under the Confederation.

This Constitution, and the Laws of the United States which shall be made in Pursuance thereof; and all Treaties made, or which shall be made, under the Authority of the United States, shall be the supreme Law of the Land; and the Judges in every State shall be bound thereby, any Thing in the Constitution or Laws of any State to the Contrary notwithstanding.

The Senators and Representatives before mentioned, and the Members of the several State Legislatures, and all executive and judicial Officers, both of the United States and of the several States, shall be bound by Oath or Affirmation, to support this Constitution; but no religious Test shall ever be required as a Qualification to any Office or public Trust under the United States.

Article VII - Ratification

The Ratification of the Conventions of nine States, shall be sufficient for the Establishment of this Constitution between the States so ratifying the Same.

Done in Convention by the Unanimous Consent of the States present the Seventeenth Day of September in the Year of our Lord one thousand seven hundred and Eighty seven and of the Independence of the United States of America the Twelfth. In Witness whereof We have hereunto subscribed our Names.

Go Washington - President and deputy from Virginia
New Hampshire - John Langdon, Nicholas Gilman
Massachusetts - Nathaniel Gorham, Rufus King
Connecticut - Wm Saml Johnson, Roger Sherman
New York - Alexander Hamilton
New Jersey - Wil Livingston, David Brearley, Wm Paterson, Jona. Dayton
Pensylvania - B Franklin, Thomas Mifflin, Robt Morris, Geo. Clymer, Thos FitzSimons, Jared Ingersoll,
James Wilson, Gouv Morris
Delaware - Geo. Read, Gunning Bedford jun, John Dickinson, Richard Bassett, Jaco. Broom
Maryland - James McHenry, Dan of St Tho Jenifer, Danl Carroll
Virginia - John Blair, James Madison Jr.
North Carolina - Wm Blount, Richd Dobbs Spaight, Hu Williamson
South Carolina - J. Rutledge, Charles Cotesworth Pinckney, Charles Pinckney, Pierce Butler
Georgia - William Few, Abr Baldwin
Attest: William Jackson, Secretary

The Amendments

The following are the Amendments to the Constitution. The first ten Amendments collectively are commonly known as the Bill of Rights.

Amendment 1 - Freedom of Religion, Press, Expression. Ratified 12/15/1791.

Congress shall make no law respecting an establishment of religion, or prohibiting the free exercise thereof; or abridging the freedom of speech, or of the press; or the right of the people peaceably to assemble, and to petition the Government for a redress of grievances.

Amendment 2 - Right to Bear Arms. Ratified 12/15/1791.

A well regulated Militia, being necessary to the security of a free State, the right of the people to keep and bear Arms, shall not be infringed.

Amendment 3 - Quartering of Soldiers. Ratified 12/15/1791.

No Soldier shall, in time of peace be quartered in any house, without the consent of the Owner, nor in time of war, but in a manner to be prescribed by law.

Amendment 4 - Search and Seizure. Ratified 12/15/1791.

The right of the people to be secure in their persons, houses, papers, and effects, against unreasonable searches and seizures, shall not be violated, and no Warrants shall issue, but upon probable cause, supported by Oath or affirmation, and particularly describing the place to be searched, and the persons or things to be seized.

Amendment 5 - Trial and Punishment, Compensation for Takings. Ratified 12/15/1791.

No person shall be held to answer for a capital, or otherwise infamous crime, unless on a presentment or indictment of a Grand Jury, except in cases arising in the land or naval forces, or in the Militia, when in actual service in time of War or public danger; nor shall any person be subject for the same offense to be twice put in jeopardy of life or limb; nor shall be compelled in any criminal case to be a witness against himself, nor be deprived of life, liberty, or property, without due process of law; nor shall private property be taken for public use, without just compensation.

Amendment 6 - Right to Speedy Trial, Confrontation of Witnesses. Ratified 12/15/1791.

In all criminal prosecutions, the accused shall enjoy the right to a speedy and public trial, by an impartial jury of the State and district wherein the crime shall have been committed, which district shall have been previously ascertained by law, and to be informed of the nature and cause of the accusation; to be confronted with the witnesses against him; to have compulsory process for obtaining witnesses in his favor, and to have the Assistance of Counsel for his defence.

Amendment 7 - Trial by Jury in Civil Cases. Ratified 12/15/1791.

In Suits at common law, where the value in controversy shall exceed twenty dollars, the right of trial by jury shall be preserved, and no fact tried by a jury, shall be otherwise re-examined in any Court of the United States, than according to the rules of the common law.

Amendment 8 - Cruel and Unusual Punishment. Ratified 12/15/1791.

Excessive bail shall not be required, nor excessive fines imposed, nor cruel and unusual punishments inflicted.

Amendment 9 - Construction of Constitution. Ratified 12/15/1791.

The enumeration in the Constitution, of certain rights, shall not be construed to deny or disparage others retained by the people.

Amendment 10 - Powers of the States and People. Ratified 12/15/1791.

The powers not delegated to the United States by the Constitution, nor prohibited by it to the States, are reserved to the States respectively, or to the people.

Amendment 11 - Judicial Limits. Ratified 2/7/1795.

The Judicial power of the United States shall not be construed to extend to any suit in law or equity, commenced or prosecuted against one of the United States by Citizens of another State, or by Citizens or Subjects of any Foreign State.

Amendment 12 - Choosing the President, Vice-President. Ratified 6/15/1804.

The Electors shall meet in their respective states, and vote by ballot for President and Vice-President, one of whom, at least, shall not be an inhabitant of the same state with themselves; they shall name in their ballots the person voted for as President, and in distinct ballots the person voted for as Vice-President, and they shall make distinct lists of all persons voted for as President, and of all persons voted for as Vice-President and of the number of votes for each, which lists they shall sign and certify, and transmit sealed to the seat of the government of the United States, directed to the President of the Senate;

The President of the Senate shall, in the presence of the Senate and House of Representatives, open all the certificates and the votes shall then be counted;

The person having the greatest Number of votes for President, shall be the President, if such number be a majority of the whole number of Electors appointed; and if no person have such majority, then from the persons having the highest numbers not exceeding three on the list of those voted for as President, the House of Representatives shall choose immediately, by ballot, the President. But in choosing the President, the votes shall be taken by states, the representation from each state having one vote; a quorum for this purpose shall consist of a member or members from two-thirds of the states, and a majority of all the states shall be necessary to a choice. And if the House of Representatives shall not choose a President whenever the right of choice shall devolve upon them, before the fourth day of March next following, then the Vice-President shall act as President, as in the case of the death or other constitutional disability of the President.

The person having the greatest number of votes as Vice-President, shall be the Vice-President, if such number be a majority of the whole number of Electors appointed, and if no person have a majority, then from the two highest numbers on the list, the Senate shall choose the Vice-President; a quorum for the purpose shall consist of two-thirds of the whole number of Senators, and a majority of the whole number shall be necessary to a choice. But no person constitutionally ineligible to the office of President shall be eligible to that of Vice-President of the United States.

Amendment 13 - Slavery Abolished. Ratified 12/6/1865.

1. Neither slavery nor involuntary servitude, except as a punishment for crime whereof the party shall have been duly convicted, shall exist within the United States, or any place subject to their jurisdiction.

2. Congress shall have power to enforce this article by appropriate legislation.

Amendment 14 - Citizenship Rights. Ratified 7/9/1868.

1. All persons born or naturalized in the United States, and subject to the jurisdiction thereof, are citizens of the United States and of the State wherein they reside. No State shall make or enforce any law which shall abridge the privileges or immunities of citizens of the United States; nor shall any State deprive any person of life, liberty, or property, without due process of law; nor deny to any person within its jurisdiction the equal protection of the laws.

2. Representatives shall be apportioned among the several States according to their respective numbers, counting the whole number of persons in each State, excluding Indians not taxed. But when the right to vote at any election for the choice of electors for President and Vice-President of the United States, Representatives in Congress, the Executive and Judicial officers of a State, or the members of the Legislature thereof, is denied to any of the male inhabitants of such State, being twenty-one years of age, and citizens of the United States, or in any way abridged, except for participation in rebellion, or other crime, the basis of representation therein shall be reduced in the

proportion which the number of such male citizens shall bear to the whole number of male citizens twenty-one years of age in such State.

3. No person shall be a Senator or Representative in Congress, or elector of President and Vice-President, or hold any office, civil or military, under the United States, or under any State, who, having previously taken an oath, as a member of Congress, or as an officer of the United States, or as a member of any State legislature, or as an executive or judicial officer of any State, to support the Constitution of the United States, shall have engaged in insurrection or rebellion against the same, or given aid or comfort to the enemies thereof. But Congress may by a vote of two-thirds of each House, remove such disability.

4. The validity of the public debt of the United States, authorized by law, including debts incurred for payment of pensions and bounties for services in suppressing insurrection or rebellion, shall not be questioned. But neither the United States nor any State shall assume or pay any debt or obligation incurred in aid of insurrection or rebellion against the United States, or any claim for the loss or emancipation of any slave; but all such debts, obligations and claims shall be held illegal and void.

5. The Congress shall have power to enforce, by appropriate legislation, the provisions of this article.

Amendment 15 - Race No Bar to Vote. Ratified 2/3/1870.

1. The right of citizens of the United States to vote shall not be denied or abridged by the United States or by any State on account of race, color, or previous condition of servitude.

2. The Congress shall have power to enforce this article by appropriate legislation.

Amendment 16 - Status of Income Tax Clarified. Ratified 2/3/1913.

The Congress shall have power to lay and collect taxes on incomes, from whatever source derived, without apportionment among the several States, and without regard to any census or enumeration.

Amendment 17 - Senators Elected by Popular Vote. Ratified 4/8/1913.

The Senate of the United States shall be composed of two Senators from each State, elected by the people thereof, for six years; and each Senator shall have one vote. The electors in each State shall have the qualifications requisite for electors of the most numerous branch of the State legislatures.

When vacancies happen in the representation of any State in the Senate, the executive authority of such State shall issue writs of election to fill such vacancies: Provided, That the legislature of any State may empower the executive thereof to make temporary appointments until the people fill the vacancies by election as the legislature may direct.

This amendment shall not be so construed as to affect the election or term of any Senator chosen before it becomes valid as part of the Constitution.

Amendment 18 - Liquor Abolished. Ratified 1/16/1919.
Repealed by Amendment 21, 12/5/1933.

1. After one year from the ratification of this article the manufacture, sale, or transportation of intoxicating liquors within, the importation thereof into, or the exportation thereof from the United States and all territory subject to the jurisdiction thereof for beverage purposes is hereby prohibited.

2. The Congress and the several States shall have concurrent power to enforce this article by appropriate legislation.

3. This article shall be inoperative unless it shall have been ratified as an amendment to the Constitution by the legislatures of the several States, as provided in the Constitution, within seven years from the date of the submission hereof to the States by the Congress.

Amendment 19 - Women's Suffrage. Ratified 8/18/1920.

The right of citizens of the United States to vote shall not be denied or abridged by the United States or by any State on account of sex.

Congress shall have power to enforce this article by appropriate legislation.

Amendment 20 - Presidential, Congressional Terms. Ratified 1/23/1933.

1. The terms of the President and Vice President shall end at noon on the 20th day of January, and the terms of Senators and Representatives at noon on the 3d day of January, of the years in which such terms would have ended if this article had not been ratified; and the terms of their successors shall then begin.

2. The Congress shall assemble at least once in every year, and such meeting shall begin at noon on the 3d day of January, unless they shall by law appoint a different day.

3. If, at the time fixed for the beginning of the term of the President, the President elect shall have died, the Vice President elect shall become President. If a President shall not have been chosen before the time fixed for the beginning of his term, or if the President elect shall have failed to qualify, then the Vice President elect shall act as President until a President shall have qualified; and the Congress may by law provide for the case wherein neither a President elect nor a Vice President elect shall have qualified, declaring who shall then act as President, or the manner in which one who is to act shall be selected, and such person shall act accordingly until a President or Vice President shall have qualified.

4. The Congress may by law provide for the case of the death of any of the persons from whom the House of Representatives may choose a President whenever the right of choice shall have devolved upon them, and for the case of the death of any of the persons from whom the Senate may choose a Vice President whenever the right of choice shall have devolved upon them.

5. Sections 1 and 2 shall take effect on the 15th day of October following the ratification of this article.

6. This article shall be inoperative unless it shall have been ratified as an amendment to the Constitution by the legislatures of three-fourths of the several States within seven years from the date of its submission.

Amendment 21 - Amendment 18 Repealed. Ratified 12/5/1933.

1. The eighteenth article of amendment to the Constitution of the United States is hereby repealed.

2. The transportation or importation into any State, Territory, or possession of the United States for delivery or use therein of intoxicating liquors, in violation of the laws thereof, is hereby prohibited.

3. The article shall be inoperative unless it shall have been ratified as an amendment to the Constitution by conventions in the several States, as provided in the Constitution, within seven years from the date of the submission hereof to the States by the Congress.

Amendment 22 - Presidential Term Limits. Ratified 2/27/1951.

1. No person shall be elected to the office of the President more than twice, and no person who has held the office of President, or acted as President, for more than two years of a term to which some other person was elected President shall be elected to the office of the President more than once. But this Article shall not apply to any person holding the office of President, when this Article was proposed by the Congress, and shall not prevent any person who may be holding the office of President, or acting as President, during the term within which this Article becomes operative from holding the office of President or acting as President during the remainder of such term.

2. This article shall be inoperative unless it shall have been ratified as an amendment to the Constitution by the legislatures of three-fourths of the several States within seven years from the date of its submission to the States by the Congress.

Amendment 23 - Presidential Vote for District of Columbia. Ratified 3/29/1961.

1. The District constituting the seat of Government of the United States shall appoint in such manner as the Congress may direct: A number of electors

of President and Vice President equal to the whole number of Senators and Representatives in Congress to which the District would be entitled if it were a State, but in no event more than the least populous State; they shall be in addition to those appointed by the States, but they shall be considered, for the purposes of the election of President and Vice President, to be electors appointed by a State; and they shall meet in the District and perform such duties as provided by the twelfth article of amendment.

2. The Congress shall have power to enforce this article by appropriate legislation.

Amendment 24 - Poll Tax Barred. Ratified 1/23/1964.

1. The right of citizens of the United States to vote in any primary or other election for President or Vice President, for electors for President or Vice President, or for Senator or Representative in Congress, shall not be denied or abridged by the United States or any State by reason of failure to pay any poll tax or other tax.

2. The Congress shall have power to enforce this article by appropriate legislation.

Amendment 25 - Presidential Disability and Succession. Ratified 2/10/1967.

1. In case of the removal of the President from office or of his death or resignation, the Vice President shall become President.

2. Whenever there is a vacancy in the office of the Vice President, the President shall nominate a Vice President who shall take office upon confirmation by a majority vote of both Houses of Congress.

3. Whenever the President transmits to the President pro tempore of the Senate and the Speaker of the House of Representatives his written declaration that he is unable to discharge the powers and duties of his office, and until he transmits to them a written declaration to the contrary, such powers and duties shall be discharged by the Vice President as Acting President.

4. Whenever the Vice President and a majority of either the principal officers of the executive departments or of such other body as Congress may by law provide, transmit to the President pro tempore of the Senate and the Speaker of the House of Representatives their written declaration that the President is unable to discharge the powers and duties of his office, the Vice President shall immediately assume the powers and duties of the office as Acting President.

Thereafter, when the President transmits to the President pro tempore of the Senate and the Speaker of the House of Representatives his written declaration that no inability exists, he shall resume the powers and duties of his office unless the Vice President and a majority of either the principal officers of the executive department or of such other body as Congress may by law provide, transmit within four days to the President pro tempore of the Senate and the Speaker of the House of Representatives their written declaration that the President is unable to discharge the powers and duties of his office. Thereupon Congress shall decide the issue, assembling within forty eight hours for that purpose if not in session. If the Congress, within twenty one days after receipt of the latter written declaration, or, if Congress is not in session, within twenty one days after Congress is required to assemble, determines by two thirds vote of both Houses that the President is unable to discharge the powers and duties of his office, the Vice President shall continue to discharge the same as Acting President; otherwise, the President shall resume the powers and duties of his office.

Amendment 26 - Voting Age Set to 18 Years. Ratified 7/1/1971.

1. The right of citizens of the United States, who are eighteen years of age or older, to vote shall not be denied or abridged by the United States or by any State on account of age.

2. The Congress shall have power to enforce this article by appropriate legislation.

Amendment 27 - Limiting Changes to Congressional Pay. Ratified 5/7/1992.

No law, varying the compensation for the services of the Senators and Representatives, shall take effect, until an election of Representatives shall have intervened.

ABOUT THE AUTHOR

Eric Hines lives in a metroplex in north Texas with his wife and two cats. He has the good fortune to have his daughter, son-in-law, and grandson nearby; they have the good fortune of living in a separate house. Hines is an ex-USAF officer, a quasi-retired systems engineer, a never hired network engineer, a writer, and a blogger.

Hines blogs at *APlebesSite.com*.

Edwards Brothers, Inc.
Thorofare, NJ USA
March 1, 2012